The Data Warehouse Workshop

Brian Ciampa

ISBN: 1494926962
ISBN-13: 978-1494926960

DEDICATION

This book is dedicated to my beautiful wife Amanda and my extraordinary kids Braden, Abby, and Cora. I also want to dedicate this to my late baby nephew and niece, Hazen and Julia. Their lives were too short, but the memories will last forever.

CONTENTS

1
INTRODUCTION

As of this writing, a Google search on "Data Warehousing" will result in almost 15 million hits. There is no lack of books, blogs, tweets, consultants, and conferences on the subject of data warehousing. The resources that have been poured into this discipline over the last couple of decades have been immense…and that is not expected to change. The technologies may change, but the need to provide decision makers with a way to quickly determine the direction of their organization and/or the direction of the environment in which that organization exists will only grow. From the recent college graduate looking to find his first job to the experienced professional looking to make a career change, this field offers great potential for those wishing to enter. It also may seem a bit overwhelming. That is why this book is written specifically for the extract, transform, and load (ETL) novice. While the experienced data warehousing professional is welcome to read and glean anything that he may find valuable, providing a pathway to some hands-on experience writing ETL for the beginner is the goal. While this book is specifically written with the aspiring ETL developer in mind, even those wishing to move into a less technical area such as business analysis or project management can benefit from experiencing the details of how a data warehouse is populated.

A developer wishing to begin a career in a web based technology such as ColdFusion can fairly easily build a website to display her skills. While the skill itself is both valuable and complex, the amount of data needed to display such an aptitude is fairly small. A realistic data warehouse, however, will move data from source system tables that contain millions of records (or more) and restructure that data so that it is optimal for analysis by a decision maker. Creating a Microsoft Access database with a few thousand records of financial transactions will probably not be enough data to adequately learn ETL concepts. Furthermore, in our HIPPA and Sarbanes-Oxley society, the chances of contacting an organization and gaining access to millions of records worth of production data in order to learn ETL concepts are slim to none. So, those wishing to break into this industry can find themselves in a bit of a quandary.

That is the gap that this book is designed to fill. A series of SQL files will be provided (the location of the files will be provided later) that will in essence create a source system in an Oracle environment. The smallest of these tables contains 3 rows and the largest contains 3,563,048 rows. If you do not have an existing Oracle environment available to you, a suggested solution to that will be provided as well. This book will, then, take you through the process of writing the ETL jobs (in

Oracle PL/SQL) necessary to create five star schemas. Practice with techniques such as these will be provided:

1.) Populating conformed dimensions
2.) Populating type one and type two slowly changing dimensions
3.) Populating junk dimensions
4.) When it is appropriate to refresh a table entirely as opposed to updating existing records and inserting new ones
5.) Creating a job so that the data in a star schema can be refreshed entirely, refreshed according to a default timeframe (only the current month, for example), or refreshed with dates provided
6.) Comparing the newly warehoused data to the source system to ensure that the ETL job is working correctly
7.) Creating tables in the staging area to make the job optimal for debugging when the data warehouse does not match the source
8.) Using the staging tables in number seven above to identify where in the ETL a problem may lie and possible solutions
9.) Changing the grain of a fact table
10.) Considering ways to make a job run more efficiently when it is discovered that it is taking too much time to complete

This book is not intended to rewrite any of the invaluable guides that explain the ins and outs of data warehouse design. In fact, discussions regarding architecture of the data warehouse are outside of the scope of this book. This book assumes that the design has been completed by either a dedicated architect or by the ETL developer herself and, from that point, will walk the reader through the process of writing the ETL to populate that design. Having said that, it is important that you have at least a basic knowledge of data warehouse design, including:

1.) Familiarity with a fact table and the purpose that it serves
2.) Familiarity with a dimension table and the purpose that it serves
3.) Difference between a dimension's natural key and its surrogate key
4.) The meaning of the term "grain" in the context of a fact table

This book will give a brief overview of some of these items in chapter three and then jump right into the hands-on practice for writing ETL. If you were familiar with these items at one time and need a refresher, chapter three should provide an adequate refresher. If they are completely new, you will probably need to refer to some additional resources to become familiar with them at a basic level before continuing.

Here are a few things to keep in mind as you read:

1.) As mentioned above, the ETL practice will involve Oracle PL/SQL. While some data warehouse implementations use PL/SQL to write ETL jobs, it is probably most typical for an organization to purchase some data integration software to use in writing ETL. The purpose is not to teach you how to use PL/SQL to write your ETL. That is just the language chosen for these exercises to help you become familiar with the thought process needed to restructure the data. You can, then, take that knowledge and use it in conjunction with a data integration tool.

2.) These examples will involve moving data from one set of Oracle tables to another set of Oracle tables in the same database and schema. A data warehouse will most likely pull data from various sources and various vendors (e.g., an ETL job may pull data from a source system using Microsoft SQL Server and load an Oracle database, etc.). Again, the purpose is to help you become familiar with the thought process needed to restructure data, as opposed to providing experience with pulling data from a database purchased from one vendor and populating a database purchased from another.

3.) The intent is not to tell you how to write each line of code. It would be rare (probably impossible) to find two ETL developers who will write a complex ETL job in exactly the same way. The solutions that are provided in this book are not the only solutions available. They are possible solutions to help get you thinking in a good direction about writing ETL.

Along with some familiarity with data warehouse design, as described above, this book assumes that you have a basic knowledge of SQL as well. While everyone is welcome to dive in and learn, the most ideal readers will be those who (1) have had hands-on exposure to a relational database (not necessarily a data warehouse) through an employer, self-study, or school, (2) have a general understanding of data warehouse design as explained above, and (3) wish to take that aptitude into the direction of ETL development.

2
WHAT IS DATA WAREHOUSING?

When I was in college I worked part-time in a fast food restaurant. If I was lucky, I was assigned to the drive-thru window instead of the heat of the kitchen, through which I would transact business with a customer. The cash register told me how much cash I should expect from the customer (this was before debit cards were accepted at fast food joints). The customer would give me that amount in some combination of bills and/or coins. The drawer would open and I had a specific area for each type of bill and coin. After placing the money into the correct place, the cash register would tell me how much was due in change. I would take that amount in some combination (often the combination that resulted in me touching the smallest number of bills and coins) from the appropriate place(s) in the drawer and place it into the customer's hand.

Because each bill and coin had its own place in the drawer I was able to get pretty good at taking money out and placing money into the drawer. In other words, the money was structured so that I could transact business quickly. It was optimal for operational use. However, as the day went on I usually had no idea how much money was in that drawer. If the boss had come by and asked how much was in the drawer I would not have been able to answer that question very easily. When I opened the drawer all I saw were stacks of bills and piles of coins in their respective places. The cash register did not make the analysis of that cash very easy. It was not optimal for analysis.

When the shift was over, I collected the drawers and took them to the office to count the money. This involved placing 50 pennies into the appropriate roll, 40 nickels into the appropriate roll, etc. and wrapping 10 of each type of bill. In other words, I was restructuring the money. Placing the coins into the rolls and placing the wraps around the bills took longer than placing them into the appropriate places in the drawer but at this point in the process, I was interested in analyzing the money (how much do we have) as opposed to conducting business transactions quickly.

At that point, without too much effort, I could scan the desk and know that two wraps of $50 bills (each wrap contained 10 bills) equated to $1,000, three rolls of quarters equated to $30 dollars, etc. Restructuring the money was a bit tedious but the counting was a piece of cake. When I placed that money into a bank bag and dropped it off at the bank the teller could also verify that the amount that I placed on the deposit slip was consistent with the actual amount in the bag. The fact that I had restructured that money from the drawer to the rolled coins and stacked bills allowed for that quick analysis.

In much the same way, operational systems are built so that data can be entered quickly. The consequence of this is that analyzing the data in that system is not easy. In the example above, this would equate to the cash register drawer. A data warehouse is a different type of system. Its sole purpose is to allow for the ease of data analysis as opposed to the operational use of data. In the example above, this would equate to the rolls that hold the coins and the wraps that hold the bills.

We've looked at a theoretical example, now consider this practical example. When you purchase a shirt at a retail store you don't want to have to stand at the register for a long time waiting for the computer to process the transaction. As a result, those systems are built so that the data can be placed into the system quickly and you can be on your way. The data produced by the transaction may look something like this:

Date	Item Number	Item Description	Department	Amount Paid
11/14/2011	876FTR	Men's Polo	Men's Dept	$12.99

What if 100,000 items were sold in one day? There would be 100,000 records like this in the system (with different data of course). Multiply that by 365 (days in a year) and you see the amount of data that we are talking about. Suppose an executive is wondering when Men's Polo shirts are most often sold? Summer? Spring? October? July? Examining all of those thousands of records is not practical much like trying to determine how much money is in the cash register drawer without rolling the coins or wrapping the bills. However, if a program ran each night that copied this data into a data warehouse and structured it in such a way that you can easily see into which year, quarter, season, and month this transaction fell, it would be much easier to answer those questions for upper management.

3
THE STRUCTURE OF A DATA WAREHOUSE

Fact Table

A fact table is a table that contains the numeric measures. In other words, the amounts that represent counts, summations, averages, etc. are stored in the fact table. In order to understand the context of these measures, the fact table also contains foreign keys that point to another type of table called a dimension table (explained below). A term that is often used when describing a fact table is the grain. A fact table's grain refers to the level of detail included. So, for a fact table that contains sales data, the grain may be one row per invoice. Another fact table that contains sales data may contain one row per invoice, per transaction. In other words, this second table contains a finer grain than the first.

From a technical perspective, the foreign keys and degenerate dimensions in the fact table define the grain. The combination of foreign keys and degenerate dimensions for each record acts as a composite primary key for that record. Although there may or may not be some sort of unique constraint on that combination of columns in the database, that combination should in fact be unique.

Dimension Table

A dimension table is a table that describes a piece of the context of the measures in the fact table. If you are looking to see sales revenue per person, per month, the data that specifies people and months will exist in the dimension tables (revenue will be in the fact table). In that example one dimension table will exist that contains date related data and another dimension table will exist that contains data about people. Each row in the fact table will contain a foreign key to the person dimension and another foreign key to the date dimension, along with any other foreign keys that may exist.

Each record in the dimension table will contain an arbitrary number (often an auto-generated number) which will serve as its primary key. This is referred to as a surrogate key. It means nothing to the business and is only useful within the data warehouse. The unique identifier that does mean something to the business is called the natural key. There is a reason that the natural key should not serve as the primary key of the dimension. That will be explained later.

Dimension tables are designed to either incorporate history or not incorporate history. Consider the following types of slowly changing dimensions:

Type 0: This type of dimension table contains data that will never change. A date dimension of some sort is a good example of a type 0 dimension.

Type 1: This type of dimension table overwrites historical data with the most current data. If an employee in the person dimension was hired as a Junior Analyst and then promoted to Senior Analyst, the title column will be overwritten to reflect a title of Senior Analyst. The description of Senior Analyst will be associated with all of this person's data, including the data that pertains to the time during which he was a Junior Analyst.

Type 2: This type of dimension table contains historical rows. To continue with the example above, if an individual is hired as a Junior Analyst a row will exist in the person dimension that reflects that he has that title. When he is promoted to a Senior Analyst, an additional row will be added to the dimension table to reflect that he is a Senior Analyst. All of the fact table rows that apply to the time frame during which he was a Junior Analyst, will reference that row in the person dimension. Those that apply to his timeframe as a Senior Analyst will reference that row.

Although other types of slowly changing dimensions exist, they are outside of the scope of this book.

Star Schema

When a fact table and its dimension tables are displayed in an entity relationship diagram, the fact table will typically be displayed as the table in the middle with the dimension tables surrounding it. As a result, this looks like a star. The data warehouse is basically a combination of star schemas. These star schemas can be "related" to each other via something called Conformed Dimensions. In other words, data from the salary fact table can be compared to data from the productivity fact table via these Conformed Dimensions.

Conformed Dimensions are dimensions that are based on the same definitions throughout the data warehouse. For example, if the fact table that contains salary data contains a reference to a department dimension table and the fact table that contains sales revenue also contains a reference to a department dimension table, the definition of department should be consistent between the two tables. If the definition is not the same (i.e., salary data is linked to individual departments and sales data is linked to what amounts to groups of departments) then those are not conformed dimensions. A conformed dimension may exist as different physical tables as long as the tables are based on the same data definitions and the same surrogate keys. The best strategy may be to plan on having one physical table for each dimension, although this is not required.

Snowflake Schema

While a data warehouse is intended to denormalize data, some architects choose to normalize dimension tables. When this happens, several dimension tables are joined to each other with one of them being joined to the fact table. Due to the multiple layers of dimension tables, the star now looks more like a snowflake. Snowflake schemas are outside of the scope of this book.

Extract, Transform, and Load (ETL)

We have examined the structure of a data warehouse but not how to populate a data warehouse. That is where an extract, transform, and load (ETL) job comes in. This job pulls data from the source system, restructures the data, and loads it into the data warehouse.

Math students (who do not use calculators) often use a piece of scrap paper to work out the answer to a math problem. This scrap paper, in a way, sits between the source (the problem in the textbook) and the target (the paper with the final answer). ETL developers also have an area that sits between the source system and the data warehouse, called the staging area. Data is often pulled from the source, placed into the staging area (to which only the ETL developer has access) so that it can be restructured, and then loaded into the appropriate fact or dimension table. This process of writing an ETL job, as opposed to designing the tables into which that job will place data, will be the main subject of this book.

4
INTRODUCTION TO EXAMPLES

Introduction

Visiting http://www.brianciampa.com will allow you to download several SQL scripts that, when run, create and populate Oracle tables that represent a human resources system. Although the data is entirely fictitious, it is designed to create a fairly realistic data set from which five star schemas can be populated. This book will walk you through the process of writing the ETL to populate those schemas.

As discussed earlier, this hands-on training is designed to be completed in Oracle. If an existing Oracle instance is not available to you, a free product called Oracle Database Express Edition may be used. This is a smaller version of Oracle that may be loaded onto a local computer. As of this writing, Oracle Database Express Edition can be downloaded from http://www.oracle.com/technetwork/database/express-edition/overview/index.html. If this link becomes unusable, typing "Oracle Express Edition" into a search engine should direct you to the appropriate location.

For those planning to use Oracle Database Express Edition, I would also recommend using an integrated development environment (IDE) called Oracle SQL Developer (also free). As of this writing it can be downloaded from http://www.oracle.com/technetwork/developer-tools/sql-developer/overview/index.html. If this link becomes unusable, typing "Oracle SQL Developer" into a search engine should direct you to the appropriate location.

While there may be multiple ways of loading this data into your instance of Oracle I will suggest two ways. Before loading the data, I would recommend logging into the schema in which you plan to load this data and running the two select statements in the checks.txt file (also below).

```
SELECT    CONSTRAINT_NAME,
          TABLE_NAME
FROM      ALL_CONSTRAINTS
WHERE     OWNER =
          (
              SELECT        SYS_CONTEXT( 'USERENV', 'CURRENT_SCHEMA' )
              FROM          DUAL
          )
          AND CONSTRAINT_NAME IN
          (
              'EVAL_ITEM_FK',
              'EVAL_HEADER_FK',
              'EVAL_REASON_FK',
              'APPOINTMENT_FK2',
              'PAY_TYPE_ID_FK',
              'PAYCHECK_HEADER_ID_FK',
              'APPOINTMENT_FK1',
              'LEAVE_TYPE_FK',
              'APPOINTMENT_FK',
              'DEPARTMENT_FK',
              'TITLE_FK',
              'EMPLOYEE_FK',
              'DEPARTMENT_PK',
              'LEAVE_TYPE_PK',
              'PAY_TYPE_PK',
              'TITLE_PK',
              'EVAL_REASON_PK',
              'EVAL_NAME_PK',
              'EMPLOYEE_PK',
              'APPOINTMENT_PK',
              'ACTUAL_LEAVE_PK',
              'PAYCHECK_HEADER_PK',
              'PAYCHECK_DETAIL_PK',
              'EVAL_HEADER_PK',
              'EVAL_DETAIL_PK'
          )
```

This select statement will return the name(s) of any existing constraint(s) in your schema that will conflict with the name of a constraint that needs to be created using these SQL scripts. If this select statement returns anything, your options are to load the data into a different schema or to rename or drop the existing constraint so that the name will not conflict with the script.

```
SELECT    TABLE_NAME
FROM      ALL_TABLES
WHERE     OWNER =
          (
            SELECT   SYS_CONTEXT( 'USERENV', 'CURRENT_SCHEMA' ) FROM
            DUAL
          )
          AND TABLE_NAME IN
          (
            'DEPARTMENT',
            'LEAVE_TYPE',
            'PAY_TYPE',
            'TITLE',
            'EVAL_REASON',
            'EVALUATION_ITEM',
            'EMPLOYEE',
            'APPOINTMENT',
            'ACTUAL_LEAVE',
            'PAYCHECK_HEADER',
            'PAYCHECK_DETAIL',
            'EVALUATION_HEADER',
            'EVALUATION_DETAIL'
          )
```

This select statement will return the name(s) of any existing table(s) in your schema that will conflict with the name of a table that needs to be created using these SQL scripts. If this select statement returns anything, your options are to load the data into a different schema or to rename or drop the existing table so that the name will not conflict with the script.

Once those conflicts have been resolved, or if neither statement returns anything, you are ready to load the data.

Load Data One Table At A Time

From an IDE (such as Oracle SQL Developer although others may be used) open the following provided SQL files and run them in the following order.

1.)   Create_Tables_SQL.sql
2.)   Department_Data.sql
3.)   Employee_Data.sql
4.)   Leave_Type_Data.sql
5.)   Title_Data.sql
6.)   Appointment_Data.sql
7.)   Actual_Leave_Data.sql
8.)   Eval_Reason_Data.sql
9.)   Evaluation_Item_Data.sql
10.) Evaluation_Header_Data.sql
11.) Evaluation_Detail_Data.sql
12.) Pay_Type_Data.sql

13.) Paycheck_Header_Data.sql
14.) Paycheck_Detail_Data.sql

Load Data In Bulk Using SQLPlus

If you wish to use a more automated approach to loading the data, SQLPlus may work well. Perform the following steps:

1.) Place ALL of the SQL files that were provided to you into the same directory.
2.) From the command line navigate to the directory into which you placed the scripts in the previous step.
3.) Type the following:
sqlplus {schema name}/{password} @Run_In_SQLPLUS
So, if you are loading this into a schema called "myschema" with the password being "mypassword", the command would look like this:
sqlplus myschema/mypassword @Run_In_SQLPLUS
Including the ".sql" extension with the filename is not necessary.
4.) Press Enter.

By using the SQLPlus approach, the Run_In_SQLPLUS.sql file will run the other scripts in the appropriate order.

Independent of the approach used to load the data, a successful execution of the load will result in 13 tables that will serve as a source system from which star schemas can be created. The tables are:

Table Name	Number of Rows
ACTUAL_LEAVE	355,861
APPOINTMENT	55,544
DEPARTMENT	15
EMPLOYEE	55,524
EVAL_REASON	3
EVALUATION_DETAIL	3,563,048
EVALUATION_HEADER	445,381
EVALUATION_ITEM	8
LEAVE_TYPE	4
PAY_TYPE	12
PAYCHECK_DETAIL	1,314,912
PAYCHECK_HEADER	112,743
TITLE	220

As you can probably tell by the names, this data represents a Human Resources system that needs to be warehoused. Three business processes for which we will build star schemas are:

1.) Payroll
2.) Leave
3.) Employee Evaluations

Payroll

This business process involves cutting the checks for employee compensation. Each employee receives one paycheck per appointment per pay period. The payroll data is stored in the source system as follows:

PAYCHECK_HEADER: This table contains the high-level data for each paycheck.

PAYCHECK_DETAIL: This table contains the detail for each paycheck. The dollars associated with each type of pay (i.e., wages, benefits, etc.) are available in this table.

PAY_TYPE: This table contains a list of all possible types of pay. The PAYCHECK_DETAIL table contains a foreign key that points to the PAY_TYPE table.

Leave

This business process involves logging the amount of leave taken by each employee. When an employee takes leave, he charges it to a "leave bank" that is attached to each appointment. This data is stored in the source system as follows:

ACTUAL_LEAVE: This table contains the amount of leave taken and the dates on which the leave was taken for each instance of leave.

LEAVE_TYPE: This table contains a list of all possible types of leave. The ACTUAL_LEAVE table contains a foreign key that points to the LEAVE_TYPE table.

Employee Evaluations

This business process involves a formal evaluation of each employee's performance by her supervisor. A number of items are available on each evaluation and the employee is scored on a scale of one (lowest) to five (highest). An evaluation can be given for a number of reasons, such as an annual evaluation, manager's discretion, etc. This data is stored in the source system as follows:

EVALUATION_HEADER: This table contains the high-level data for each evaluation

EVALUATION_DETAIL: This table contains the detail for each evaluation. The items that make up that particular evaluation as well as the individual scores are included.

EVALUATION_ITEM: This table contains a list of all of the items that comprise an evaluation.

EVAL_REASON: This table contains a list of all of the possible reasons that an evaluation can be administered. Each evaluation is associated with only one reason. The EVALUATION_HEADER table contains a foreign key that points to the EVAL_REASON table.

Additional Tables

The tables that touch all three business processes are:

APPOINTMENT: This table contains a record for each appointment in the organization. An appointment basically refers to a job. If I am appointed in the Marketing department, then I am employed by the Marketing department. If I am appointed part-time by Marketing and then part-time by Information Systems, then I have two appointments. If I am hired by Marketing and then move to the Human Resources department, I have ended one appointment and begun another.

DEPARTMENT: This table contains a record for each department in the organization. The APPOINTMENT table contains a foreign key that points to the DEPARTMENT table.

EMPLOYEE: This table contains a record for each employee in the organization. The APPOINTMENT table contains a foreign key that points to the EMPLOYEE table.

TITLE: This table contains a record for each job title in the organization. The APPOINTMENT table contains a foreign key that points to the TITLE table.

Source System ERD

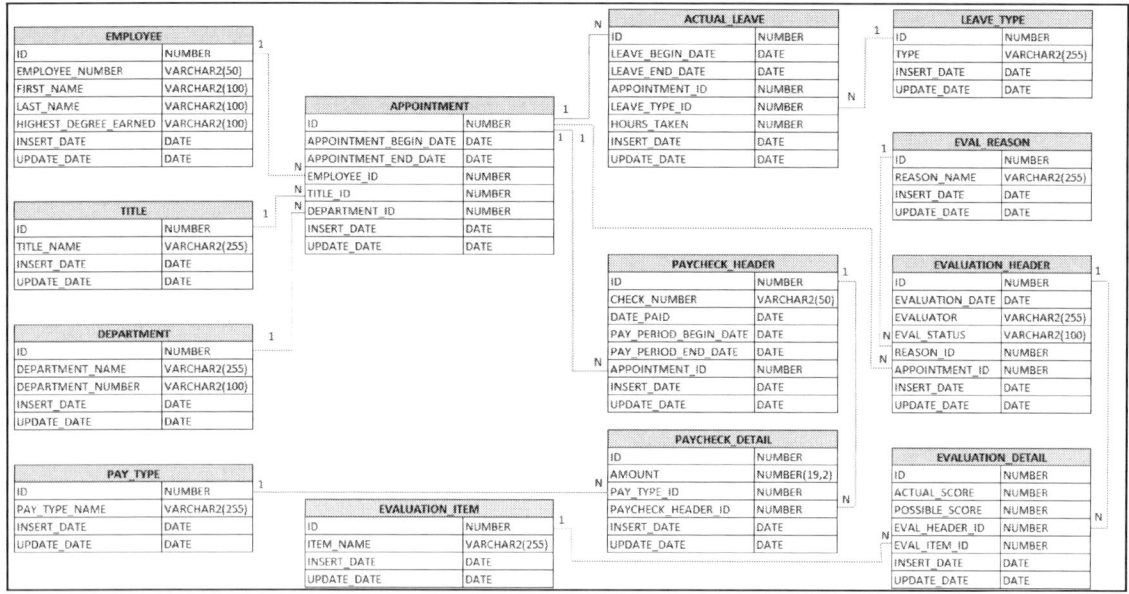

Disclaimer

The purpose of both this data and the exercises that follow is to share some best practices and provide a way to practice warehousing data. While the data is intended to produce a fairly realistic source system I will encourage you not to read too much into the data. For example, the results of the following select statement, which show the amounts paid to two individuals on July 29, 1994, show that a Human Resources Generalist made considerably more than the Chief Executive Officer.

```
SELECT      B.FIRST_NAME,
            B.LAST_NAME,
            C.TITLE_NAME,
            SUM(E.AMOUNT)
FROM        APPOINTMENT A,
            EMPLOYEE B,
```

```
                   TITLE C,
                   PAYCHECK_HEADER D,
                   PAYCHECK_DETAIL E,
                   PAY_TYPE F
   WHERE           A.EMPLOYEE_ID = B.ID
                   AND A.TITLE_ID = C.ID
                   AND A.ID = D.APPOINTMENT_ID
                   AND D.ID = E.PAYCHECK_HEADER_ID
                   AND E.PAY_TYPE_ID = F.ID
                   AND D.DATE_PAID = '29-JUL-1994'
                   AND B.ID IN (641, 2014)
   GROUP BY        B.FIRST_NAME,
                   B.LAST_NAME,
                   C.TITLE_NAME
```

First Name	Last Name	Title Name	Sum(Amount)
Rodney	Albright	Human Resources Generalist	$8,166.08
George	Adam	Chief Executive	$961.80

Although this particular example is probably not realistic from a business perspective, that's ok. Our purpose is to consider ways to warehouse the data which can still be done.

Star Schema Design

As discussed already, the purpose of this book is to examine some of the methods of populating a star schema and not to examine how to design such a schema. While those two tasks can be somewhat interconnected, we will assume that the stars have been designed and we have been tasked with writing the ETL. The rest of the book will be devoted to explaining how to populate each of the star schema designs provided in the chapters that follow. Before we begin this in-depth practice, let us examine some of the techniques used when writing ETL.

5
APPROACH TO WRITING ETL

Any craftsman uses a three-pronged approach to creating a product. The point is not that every job only has three steps but that each job generally accomplishes three things once the requirements have been finalized. Consider the process of a carpenter building a table. The raw materials are purchased and taken to the carpenter's workshop (step one). The workshop is the place in which the raw materials are measured, trimmed, and sanded. In the workshop, the carpenter molds the raw materials according to the design (step two). The workshop is not a place in which the customer belongs. The customer is only allowed to see the final product once it has been delivered to the store from which it will be sold (step three).

Data Warehouse developers take a similar approach when they restructure data to make it optimal for analysis. As the name suggests, an ETL job (Extract, Transform, and Load) uses a three-pronged approach to place data into a data warehouse. Data will be extracted from the source system, transformed so that it is appropriate for the type of analysis needed by the customer, and loaded into the data warehouse. Just as in the example of the carpenter working, the ETL developer needs a similar intermediate area (workshop) called a staging area in which the data is transformed (step two of the three-pronged approach). The raw data, from the source system, is placed into this area so that the data can be restructured and then placed into the data warehouse for analysis by the customer. As with the carpenter in his workshop, the staging area is only for the ETL developer to use. Customers only have access to the data once it has been delivered from the staging area into the area used for presentation.

Basic ETL Steps

The steps below are designed to lay out the basic thought process associated with designing an ETL job that will populate a fact or a dimension table. As with any application development effort, no two developers will take exactly the same approach. That is perfectly fine. There may be (actually, there WILL be) variations within each step.

For example, if a job is pulling data from two different source systems, the extract portion of the job will probably be completed twice. The data from one system will be extracted and staged and then the data from the other system will be extracted and staged. From there it will be transformed and eventually loaded into the data warehouse.

When populating a fact or dimension table, the following things need to occur. The order may be a bit different from job to job but will probably follow this general flow.

Fact Table

1.) Select all necessary data from the source
   a. Measures
   b. Natural keys of the dimension objects
   c. Degenerate dimension objects
2.) Transform the data as needed
   a. Aggregate measures and group by the appropriate objects
   b. Add foreign keys to dimension tables
3.) Delete any existing rows from the fact table that will be replaced by the new data
4.) Load the fact table

Dimension Table

1.) Select all of the necessary dimension attributes from the source
2.) Transform the data as needed
3.) Update any existing records
   a. Existing records are defined as records for which the natural key already exists in the dimension table but having data that changed in the source system
4.) Add the surrogate key to any new records
   a. New records are defined as records for which the natural key does not exist in the dimension table
5.) Add the new records to the dimensions

ETL Step 1 – Extracting Data

One of the interesting challenges of an ETL developer is to determine how to identify the data that needs to be loaded into the data warehouse today. In other words, if data was successfully loaded into the data warehouse yesterday how do we identify the records that need to be loaded into the data warehouse today? Using the salary star that we have been tasked to build, let us consider a few options.

Entire Refresh

From an extraction perspective, this is the simplest method to use. The developer will simply pull everything into the staging area. Please note that this does not necessarily mean that the developer will delete all of the existing data from the target table and reload the entire table. That approach may be taken, although the developer may choose to compare this source data with the data that has already been loaded and only update or insert the delta. The scope of this discussion involves the initial extraction from the source system. Techniques used to populate the target tables in the data warehouse will be discussed later. Consider the following example:

```
DECLARE
    SQLSTMT    VARCHAR2(300);
    TBLCOUNT NUMBER := 0;


BEGIN
```

```
SELECT       COUNT(*) INTO TBLCOUNT
FROM         ALL_TABLES
WHERE        TABLE_NAME = 'STAGE_SALARY_DATA'
             AND OWNER =
             (
                 SELECT       SYS_CONTEXT( 'USERENV', 'CURRENT_SCHEMA' )
                 FROM         DUAL
             );

IF TBLCOUNT > 0 THEN
     EXECUTE IMMEDIATE 'DROP TABLE STAGE_SALARY_DATA';
END IF;

SQLSTMT := 'CREATE TABLE STAGE_SALARY_DATA ';
SQLSTMT := SQLSTMT || 'AS (';
SQLSTMT := SQLSTMT || 'SELECT A.AMOUNT, ';
SQLSTMT := SQLSTMT || 'A.PAY_TYPE_ID, ';
SQLSTMT := SQLSTMT || 'B.CHECK_NUMBER, ';
SQLSTMT := SQLSTMT || 'B.DATE_PAID, ';
SQLSTMT := SQLSTMT || 'B.PAY_PERIOD_BEGIN_DATE, ';
SQLSTMT := SQLSTMT || 'B.PAY_PERIOD_END_DATE, ';
SQLSTMT := SQLSTMT || 'B.APPOINTMENT_ID ';
SQLSTMT := SQLSTMT || 'FROM PAYCHECK_DETAIL A, ';
SQLSTMT := SQLSTMT || 'PAYCHECK_HEADER B ';
SQLSTMT := SQLSTMT || 'WHERE A.PAYCHECK_HEADER_ID = B.ID)';

     EXECUTE IMMEDIATE SQLSTMT;
END;
```

Additional steps are needed to place this data into the fact and dimension tables, which we will examine later. At this point, we are pulling all salary data from the source system into the STAGE_SALARY_DATA table, which is located in the staging area, so that it can be restructured. When the job runs again it will replace the contents of the STAGE_SALARY_DATA table with the updated extract. The updated extract should contain everything that the previous extract contained (assuming that nothing was deleted in the source system since the last time the job ran) plus any additions to the data.

For example, assume that this job runs every night at 10:00 PM. On Sunday night suppose that it pulls in 100,000 records (the entire contents of the PAYCHECK_HEADER and PAYCHECK_DETAILS tables). During business hours on Monday 1,000 records worth of paycheck data are added. On Monday night 101,000 records (the original 100,000 plus the new 1,000) will be pulled. The extract will always include the entire population of data.

The advantages of this approach are:

1.) All data will be pulled. There are no cracks through which the data can fall.
2.) The extraction portion of the ETL logic is fairly simple to write.

The disadvantage of this approach is that

1.)   The size of the extract will grow as time goes on. The time and resources needed to complete the load will only increase. If only a small window of time exists during which this job can be run, it is likely that the job will eventually require more time than that window offers.

Partial Refresh

If an entire extract each day is not practical, a partial refresh is possible, depending on the structure of your source system. A couple of options within this strategy exist.

Based on Timestamp

This approach is only possible if a source system was built so that each record is logged with the date on which it was inserted and updated. So that this example can be used, the source system data in the sample HR system was created this way. In order for this approach to work, a table must be created that will log the date of the last successful refresh for each job. A table such as the following will work:

```
CREATE TABLE LATEST_ETL_REFRESH
(
    ETL_JOB_NAME                    VARCHAR2(100),
    LAST_SUCCESSFUL_REFRESH         DATE
);
```

All records inserted or updated as of the LAST_SUCCESSFUL_REFRESH field will be pulled into the staging area. Consider this example:

```
DECLARE
    SQLSTMT         VARCHAR2(400);
    TBLCOUNT        NUMBER := 0;
    JOBNAME         NUMBER := 0;
    AS_OF_DATE      DATE;

BEGIN
    SELECT      COUNT(*) INTO TBLCOUNT
    FROM        ALL_TABLES
    WHERE       TABLE_NAME = 'STAGE_SALARY_DATA'
                AND OWNER =
                (
                    SELECT      SYS_CONTEXT( 'USERENV', 'CURRENT_SCHEMA' )
                    FROM        DUAL
                );

    IF TBLCOUNT > 0 THEN
            EXECUTE IMMEDIATE 'DROP TABLE STAGE_SALARY_DATA';
    END IF;
```

```
SELECT      COUNT(*) INTO JOBNAME
FROM        LATEST_ETL_REFRESH
WHERE       ETL_JOB_NAME = 'SALARY_DATA_JOB';

IF JOBNAME = 0 THEN
        INSERT INTO LATEST_ETL_REFRESH
        (
            ETL_JOB_NAME,
            LAST_SUCCESSFUL_REFRESH
        )
        VALUES
        (
            'SALARY_DATA_JOB',
            NULL
        );
        COMMIT;
END IF;

SELECT      LAST_SUCCESSFUL_REFRESH INTO AS_OF_DATE
FROM        LATEST_ETL_REFRESH
WHERE       ETL_JOB_NAME = 'SALARY_DATA_JOB';

SQLSTMT := 'CREATE TABLE STAGE_SALARY_DATA ';
SQLSTMT := SQLSTMT || 'AS (';
SQLSTMT := SQLSTMT || 'SELECT A.AMOUNT, ';
SQLSTMT := SQLSTMT || 'A.PAY_TYPE_ID, ';
SQLSTMT := SQLSTMT || 'B.CHECK_NUMBER, ';
SQLSTMT := SQLSTMT || 'B.DATE_PAID, ';
SQLSTMT := SQLSTMT || 'B.PAY_PERIOD_BEGIN_DATE, ';
SQLSTMT := SQLSTMT || 'B.PAY_PERIOD_END_DATE, ';
SQLSTMT := SQLSTMT || 'B.APPOINTMENT_ID ';
SQLSTMT := SQLSTMT || 'FROM PAYCHECK_DETAIL A, ';
SQLSTMT := SQLSTMT || 'PAYCHECK_HEADER B ';
SQLSTMT := SQLSTMT || 'WHERE A.PAYCHECK_HEADER_ID = B.ID ';

IF AS_OF_DATE IS NOT NULL THEN
    SQLSTMT := SQLSTMT || 'AND (A.INSERT_DATE >= ''' ||
    TO_CHAR(AS_OF_DATE,'DD-MON-YYYY') || ''' ';
    SQLSTMT := SQLSTMT || 'OR A.UPDATE_DATE >= ''' ||
    TO_CHAR(AS_OF_DATE,'DD-MON-YYYY') || ''' ';
    SQLSTMT := SQLSTMT || 'OR B.INSERT_DATE >= ''' ||
    TO_CHAR(AS_OF_DATE,'DD-MON-YYYY') || ''' ';
    SQLSTMT := SQLSTMT || 'OR B.UPDATE_DATE >= ''' ||
    TO_CHAR(AS_OF_DATE,'DD-MON-YYYY') || ''')';
END IF;

SQLSTMT := SQLSTMT || ')';
```

```
        EXECUTE IMMEDIATE SQLSTMT;

END;
```

Again, additional steps are needed to place this data into the fact table, which we will examine later. Also, the end of the larger job (not only this piece) will need to update the table holding the date of the last successful refresh for each job if the job is successful.

This code will pull all new or updated records as of the last time that the job ran successfully. Some developers may choose to load all records as of one or two days before the last refresh date to make sure that nothing is accidentally overlooked. It is possible that in an early step of the job, the records are pulled and one hour later, when the job is complete, the date and timestamp is written to the log table. If records were inserted or updated in the source system between this early step of the job (the time that the data was extracted) and the time that the job completed, they may not be picked up the next day. That logic can be incorporated into an ETL job (written in PL/SQL or otherwise) based on the ETL developer's preference or the business requirements.

The advantages of this approach are:

1.) Only the data that is important to the data warehouse is being pulled. With the exception of an intentional overlap to make sure that nothing falls through the cracks, everything that is selected from the source system should be new (or updated) data.
2.) Assuming that there are no massive peaks and valleys in the business process, the amount of data pulled into the staging area each time should remain roughly the same.

The disadvantages of this approach are:

1.) The job is a bit more complex. Additional logic has been added to interact with the table holding the date of the latest refresh in order to identify those records that need to be loaded.
2.) Because of the complexity of number one, this step of the job may take a bit longer to run, although the advantages of pulling in a smaller record set may counterbalance that.
3.) Because the table that contains the date of the latest refresh (the LATEST_ETL_REFRESH table in the example above) will probably be shared by multiple jobs, this job is dependent on the structure of that table to remain unchanged. If that table is altered, it may cause this job to fail.
4.) This is assuming that the source system is structured so that the insert and update dates are stored for each record. If that is not the case, this approach will not work.

Based on Timeframe

While this approach is similar in nature to the Based on Timestamp approach, some differences exist. The Based on Timestamp approach examines the point in time at which a record was inserted or updated while the Based on Timeframe approach examines the point in time for which the transaction applies. An ETL job that uses the Based on Timeframe approach will specify a timeframe (i.e., one month, six months, one year, etc.) and reload all transactions that apply to that timeframe, whether or not they have recently been inserted or updated. Consider this example:

The following record exists in the PAYCHECK_HEADER table, which can be examined with the following SQL statement.

```
SELECT    ID,
          CHECK_NUMBER,
          DATE_PAID,
          PAY_PERIOD_BEGIN_DATE AS PP_BEGIN,
          PAY_PERIOD_END_DATE AS PP_END,
          INSERT_DATE
FROM      PAYCHECK_HEADER
WHERE     ID = 15
```

ID	CHECK_NO	DT_PAID	PP_BEGIN	PP_END	INSERT_DATE
15	000000016	12/7/2001	11/19/2001	12/2/2001	11/30/2001

If an ETL job is using the Based on Timestamp approach, and the job had been successfully run on 12/2/2001, then this record would not be pulled in on or after 12/3/2001 (assuming it had not been updated and assuming there is no logic to pull in a prior day's data). However, if the ETL job is using the Based on Timeframe approach for the DATE_PAID column and that timeframe is 12/1/2001 through 12/31/2001 then this record will be pulled into the staging area each time that the job is run for this timeframe. Even if this record had not been updated since the last time the job ran, if it falls within the specified timeframe it will be loaded again.

A PL/SQL block that uses this approach may look something like this:

```
DECLARE
    SQLSTMT          VARCHAR2(400);
    TBLCOUNT         NUMBER := 0;
    BEGIN_DATE       DATE;
    END_DATE         DATE;
    JOB_DATE         DATE := TRUNC(SYSDATE);

BEGIN
    SELECT      COUNT(*) INTO TBLCOUNT
    FROM        ALL_TABLES
    WHERE       TABLE_NAME = 'STAGE_SALARY_DATA'
                AND OWNER =
                (
                    SELECT      SYS_CONTEXT( 'USERENV', 'CURRENT_SCHEMA' )
                    FROM        DUAL
                );

    IF TBLCOUNT > 0 THEN
            EXECUTE IMMEDIATE 'DROP TABLE STAGE_SALARY_DATA';
    END IF;

    SELECT      TRUNC(CURRENT_DATE,'YEAR'),
                ADD_MONTHS(TRUNC(CURRENT_DATE,'YEAR'),12)-1
                INTO
                BEGIN_DATE,
                END_DATE
```

```
    FROM          DUAL;

    IF TO_CHAR(BEGIN_DATE, 'MONTH') = 'JANUARY' THEN
        BEGIN_DATE := ADD_MONTHS(TRUNC(BEGIN_DATE,'YEAR'),-12);
    END IF;

    SQLSTMT := 'CREATE TABLE STAGE_SALARY_DATA ';
    SQLSTMT := SQLSTMT || 'AS (';
    SQLSTMT := SQLSTMT || 'SELECT A.AMOUNT, ';
    SQLSTMT := SQLSTMT || 'A.PAY_TYPE_ID, ';
    SQLSTMT := SQLSTMT || 'B.CHECK_NUMBER, ';
    SQLSTMT := SQLSTMT || 'B.DATE_PAID, ';
    SQLSTMT := SQLSTMT || 'B.PAY_PERIOD_BEGIN_DATE, ';
    SQLSTMT := SQLSTMT || 'B.PAY_PERIOD_END_DATE, ';
    SQLSTMT := SQLSTMT || 'B.APPOINTMENT_ID ';
    SQLSTMT := SQLSTMT || 'FROM PAYCHECK_DETAIL A, ';
    SQLSTMT := SQLSTMT || 'PAYCHECK_HEADER B ';
    SQLSTMT := SQLSTMT || 'WHERE A.PAYCHECK_HEADER_ID = B.ID ';
    SQLSTMT := SQLSTMT || 'AND B.DATE_PAID BETWEEN ''' ||
TO_CHAR(BEGIN_DATE,'DD-MON-YYYY') || ''' AND ''' || TO_CHAR(END_DATE,'DD-
MON-YYYY') || ''')';

    EXECUTE IMMEDIATE SQLSTMT;
END;
```

This PL/SQL block pulls data for all salary dollars paid in the current calendar year. Each subsequent time that the job is run, all records that were pulled previously are pulled again in addition to any new records pertaining to the current calendar year (independent of when those records were added to or updated in the source system). This will require that the later stages of the job delete the current year's records from the fact table so that they can be replaced with this latest extract, which will be examined a bit later.

The advantages of this approach are:

1.) A smaller subset of data is being pulled into the staging area than is needed for the Entire Refresh approach
2.) Because data that pertains to an entire timeframe is being pulled into the data warehouse, there is a lower chance of data within that timeframe falling through the cracks.

The disadvantages of this approach are:

1.) Any data that changed in the source system outside of the timeframe being pulled for which the job is running (i.e., older data that has been corrected in some way) will not be pulled into the staging area.
2.) The ETL must process the date logic which may be a bit complex. However, as with the Based on Timestamp approach, the advantages of extracting a smaller data set than the Entire Refresh approach may counterbalance that.

3.) This approach requires that the timeframe to which the data applies is stored in the applicable tables in the data warehouse. An ETL job can easily delete rows that pertain to a given timeframe from a fact table that is at a monthly grain. The reference to the month dimension can be used to identify those rows. However, if a dimension table contains product attributes (i.e., product group, product name, product location, product size, etc.) then there is nothing in this table that attaches a product to a particular timeframe. The very purpose of the fact table is to tie an instance of one of the products to a timeframe and to other dimension attributes as well. While this approach can be used to load the fact table, in this example, it cannot be used to load the dimension tables.

ETL Step 1 – Extracting Data Observations

While other approaches exist, these are three approaches that typically work well. It is not necessary to select one approach and use it to populate each table in a given star. As we will see in later sections, it is entirely appropriate to use a hybrid. For example, perhaps the data for the dimension tables is pulled using the Entire Refresh approach and the data for the fact is pulled using the Based on Timestamp approach.

Notice that in each of the three cases, a couple of things happen. First, the data as it exists in the source system is dumped into the staging area. It is a good idea to touch the source system for as short of a time as possible when pulling this data. If a select statement aggregates, groups by, etc. within the source system itself, it may return results in a slower duration. While there is no technical issue with this, the source system owners may not appreciate the resources required on their end to return the results of such a large select statement. Also, if, while testing the data, the star schema is found to contain something that is incorrect it is helpful to examine that data in the original staging table. If this table is truly a copy as it appeared in the source system, it will help to see if the data looked this way in the source system at the time of the load or if a downstream piece of the ETL job caused the error.

Second, notice how this original staging table is always dropped and recreated by the ETL job. While this book is not attempting to advocate a certain syntax, it is suggesting the concept. This will ensure that when the ETL job is implemented, it will not be dependent on separate create table statements for those particular tables. All of that create table logic is already a part of the job. While the contents of the job are a little more complex, the use of the job has been simplified so that it is not dependent on any other database activities before running successfully. The job can be run and as a part of that, the appropriate table will be created, populated, and used. Some examples of this approach will be presented in the chapters that follow.

One potential difficulty with this is that any indexes or permissions that are associated with this table will have to be recreated or re-granted, respectively, each time that it is rebuilt. However, this logic can also be placed into the job. This practice may also make it difficult for a database administrator (DBA) to acquire statistics on these particular tables. As a result, it is probably a good practice to discuss this with a DBA before taking this approach.

ETL Step 2 – Transforming Data

This portion of the job is done in the staging area and is pretty wide open. Whatever needs to be done in order to transform the data so that it fits the data warehouse design can be done here. This staging area is the ETL developer's work area which is off limits to the user. Typically, data is extracted from the source system (step 1) and loaded into a table (or tables) in this area. From here, additional tables may be created to hold the intermediate data as needed until it is ready to be loaded into the data warehouse. The ETL developer will probably spend most of his time creating this piece of the job.

ETL Step 3 – Loading Data

Just as options exist when it comes to extracting data from the source system, options also exist when it comes to loading data into the target table. Generally speaking, one of two approaches can be taken. The decision between the approaches mainly depends on the type of table that is being populated.

Delete Rows and Re-Insert Rows

Using this approach, data from the target table is deleted and then re-inserted. This may refer to all rows that currently exist in the table being deleted and replaced or only a portion of the rows being deleted and replaced. This approach is usually simple when being used to populate fact tables (simply delete and repopulate) and complex when being used to populate dimension tables. Here's why:

Because fact tables contain foreign keys that point to dimensions, truncating a dimension table may not be allowed by the database if foreign key constraints exist and are enabled. Even if the constraints do not exist or are not enabled, the fact table relies on the static nature of the surrogate keys, which should act as each dimension's primary key. For example, suppose that a fact table contains a KEY_EMPLOYEE field that serves as a foreign key pointing to the KEY_EMPLOYEE field (which is the primary key) in the DIM_EMPLOYEE dimension table. If the DIM_EMPLOYEE table contains these two rows (among others) then any rows in a fact table having a KEY_EMPLOYEE value of 6 will refer to John Smith. Those having a KEY_EMPLOYEE value of 7 will refer to Mary Jones.

KEY_EMPLOYEE	EMPLOYEE_NUMBER	FIRST_NAME	LAST_NAME
6	12398457	John	Smith
7	88754123	Mary	Jones

In other words, the integrity of the data warehouse depends on the reassignment of a KEY_EMPLOYEE value of 6 to John Smith and a value of 7 to Mary Jones. If the dimension table is truncated and then repopulated, an additional table, usually referred to as a lookup table, will need to exist that will act as a cross reference between a dimension record's natural key and its surrogate key. The ETL job will compare the incoming EMPLOYEE_NUMBER (assuming that is the natural key) to the EMPLOYEE_NUMBER value in this lookup table and then place the associated KEY_EMPLOYEE value from the lookup table into the KEY_EMPLOYEE column in the dimension table.

One way around this level of complexity for dimension tables involves refreshing both the fact and the dimension table entirely in the same ETL job. This will only work if the dimension is not a conformed dimension. However, due to the large size of some fact tables, it may not be practical to refresh an entire star (perhaps several years' worth of data with millions of rows pertaining to each year) on a regular basis.

Update Existing Rows and Insert New Rows

Using this approach, data from the source system that already exists in the data warehouse is updated if it has changed since the last refresh. If the data is new to the source system as of the time of the last refresh, meaning that it does not yet exist in the data warehouse, it will be inserted.

This approach is simple to implement but may be taxing on system resources. Because a dimension table typically has fewer rows and needs to maintain static surrogate keys, this approach is usually more appropriate for populating a dimension table than a fact table.

Using the same example as above, assume that the EMPLOYEE_NUMBER field is the natural key.

From DIM_EMPLOYEE

KEY_EMPLOYEE	EMPLOYEE_NUMBER	FIRST_NAME	LAST_NAME
6	12398457	John	Smith
7	88754123	Mary	Jones

If Mary Jones gets married and Jason Rogers is hired since the last refresh, then the source system extract will contain the following rows, among others.

From Source System

EMPLOYEE_NUMBER	FIRST_NAME	LAST_NAME
12398457	John	Smith
88754123	Mary	Allen
65987425	Jason	Rogers

The FIRST_NAME and LAST_NAME values from the row having an EMPLOYEE_NUMBER value of 12398457 in the source system extract will be compared to the FIRST_NAME and LAST_NAME values from the row having an EMPLOYEE_NUMBER value of 12398457 in the dimension table. The ETL job will notice that there is no difference between the FIRST_NAME and the LAST_NAME values and will do nothing (or will replace the "old" values with the "new" values, which results in no change).

The FIRST_NAME and LAST_NAME values from the row having an EMPLOYEE_NUMBER value of 88754123 in the source system extract will be compared to the FIRST_NAME and LAST_NAME values from the row having an EMPLOYEE_NUMBER value of 88754123 in the dimension table. The ETL job will notice that the LAST_NAME is different and will replace the value of Jones with the value of Allen.

The ETL job will notice that a row in the dimension table with an EMPLOYEE_NUMBER value of 65987425 does not exist and will insert one. The updated DIM_EMPLOYEE table will now contain the following rows, among others.

DIM_EMPLOYEE (after update)

KEY_EMPLOYEE	EMPLOYEE_NUMBER	FIRST_NAME	LAST_NAME
6	12398457	John	Smith
7	88754123	Mary	Allen
8	65987425	Jason	Rogers

From a technical perspective, this approach can be taken when populating a fact table but will probably be much less efficient than deleting rows and re-inserting.

6
SALARY DATA MONTHLY

Description of the Salary Business Process

Salary dollars are funneled through the payroll system on a bi-weekly basis. The pay period begins on Monday, ends on Sunday (14 days later), and the check is cut the following Friday. The source system contains the salary dollars in the PAYCHECK_DETAIL table, grouped by pay type. The PAYCHECK_DETAIL table contains the total gross wages for each paycheck as well as the breakdown of the taxes and benefits paid. In other words, the system stores the total paid before any deductions and it also stores some (but not all) of the detail that makes up that total. Also, one paycheck will be cut per person, per appointment. In other words, if an individual were to have two concurrent appointments, he will receive two paychecks.

Requirements

The users wish to view salary dollars at a monthly level, based on date paid, for each employee and appointment. Also, because net pay has to be calculated each time that they extract data from the PAYCHECK_DETAIL table, the users are requesting that the data warehouse allow an analyst to easily see the net pay, employee paid benefits, employer paid benefits, and taxes as components of total compensation. The source system stores the total gross wages along with the individual components of gross wages as well as some salary pieces that fall outside of gross wages. The elements that are a part of gross wages but that are withheld from an employee's paycheck are:

- Federal Withholding
- Employee Paid – Health Insurance
- Employee Paid – Dental Insurance
- 401K Employee Contribution
- Employee Paid – FICA OASDI
- Employee Paid – FICA Med

For any given paycheck, the gross wages minus the sum of these elements should result in the net pay. The elements that are given to the employee outside of the gross wages are:

- Employer Paid – FICA OASDI
- Employer Paid – FICA Med
- Employer Paid – Health Insurance
- Employer Paid – Dental Insurance
- 401K Employer Contribution

Based on these requirements, this is the design of this star schema that our ETL will need to populate.

Figure 6-1

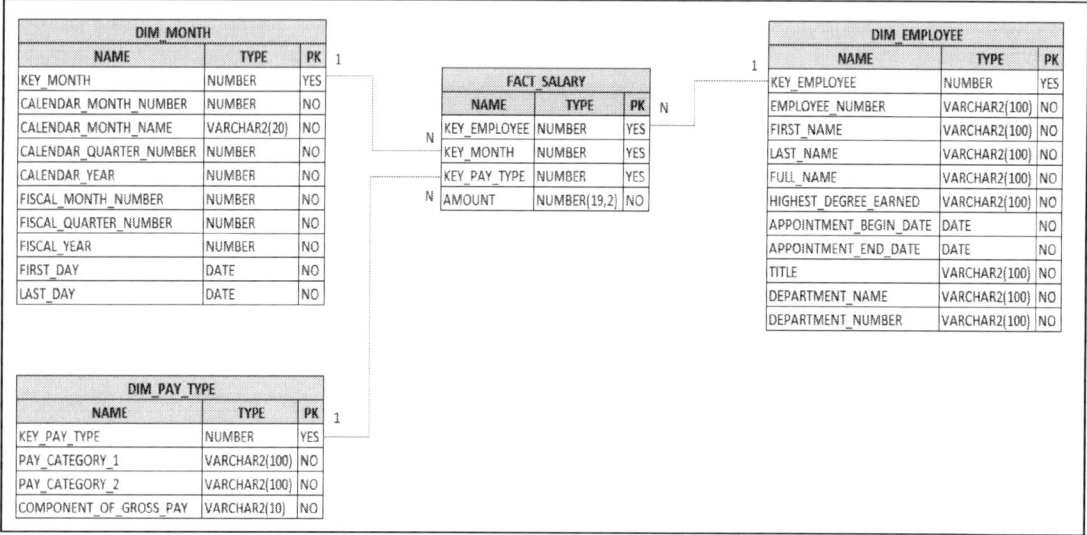

DIM_EMPLOYEE: This dimension table is a type two slowly changing dimension that contains the employee data. The natural key is defined as the combination of:

1.) EMPLOYEE_NUMBER
2.) APPOINTMENT_BEGIN_DATE
3.) TITLE
4.) DEPARTMENT_NUMBER

If any of these four values change for an employee, a new row is added. The source of each column in the ERD above is in the table below.

Column Name	Source
KEY_EMPLOYEE	Not Applicable (Surrogate Key)
EMPLOYEE_ID	EMPLOYEE. ID
APPOINTMENT_ID	APPOINTMENT.ID
EMPLOYEE_NUMBER	EMPLOYEE.EMPLOYEE_NUMBER
FIRST_NAME	EMPLOYEE.FIRST_NAME

Column Name	Source
LAST_NAME	EMPLOYEE.LAST_NAME
FULL_NAME	Derived - Combination of EMPLOYEE.FIRST_NAME and EMPLOYEE.LAST_NAME
HIGHEST_DEGREE_ EARNED	EMPLOYEE.HIGHEST_DEGREE_EARNED
APPOINTMENT_ BEGIN_ DATE	APPOINTMENT.APPOINTMENT_BEGIN_DATE
APPOINTMENT_ END_ DATE	APPOINTMENT.APPOINTMENT_END_DATE
TITLE	TITLE.TITLE_NAME
DEPARTMENT_NAME	DEPARTMENT.DEPARTMENT_NAME
DEPARTMENT_NUMBER	DEPARTMENT.DEPARTMENT_NUMBER

DIM_PAY_TYPE: This dimension table is a type one slowly changing dimension that is based somewhat off of the PAY_TYPE table. The users have defined additional categories to be used in their analysis of the salary data. The source system stores the total wages and then it stores some of the details that make up that total. For example, it does not store the net pay. From the requirements outlined in the section above, this table will be designed so that ALL of the individual components will be stored in the star schema and those elements that make up the gross pay will be flagged as such. Because these categories are not expected to change frequently and since the source system does not contain the categories as they need to exist in the data warehouse, this table will not be populated via ETL. The following data will be placed there manually.

PAY_CATEGORY_1	PAY_CATEGORY_2	COMPONENT_OF _GROSS_PAY
Net Pay	Wages	Yes
Federal Withholding	Federal Withholding	Yes
Employer Paid Benefit	Employer Paid FICA OASDI	No
Employer Paid Benefit	Employer Paid FICA MED	No
Employer Paid Benefit	Employer Paid Health Insurance	No
Employee Paid Benefit	Employee Paid Health Insurance	Yes
Employer Paid Benefit	Employer Paid Dental Insurance	No
Employee Paid Benefit	Employee Paid Dental Insurance	Yes
Employee Paid Benefit	Employee Paid 401K Contribution	Yes
Employer Paid Benefit	Employer Paid 401K Contribution	No
Employee Paid Benefit	Employee Paid FICA OASDI	Yes
Employee Paid Benefit	Employee Paid FICA MED	Yes
Unknown	Unknown	Unknown

DIM_MONTH: This is a standard type zero date dimension table at the monthly level. This dimension has no system source and will be populated by the ETL developer.

FACT_SALARY: This is a basic fact table that allows the user to analyze salary dollars by month, pay type, and employee. The FACT_SALARY.AMOUNT value will come from the PAYCHECK_DETAIL.AMOUNT column. The three key values will refer to their associated dimension tables. It is important to remember from the requirements that the "users wish to view salary dollars at a monthly level, based on date paid." This means that the KEY_MONTH in this fact table must be derived from the PAYCHECK_HEADER.DATE_PAID column.

Strategy for ETL

This salary data star contains one fact table and three dimension tables. Because the addition of new rows into the fact table will require references to their respective dimension tables, the dimension tables must be created and updated first. While it is possible to populate the three dimension tables and the fact table as one PL/SQL procedure, it is probably smarter to write a separate procedure for each table. If a dimension is a conformed dimension (referred to by multiple fact tables) the procedure to populate it can be called by other procedures.

Populating the DIM_EMPLOYEE Dimension

We will begin by populating the DIM_EMPLOYEE table. Remember from chapter five that the goal of an ETL job that populates a dimension table is to accomplish the following.

      1.) Select all of the necessary dimension attributes from the source
      2.) Transform the data as needed
      3.) Update any existing records
          a. Defined as records for which the natural key already exists in the dimension table but having data that changed in the source system
      4.) Add the surrogate key to any new rows
          a. Defined as records for which the natural key does not exist in the dimension table
      5.) Add the new rows to the dimensions

In order to accomplish number one, we need to consider our approach to pulling the data for this dimension. Because the source system provides the date inserted, let's move forward with what we have been calling the "Based on Timestamp" approach. Remember from chapter five that this will be best implemented with a table to log the last successful refresh date.

As we consider creating this log table, let's also remember that it will be important to log any errors raised by the procedure. As a result, perhaps these two requirements (log the last successful refresh date and log any errors) can be accomplished using the same table. We can create one table into which a row will be inserted each time that a job (1) begins, (2) completes successfully, and (3) completes unsuccessfully. In each case, the date and time of each event will be stored in the table. In the case of number three, the exception that is raised should be stored in the table as well. This table can be used to both find the last successful refresh date and time as well as to identify the reason as to why a job resulted in an error for any job (not only this job). Consider the following script:

```
CREATE TABLE ETL_JOB_STATUS
(
    ID                   NUMBER,
    ETL_JOB_NAME         VARCHAR2(100),
    STATUS_NAME          VARCHAR2(100),
    STATUS_TIMESTAMP     TIMESTAMP(9),
    ERROR_MESSAGE        VARCHAR2(255),
    CONSTRAINT PK_ETL_JOB_STATUS PRIMARY KEY (ID)
);
CREATE SEQUENCE SEQ_ETL_JOB_STATUS
START WITH 1
NOMAXVALUE;
CREATE OR REPLACE TRIGGER TRG_BI_ETL_JOB_STATUS
BEFORE INSERT ON ETL_JOB_STATUS
 FOR EACH ROW
  BEGIN
   SELECT SEQ_ETL_JOB_STATUS.NEXTVAL INTO :NEW.ID FROM DUAL;
  END;
```

This script will create the table, create a sequence so that a unique identifier for each record can be stored, and create a trigger that will auto increment this unique identifier. Run the script in Oracle so that these objects are created.

Unique identifiers (surrogate keys) will need to exist in the dimension table as well. While ETL tools and database vendors offer various ways of creating these surrogate keys, this job will use an Oracle sequence to increment. The ways in which the ETL job will use this sequence will be discussed later. For now, run this script to create the sequence:

```
CREATE SEQUENCE SEQ_DIM_EMPLOYEE
START WITH 0
MINVALUE 0
NOMAXVALUE
INCREMENT BY 1;
```

As a final piece of the setup, the DIM_EMPLOYEE table will need to be created so that this job can populate it. Run the following to create the DIM_EMPLOYEE table:

```
CREATE TABLE DIM_EMPLOYEE
 (
    KEY_EMPLOYEE               NUMBER,
    EMPLOYEE_NUMBER            VARCHAR2(100),
    FIRST_NAME                 VARCHAR2(100),
    LAST_NAME                  VARCHAR2(100),
    FULL_NAME                  VARCHAR2(100),
    HIGHEST_DEGREE_EARNED      VARCHAR2(100),
    APPOINTMENT_BEGIN_DATE     DATE,
    APPOINTMENT_END_DATE       DATE,
    TITLE                      VARCHAR2(100),
```

```
          DEPARTMENT_NAME              VARCHAR2(100),
          DEPARTMENT_NUMBER            VARCHAR2(100)
    );
```

Now that the infrastructure has been created, we can move forward with actually populating the dimension. We will call the procedure LOAD_EMPLOYEE_DIMENSION. Consider this code (not complete) for the preliminary portion of the job. The preliminary portion of the job may be treated as certain housekeeping activities that must occur before it can accomplish any of the five items listed on page 30.

Lines 1 – 11

Line	Code
1	CREATE OR REPLACE PROCEDURE LOAD_EMPLOYEE_DIMENSION
2	
3	AS
4	
5	SQLSTMT VARCHAR2(2000);
6	TBLCOUNT NUMBER := 0;
7	AS_OF_DATE DATE;
8	ERR_MSG VARCHAR2(200);
9	MAX_KEY_EMPLOYEE NUMBER;
10	NEXT_SEQ_VAL NUMBER;
11	

These lines contain the standard beginning of the PL/SQL procedure. The procedure is named, variables are declared, and the job begins.

Lines 12 – 30

Line	Code
12	BEGIN
13	--Log the beginning of the job
14	INSERT INTO ETL_JOB_STATUS
15	(
16	ID,
17	ETL_JOB_NAME,
18	STATUS_NAME,
19	STATUS_TIMESTAMP
20	)

Line	Code
21	VALUES
22	(
23	SEQ_ETL_JOB_STATUS.NEXTVAL,
24	'LOAD_EMPLOYEE_DIMENSION',
25	'IN PROGRESS',
26	SYSTIMESTAMP
27	);
28	
29	COMMIT;
30	

The first step, once the variables have been declared, is to log the beginning of the job. The ETL_JOB_STATUS table will show that this job is currently in progress as of the date and time. This is important to do first since there may be other areas of the Business Intelligence environment that refer to this table to see the status of the job. For example, a user may need to check to make sure that ETL is not running before accessing a certain report. Also, this table may be used to do some analysis on the duration of each job.

Lines 31 – 45

Line	Code
31	--Make sure that the sequence that populates the key_employee is set to begin
32	--at the next integer
33	SELECT NVL(MAX(KEY_EMPLOYEE), 0) INTO MAX_KEY_EMPLOYEE FROM DIM_EMPLOYEE;
34	SELECT SEQ_DIM_EMPLOYEE.NEXTVAL INTO NEXT_SEQ_VAL FROM DUAL;
35	
36	IF NEXT_SEQ_VAL <> MAX_KEY_EMPLOYEE THEN
37	SQLSTMT := 'ALTER SEQUENCE SEQ_DIM_EMPLOYEE INCREMENT BY '
38	|| ((NEXT_SEQ_VAL - MAX_KEY_EMPLOYEE) * -1)
39	|| ' MINVALUE 0';
40	EXECUTE IMMEDIATE SQLSTMT;
41	SELECT SEQ_DIM_EMPLOYEE.NEXTVAL INTO NEXT_SEQ_VAL FROM DUAL;
42	SQLSTMT := 'ALTER SEQUENCE SEQ_DIM_EMPLOYEE INCREMENT BY 1 MINVALUE 0';
43	EXECUTE IMMEDIATE SQLSTMT;

Line	Code
44	END IF;
45	

Next, the Oracle sequence used to create the KEY_EMPLOYEE value (the DIM_EMPLOYEE table's surrogate key) is set. A sequence in Oracle is basically a database object that will increment by a certain amount (one in this case) each time that it is used. Sometimes developers create a sequence that begins with the number one and then just let it go. This is not a bad idea, but what happens if this ETL gets as far as creating 100 new KEY_EMPLOYEE values and then, before inserting the records into the DIM_EMPLOYEE table, it fails? If the problem is fixed and the job is rerun, the sequence will assume that those 100 key values have been used and create 100 more with values above what was already used. In other words, the KEY_EMPLOYEE values will not be sequential. A large gap will exist. This will not cause a data integrity issue with the data warehouse, but in the interest of not letting numbers get too high too quickly this job will try to prevent that from happening. The maximum KEY_EMPLOYEE value is compared to the next value that the sequence plans to use and the sequence is adjusted to one above the maximum KEY_EMPLOYEE value if necessary.

Extract From the Source System

Now that the preliminary steps have been written, consider this code to be used when extracting data from the source system.

Lines 46 – 60

Line	Code
46	--If the table exists, drop it. If not, do nothing. The table will be
47	--created below.
48	SELECT COUNT(*) INTO TBLCOUNT
49	FROM ALL_TABLES
50	WHERE TABLE_NAME = 'STAGE_EMPLOYEE_DATA'
51	AND OWNER =
52	(
53	SELECT SYS_CONTEXT('USERENV', 'CURRENT_SCHEMA')
54	FROM DUAL
55	);
56	
57	IF TBLCOUNT > 0 THEN
58	EXECUTE IMMEDIATE 'DROP TABLE STAGE_EMPLOYEE_DATA';
59	END IF;
60	

Notice that the STAGE_EMPLOYEE_DATA table is always dropped and recreated with the data set. Although creating the table outside of this job and then designing the job to truncate the table and insert records will certainly work, it will be more tedious. A create table statement for the STAGE_EMPLOYEE_DATA table, in that case, will need to accompany the implementation instructions for this job and be executed successfully before the job is run for the first time. If at some point additional data needs to be placed into the DIM_EMPLOYEE table, the structure of the STAGE_EMPLOYEE_DATA table must be altered outside of this ETL job and then the insert statement within the job must be edited in that order. If these actions are not timed correctly, the job will fail.

With the drop and recreate approach, the job will drop the STAGE_EMPLOYEE_DATA table if it exists and then recreate it based on the structure of the data being pulled from the source system. If an additional column needs to be extracted from the source system, it is as simple as inserting it into the select list and running the job. As discussed in an earlier chapter, any permissions or indexes that must be granted or created for this table will be lost when the table is dropped. However, the logic to add these items can be placed into the job as well. While neither approach is right or wrong, dropping and recreating a staging table may make maintenance easier.

Lines 61 – 99

Line	Code
61	--The procedure will pull all records that were inserted into (or updated in) the
62	-- EMPLOYEE table or APPOINTMENT table since the date of the last successful
63	-- refresh date from the ETL_JOB_STATUS. The data from the source system is
64	-- "dumped" into the STAGE_EMPLOYEE_DATA table in the staging area.
65	SELECT MAX(TRUNC(STATUS_TIMESTAMP)) INTO AS_OF_DATE
66	FROM ETL_JOB_STATUS
67	WHERE ETL_JOB_NAME = 'LOAD_EMPLOYEE_DIMENSION'
68	AND STATUS_NAME = 'SUCCESSFULLY COMPLETED';
69	SQLSTMT := 'CREATE TABLE STAGE_EMPLOYEE_DATA '
70	|| 'AS ('
71	|| 'SELECT '
72	|| 'D.EMPLOYEE_NUMBER, '
73	|| 'D.FIRST_NAME, '
74	|| 'D.LAST_NAME, '
75	|| 'D.HIGHEST_DEGREE_EARNED, '
76	|| 'A.APPOINTMENT_BEGIN_DATE, '
77	|| 'A.APPOINTMENT_END_DATE, '
78	|| 'B.TITLE_NAME TITLE, '
79	|| 'C.DEPARTMENT_NAME, '
80	|| 'C.DEPARTMENT_NUMBER '

Line	Code
81	|| 'FROM APPOINTMENT A, '
82	|| 'TITLE B, '
83	|| 'DEPARTMENT C, '
84	|| 'EMPLOYEE D '
85	|| 'WHERE A.DEPARTMENT_ID = C.ID '
86	|| 'AND A.TITLE_ID = B.ID '
87	|| 'AND A.EMPLOYEE_ID = D.ID ';
88	
89	IF AS_OF_DATE IS NOT NULL THEN
90	SQLSTMT := SQLSTMT || 'AND (A.INSERT_DATE >= ''' || TO_CHAR(AS_OF_DATE,'DD-MON-YYYY') || ''' '
91	|| 'OR A.UPDATE_DATE >= ''' || TO_CHAR(AS_OF_DATE,'DD-MON-YYYY') || ''' '
92	|| 'OR D.INSERT_DATE >= ''' || TO_CHAR(AS_OF_DATE,'DD-MON-YYYY') || ''' '
93	|| 'OR D.UPDATE_DATE >= ''' || TO_CHAR(AS_OF_DATE,'DD-MON-YYYY') || ''')';
94	END IF;
95	
96	SQLSTMT := SQLSTMT || ')';
97	
98	EXECUTE IMMEDIATE SQLSTMT;
99	

Notice that this step is finding the latest date on which this job finished successfully (based on the ETL_JOB_STATUS table) and pulling only those records that were inserted or updated into the source system on or after that date. In other words, this is how this job is enforcing the Based on Timestamp approach. At this point, the STAGE_EMPLOYEE_DATA table contains the data that will eventually reside in the DIM_EMPLOYEE table. Some of the records in the STAGE_EMPLOYEE_DATA table are not yet in the DIM_EMPLOYEE table and will be added for the first time. Other records may already exist in the DIM_EMPLOYEE table, but will be updated (i.e., the LAST_NAME column may change due to a marriage or the HIGHEST_DEGREE_EARNED column may change due to somebody furthering their education) based on new data about those records in the STAGE_EMPLOYEE_DATA table.

Transform the Data

Remember from the design that the FULL_NAME column is a concatenation of the FIRST_NAME and LAST_NAME columns. This will be accomplished in the transform area of the job. Consider the following code.

Lines 100 – 115

Line	Code
100	--The full name field is created for each record. The data is then placed
101	--into the STAGE_EMPLOYEE_DATA_TRANSFORM table (table is dropped if
102	-- it exists and then created below).
103	SELECT COUNT(*) INTO TBLCOUNT
104	FROM ALL_TABLES
105	WHERE TABLE_NAME = 'STAGE_EMPLOYEE_DATA_TRANSFORM'
106	AND OWNER =
107	(
108	SELECT SYS_CONTEXT('USERENV', 'CURRENT_SCHEMA')
109	FROM DUAL
110	);
111	
112	IF TBLCOUNT > 0 THEN
113	EXECUTE IMMEDIATE 'DROP TABLE STAGE_EMPLOYEE_DATA_TRANSFORM';
114	END IF;
115	

This portion of the job drops the STAGE_EMPLOYEE_DATA_TRANSFORM table if it exists.

Lines 116 – 132

Line	Code
116	SQLSTMT := 'CREATE TABLE STAGE_EMPLOYEE_DATA_TRANSFORM '
117	|| 'AS ('
118	|| 'SELECT '
119	|| 'A.EMPLOYEE_NUMBER, '
120	|| 'A.FIRST_NAME, '
121	|| 'A.LAST_NAME, '
122	|| 'A.FIRST_NAME || " " || A.LAST_NAME FULL_NAME, '
123	|| 'A.HIGHEST_DEGREE_EARNED, '
124	|| 'A.APPOINTMENT_BEGIN_DATE, '
125	|| 'A.APPOINTMENT_END_DATE, '

Line	Code
126	|| 'A.TITLE, '
127	|| 'A.DEPARTMENT_NAME, '
128	|| 'A.DEPARTMENT_NUMBER '
129	|| 'FROM STAGE_EMPLOYEE_DATA A)';
130	
131	EXECUTE IMMEDIATE SQLSTMT;
132	

This portion of the job will concatenate the FIRST_NAME and LAST_NAME columns to form the FULL_NAME column. It, then, places all of the data (FULL_NAME plus the rest) into the STAGE_EMPLOYEE_DATA_TRANSFORM table.

Add Records to the Dimension Table

Once the data has been placed into the STAGE_EMPLOYEE_DATA_TRANSFORM table, it is time for the job to examine the way in which the data needs to be integrated into the DIM_EMPLOYEE table. In other words, which records are new records and which records should update existing records? There are many ways of accomplishing this and it is up to each developer to use her creativity to find the best way for that situation. In this case, the job will create two additional tables in the staging area. One will hold records that need to be inserted and the other will hold records that need to be updated. If questions arise regarding which records were inserted and which were updated, this will allow the ETL developer to refer to these tables in the staging area and easily identify those records.

Identify Records For Update

This portion of the job will identify those records that already exist in the DIM_EMPLOYEE table but have data that needs to be updated.

Lines 133 – 148

Line	Code
133	--Any records containing data that was updated (not new records) as compared
134	--to DIM_APPOINTMENT are placed into the STAGE_APPT_DATA_LOAD_UPD
135	--table (table is dropped if it exists and then created below).
136	SELECT COUNT(*) INTO TBLCOUNT
137	FROM ALL_TABLES
138	WHERE TABLE_NAME = 'STAGE_EMPLOYEE_DATA_LOAD_UPD'
139	AND OWNER =
140	(
141	SELECT SYS_CONTEXT('USERENV', 'CURRENT_SCHEMA')

Line	Code
142	FROM DUAL
143	);
144	
145	IF TBLCOUNT > 0 THEN
146	EXECUTE IMMEDIATE 'DROP TABLE STAGE_EMPLOYEE_DATA_LOAD_UPD';
147	END IF;
148	

The STAGE_EMPLOYEE_DATA_LOAD_UPD table is created using the same drop and recreate procedure as above.

Lines 149 – 179

Line	Code
149	SQLSTMT := 'CREATE TABLE STAGE_EMPLOYEE_DATA_LOAD_UPD '
150	|| 'AS ('
151	|| 'SELECT '
152	|| 'A.EMPLOYEE_NUMBER, '
153	|| 'A.FIRST_NAME, '
154	|| 'A.LAST_NAME, '
155	|| 'A.FULL_NAME, '
156	|| 'A.HIGHEST_DEGREE_EARNED, '
157	|| 'A.APPOINTMENT_BEGIN_DATE, '
158	|| 'A.APPOINTMENT_END_DATE, '
159	|| 'A.TITLE, '
160	|| 'A.DEPARTMENT_NAME, '
161	|| 'A.DEPARTMENT_NUMBER, '
162	|| 'B.KEY_EMPLOYEE '
163	|| 'FROM STAGE_EMPLOYEE_DATA_TRANSFORM A, '
164	|| 'DIM_EMPLOYEE B '
165	|| 'WHERE A.APPOINTMENT_BEGIN_DATE = B.APPOINTMENT_BEGIN_DATE '
166	|| 'AND A.TITLE = B.TITLE '
167	|| 'AND A.DEPARTMENT_NUMBER = B.DEPARTMENT_NUMBER '
168	|| 'AND A.EMPLOYEE_NUMBER = B.EMPLOYEE_NUMBER '
169	|| 'AND (NVL(A.DEPARTMENT_NAME,-1) <>

Line	Code
	NVL(B.DEPARTMENT_NAME,-1) '
170	| | 'OR NVL(TO_CHAR(A.APPOINTMENT_END_DATE),-1) <> '
171	| | 'NVL(TO_CHAR(B.APPOINTMENT_END_DATE),-1) '
172	| | 'OR NVL(A.FIRST_NAME,-1) <> NVL(B.FIRST_NAME,-1) '
173	| | 'OR NVL(A.LAST_NAME,-1) <> NVL(B.LAST_NAME,-1) '
174	| | 'OR NVL(A.FULL_NAME,-1) <> NVL(B.FULL_NAME,-1) '
175	| | 'OR NVL(A.HIGHEST_DEGREE_EARNED,-1) <> NVL(B.HIGHEST_DEGREE_EARNED,-1) '
176	| | ')) ';
177	
178	EXECUTE IMMEDIATE SQLSTMT;
179	

This SQL statement identifies those records from the extract that already exist in the DIM_EMPLOYEE table but have data that has changed. Remember that when the extract is compared to the existing data in the dimension table, a new row is added to the dimension if that natural key does not exist. Otherwise, that row is updated if any of the other data (data that is not a part of the natural key) has changed. Notice that this select statement is pulling data from two tables, STAGE_EMPLOYEE_DATA_TRANSFORM and DIM_EMPLOYEE. The two tables are being joined on the employee's natural key (lines 165 – 168) so that only those records with a natural key from the STAGE_EMPLOYEE_DATA_TRANSFORM table that also exists in the DIM_EMPLOYEE table will be included. All other data is compared between the two tables (lines 169 – 175) and only those records for which that non-natural key data differs are being placed into the STAGE_EMPLOYEE_DATA_LOAD_UPD table. Remember from the requirements that the DIM_EMPLOYEE dimension is a type two slowly changing dimension. This means that if the natural key changes for a given employee, a new row is added to the dimension table so that the historical data is made available. If this were a type one slowly changing dimension, any changes to employee data would simply be overwritten. With a type one slowly changing dimension, the select statement above would probably join on the EMPLOYEE_NUMBER field only and then compare ALL other columns to attempt to find any differences in the data.

From an ETL developer's perspective, the difference between populating a type one and a type two slowly changing dimension is in the comparison of the natural key between the extract (STAGE_EMPLOYEE_DATA_TRANSFORM table) and the dimension data as it currently exists (DIM_EMPLOYEE table). A type two slowly changing dimension has a larger natural key (larger, meaning more columns) than a type one.

Update Existing Records

Now that the records that need to be updated have been identified and placed into the STAGE_EMPLOYEE_DATA_LOAD_UPD table, it is time to update the DIM_EMPLOYEE table with this data. This portion of the job will accomplish that.

Line 180 – 187

Line	Code
180	--Because the STAGE_EMPLOYEE_DATA_LOAD_UPD table is dropped and recreated
181	--each time, the index that is necessary to make the update statement work
182	--must be rebuilt each time. An organizational rule of some sort will need
183	--to make sure that there is no conflict with the name.
184	SQLSTMT := 'CREATE INDEX INDEX_STAGE_KEY_EMPLOYEE ON '
185	|| 'STAGE_EMPLOYEE_DATA_LOAD_UPD (KEY_EMPLOYEE)';
186	EXECUTE IMMEDIATE SQLSTMT;
187	

In order to update the DIM_EMPLOYEE table, we must join the STAGE_EMPLOYEE_DATA_LOAD_UPD table to the DIM_EMPLOYEE table on the KEY_EMPLOYEE in the update statement. This will take quite a while without an index. Adding one outside of the job will be inadequate since this table is dropped and recreated. As a result, the job must add this index each time.

Other pieces of software may offer other options with regards to increasing the efficiency of your code. My intent is not to make a statement about when and how to use Oracle indexes but to encourage you to use the tools available to you to make an ETL job as efficient as possible. The duration of the ETL job must fit into a practical timeframe. If it does not, improvements need to be considered. Discussing questions like these with a DBA will probably be a good practice.

Lines 188 – 215

Line	Code
188	SQLSTMT := 'UPDATE DIM_EMPLOYEE A '
189	|| 'SET (A.APPOINTMENT_END_DATE, '
190	|| 'A.DEPARTMENT_NAME, '
191	|| 'A.FIRST_NAME, '
192	|| 'A.LAST_NAME, '
193	|| 'A.FULL_NAME, '
194	|| 'A.HIGHEST_DEGREE_EARNED) = '
195	|| '(SELECT B.APPOINTMENT_END_DATE, '
196	|| 'B.DEPARTMENT_NAME, '
197	|| 'B.FIRST_NAME, '
198	|| 'B.LAST_NAME, '
199	|| 'B.FULL_NAME, '
200	|| 'B.HIGHEST_DEGREE_EARNED '

Line	Code
201	|| 'FROM STAGE_EMPLOYEE_DATA_LOAD_UPD B '
202	|| 'WHERE A.KEY_EMPLOYEE = B.KEY_EMPLOYEE)'
203	|| 'WHERE EXISTS '
204	|| '(SELECT B.APPOINTMENT_END_DATE, '
205	|| 'B.DEPARTMENT_NAME, '
206	|| 'B.FIRST_NAME, '
207	|| 'B.LAST_NAME, '
208	|| 'B.FULL_NAME, '
209	|| 'B.HIGHEST_DEGREE_EARNED '
210	|| 'FROM STAGE_EMPLOYEE_DATA_LOAD_UPD B '
211	|| 'WHERE A.KEY_EMPLOYEE = B.KEY_EMPLOYEE)';
212	
213	EXECUTE IMMEDIATE SQLSTMT;
214	COMMIT;
215	

These lines of code are updating the DIM_EMPLOYEE table. When using a database that requires a commit, such as Oracle, there is some debate with regards to the frequency of that commit. Some say that the commit should be executed every 1,000 transactions or so, which would require that we write this job to loop through the transactions and execute the commit when the counter reaches 1,000. Others say that the transaction should only be committed at the end so that the entire transaction can be rolled back. I have chosen to go with the second option in writing this job so as not to add additional complexity while trying to simply explain the update. The ETL tools on the market will probably offer an option to commit after a certain number of records. Consider the pros and cons of each option and make a decision that best fits the needs of your organization.

Identify Records to Be Inserted

This portion of the job will identify those records that do not exist in the DIM_EMPLOYEE table and need to be inserted.

Lines 216 – 234

Line	Code
216	--Any records containing new records (not data that was updated) are placed
217	--into the STAGE_APPT_DATA_LOAD_NEW table (table is dropped if it exists
218	--and then created below). The KEY_APPOINTMENT is created using the
219	--SEQ_DIM_APPOINTMENT sequence. This sequence is incremented directly in
220	--the ETL job (see below) as opposed to using a trigger, so that it will be

Line	Code
221	--more efficient.
222	SELECT COUNT(*) INTO TBLCOUNT
223	FROM ALL_TABLES
224	WHERE TABLE_NAME = 'STAGE_EMPLOYEE_DATA_LOAD_NEW'
225	AND OWNER =
226	(
227	SELECT SYS_CONTEXT('USERENV', 'CURRENT_SCHEMA')
228	FROM DUAL
229	);
230	
231	IF TBLCOUNT > 0 THEN
232	EXECUTE IMMEDIATE 'DROP TABLE STAGE_EMPLOYEE_DATA_LOAD_NEW';
233	END IF;
234	

This portion of the job drops the STAGE_EMPLOYEE_DATA_LOAD_NEW table if it exists.

Lines 235 – 262

Line	Code
235	SQLSTMT := 'CREATE TABLE STAGE_EMPLOYEE_DATA_LOAD_NEW '
236	|| 'AS ('
237	|| 'SELECT '
238	|| 'SEQ_DIM_EMPLOYEE.NEXTVAL AS KEY_EMPLOYEE, '
238	|| 'A.EMPLOYEE_NUMBER, '
239	|| 'A.FIRST_NAME, '
240	|| 'A.LAST_NAME, '
241	|| 'A.FULL_NAME, '
242	|| 'A.HIGHEST_DEGREE_EARNED, '
243	|| 'A.APPOINTMENT_BEGIN_DATE, '
244	|| 'A.APPOINTMENT_END_DATE, '
245	|| 'A.TITLE, '
246	|| 'A.DEPARTMENT_NAME, '
247	|| 'A.DEPARTMENT_NUMBER '
248	|| 'FROM STAGE_EMPLOYEE_DATA_TRANSFORM A '

Line	Code
249	|| 'WHERE (NVL(TO_CHAR(A.APPOINTMENT_END_DATE),-1), '
250	|| 'A.TITLE, '
251	|| 'A.DEPARTMENT_NUMBER, '
252	|| 'A.EMPLOYEE_NUMBER) '
253	|| 'NOT IN '
254	|| '(SELECT '
255	|| 'NVL(TO_CHAR(APPOINTMENT_END_DATE),-1), '
256	|| 'TITLE, '
257	|| 'DEPARTMENT_NUMBER, '
258	|| 'EMPLOYEE_NUMBER '
259	|| 'FROM DIM_EMPLOYEE)) ';
260	
261	EXECUTE IMMEDIATE SQLSTMT;
262	

This SQL statement identifies those records that were pulled from the source having a natural key that does not exist in the DIM_EMPLOYEE table. Surrogate keys are assigned to those records and they are placed in the STAGE_EMPLOYEE_DATA_LOAD_NEW table. Line 238 uses the SEQ_DIM_EMPLOYEE sequence to apply the surrogate key to each new record.

Insert New Records
This portion of the job will place the new records into the DIM_EMPLOYEE table.

Lines 263 – 282

Line	Code
263	--The new records are added to the DIM_EMPLOYEE table.
264	SQLSTMT := 'INSERT INTO DIM_EMPLOYEE '
265	|| '(KEY_EMPLOYEE, '
266	|| 'EMPLOYEE_NUMBER, '
267	|| 'FIRST_NAME, '
268	|| 'LAST_NAME, '
269	|| 'FULL_NAME, '
270	|| 'HIGHEST_DEGREE_EARNED, '
271	|| 'APPOINTMENT_BEGIN_DATE, '
272	|| 'APPOINTMENT_END_DATE, '
273	|| 'TITLE, '

Line	Code
274	| | 'DEPARTMENT_NAME,'
275	| | 'DEPARTMENT_NUMBER)'
276	| | 'SELECT A.*'
277	| | 'FROM STAGE_EMPLOYEE_DATA_LOAD_NEW A';
278	
279	EXECUTE IMMEDIATE SQLSTMT;
280	COMMIT;
281	END;

The records are inserted and the transaction is committed. Running this piece of code should result in 55,544 rows being placed into the DIM_EMPLOYEE table.

Review the ETL Job

This procedure is designed to be executed in the same schema as the source system tables are located. Let us examine a few of the approaches taken with this job:

1.) Because the job is always comparing the data in the EMPLOYEE table (in the source system) to the DIM_EMPLOYEE table, it is designed to be run as often as necessary with no negative impact. In other words, running the job twice will not result in the records in the DIM_EMPLOYEE table being duplicated, which is important when designing the job.

2.) Notice that while the KEY_EMPLOYEE column (the surrogate key) in the DIM_EMPLOYEE table is that table's primary key, it is not defined as the primary key in the database. This is a judgment call on the part of the designer. While setting this column as the primary key in the database will prevent records from containing the same surrogate key (a safe precaution), it may also slow the job. Each insertion will require that the database check all of the other KEY_EMPLOYEE values to make sure that there is no duplication. This job is designed to find the highest KEY_EMPLOYEE value and set the sequence to be one more than that value. Also, this job is the only method by which the DIM_EMPLOYEE table should be populated, so the assignment of the primary key should be controlled (although that doesn't mean that a duplicate key couldn't happen somehow). In this job, we've decided to err on the side of efficiency, which may require that we write a SQL statement down the road that will alert us of duplicate primary key values.

3.) One thought that may cross the mind of an ETL developer is to design the ETL job so that it will always delete all records from the DIM_EMPLOYEE table and repopulate it each time. While this may sound good at this stage of developing the ETL job, remember that eventually a fact table will be referring to this dimension table. If the data in the DIM_EMPLOYEE table is wiped out and repopulated, the surrogate keys may not be applied to each record exactly as they were before. As a result, the foreign keys that the fact table uses to refer to the DIM_EMPLOYEE table may be incorrect, which will require that the fact table be entirely repopulated as well. Appending to the dimension table is the approach that needs to be taken, unless it is appropriate that any fact table that refers to a given dimension (which may be more than one if it is a conformed dimension) should be repopulated as well.

Updates

As we review our job, there may be some opportunities to improve.

1.) Notice that in deciding which records to pull from the EMPLOYEE table, the ETL job always pulls records that were inserted on or after the date of the latest successful refresh. While this is fine during normal operations, what happens if the table needs to be totally refreshed for some reason (i.e., it underwent a structural change or it was accidentally truncated)? As written, some false data will need to be placed into the ETL_JOB_STATUS table, which is not a good solution. As a result, the job should probably be edited to allow a user to pass a date if necessary.

2.) The users would like to see the APPOINTMENT.ID and the EMPLOYEE.ID columns added to the DIM_EMPLOYEE table. These were not a part of the original requirements.

3.) While I pointed out earlier that my intent is not to get lost in the mechanics of how the code is written, it is worth pointing out that the NOT IN statement in lines 253 through 259 is very inefficient. Searching for a more efficient option is probably a good idea.

We will take a look at this in the enhancements section that follows. As a result of number two, the ERD has been updated:

Figure 6-2

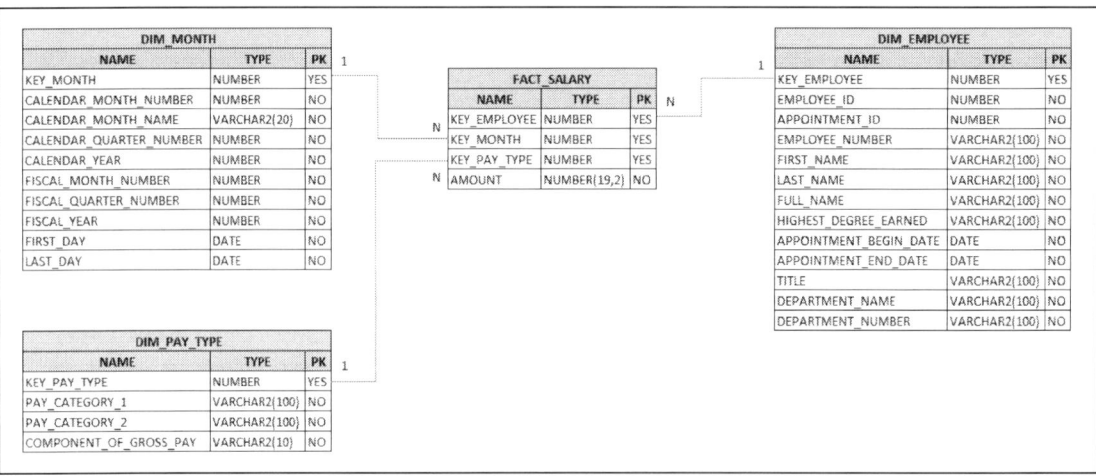

Enhancements to Populating the DIM_EMPLOYEE Dimension

Based on the updates specified in the section above, consider the following updated ETL logic. Remember that one of the requirements involved adding the APPOINTMENT.ID and the EMPLOYEE.ID columns to the DIM_EMPLOYEE table. As a result the structure of the DIM_EMPLOYEE table will need to change. Running the following statements will probably be the easiest way to accomplish this:

```
DROP TABLE DIM_EMPLOYEE;
CREATE TABLE DIM_EMPLOYEE
  (
          KEY_EMPLOYEE                NUMBER,
          EMPLOYEE_ID                 NUMBER,
          APPOINTMENT_ID              NUMBER,
          EMPLOYEE_NUMBER             VARCHAR2(100),
          FIRST_NAME                  VARCHAR2(100),
          LAST_NAME                   VARCHAR2(100),
          FULL_NAME                   VARCHAR2(100),
          HIGHEST_DEGREE_EARNED       VARCHAR2(100),
          APPOINTMENT_BEGIN_DATE      DATE,
          APPOINTMENT_END_DATE        DATE,
          TITLE                       VARCHAR2(100),
          DEPARTMENT_NAME             VARCHAR2(100),
          DEPARTMENT_NUMBER           VARCHAR2(100)
);
```

Rather than examine the entire job again with the three updates, let us look only at the changes that need to be made.

Update 1 - Allow the DIM_EMPLOYEE table to be refreshed as of a certain date

Lines 1 - 5 (New)

Line	Code
1 (new)	CREATE OR REPLACE PROCEDURE LOAD_EMPLOYEE_DIMENSION
2 (new)	(
3 (new)	DATE_OVERRIDE DATE
4 (new)	)
5 (new)	

This begins with allowing a user to pass a date to the procedure at runtime.

Lines 64 – 77

Line	Code
64 (new)	--If a date was not passed to the procedure, the procedure will pull all
65 (new)	--records that were inserted into (or updated in) the EMPLOYEE table or
66 (new)	--APPOINTMENT table since the date of the last successful refresh date from
67 (new)	--the ETL_JOB_STATUS. The data from the source system is "dumped" into the
68 (new)	--STAGE_EMPLOYEE_DATA table in the staging area.

Line	Code
69 (new)	IF DATE_OVERRIDE IS NULL THEN
70 (new)	SELECT MAX(TRUNC(STATUS_TIMESTAMP)) INTO AS_OF_DATE
71 (new)	FROM ETL_JOB_STATUS
72 (new)	WHERE ETL_JOB_NAME = 'LOAD_EMPLOYEE_DIMENSION'
73 (new)	AND STATUS_NAME = 'SUCCESSFULLY COMPLETED';
74 (new)	ELSE
75 (new)	AS_OF_DATE := DATE_OVERRIDE;
76 (new)	END IF;
77 (new)	

If a date is passed, the data will be loaded as of that date. If a null is passed the procedure will load the data as of the last successful refresh. Because the AS_OF_DATE variable is a part of the job already, we can very easily use it with this logic as well.

Update 2 - Add APPOINTMENT.ID and EMPLOYEE.ID to the DIM_EMPLOYEE table

Because of the way in which we wrote the original job this should be pretty painless. Consider this:

Lines 78 – 107 (new)

Line	Code
78 (new)	SQLSTMT := 'CREATE TABLE STAGE_EMPLOYEE_DATA '
79 (new)	|| 'AS ('
80 (new)	|| 'SELECT '
81 (new)	|| 'D.ID EMPLOYEE_ID, '
82 (new)	|| 'A.ID APPOINTMENT_ID, '
83 (new)	|| 'D.EMPLOYEE_NUMBER, '
84 (new)	|| 'D.FIRST_NAME, '
85 (new)	|| 'D.LAST_NAME, '
86 (new)	|| 'D.HIGHEST_DEGREE_EARNED, '
87 (new)	|| 'A.APPOINTMENT_BEGIN_DATE, '
88 (new)	|| 'A.APPOINTMENT_END_DATE, '
89 (new)	|| 'B.TITLE_NAME TITLE, '
90 (new)	|| 'C.DEPARTMENT_NAME, '
91 (new)	|| 'C.DEPARTMENT_NUMBER '
92 (new)	|| 'FROM APPOINTMENT A, '

Line	Code
93 (new)	|| 'TITLE B, '
94 (new)	|| 'DEPARTMENT C, '
95 (new)	|| 'EMPLOYEE D '
96 (new)	|| 'WHERE A.DEPARTMENT_ID = C.ID '
97 (new)	|| 'AND A.TITLE_ID = B.ID '
98 (new)	|| 'AND A.EMPLOYEE_ID = D.ID ';
99 (new)	
100 (new)	IF AS_OF_DATE IS NOT NULL THEN
101 (new)	SQLSTMT := SQLSTMT || 'AND (A.INSERT_DATE >= ''' || TO_CHAR(AS_OF_DATE,'DD-MON-YYYY') || ''''
102 (new)	|| 'OR A.UPDATE_DATE >= ''' || TO_CHAR(AS_OF_DATE,'DD-MON-YYYY') || ''''
103 (new)	|| 'OR D.INSERT_DATE >= ''' || TO_CHAR(AS_OF_DATE,'DD-MON-YYYY') || ''''
104 (new)	|| 'OR D.UPDATE_DATE >= ''' || TO_CHAR(AS_OF_DATE,'DD-MON-YYYY') || ''')';
105 (new)	END IF;
106 (new)	
107 (new)	SQLSTMT := SQLSTMT || ')';

Remember that we opted to take the drop and recreate approach to building our staging tables. That approach makes requirements changes like this easier. The DIM_EMPLOYEE table cannot be dropped and recreated, so it was updated manually above. Other than that, the select clause of each CREATE TABLE statement simply needs to be updated to include the APPOINTMENT.ID and the EMPLOYEE.ID (and named appropriately). This was done on lines 81 and 82 (new). Taking a different approach would require that:

1.) Each staging table is manually updated to include these new columns
2.) The job is updated to select these new columns where appropriate
3.) The changes in number one are made successfully before the updated job is run.

In contrast, our approach allows the job to execute the changes itself without any outside intervention.

We will not examine each place that needs the change, but remember that each staging table that is created will now need to include these columns. I will mention briefly that the join in the update statement on the original lines 188 – 215 will need to be updated to include these columns as well.

Update 3 - Improve the inefficiency of the NOT IN statement in the original lines 253 through 259

Lines 256 – 293 (new)

Line	Code
256 (new)	SQLSTMT := 'CREATE TABLE STAGE_EMPLOYEE_DATA_LOAD_NEW '
257 (new)	| | 'AS ('
258 (new)	| | 'SELECT '
259 (new)	| | 'SEQ_DIM_EMPLOYEE.NEXTVAL AS KEY_EMPLOYEE, '
260 (new)	| | 'A.EMPLOYEE_ID, '
261 (new)	| | 'A.APPOINTMENT_ID, '
262 (new)	| | 'A.EMPLOYEE_NUMBER, '
263 (new)	| | 'A.FIRST_NAME, '
264 (new)	| | 'A.LAST_NAME, '
265 (new)	| | 'A.FULL_NAME, '
266 (new)	| | 'A.HIGHEST_DEGREE_EARNED, '
267 (new)	| | 'A.APPOINTMENT_BEGIN_DATE, '
268 (new)	| | 'A.APPOINTMENT_END_DATE, '
269 (new)	| | 'A.TITLE, '
270 (new)	| | 'A.DEPARTMENT_NAME, '
271 (new)	| | 'A.DEPARTMENT_NUMBER '
272 (new)	| | 'FROM STAGE_EMPLOYEE_DATA_TRANSFORM A '
273 (new)	| | 'WHERE (NVL(TO_CHAR(A.APPOINTMENT_END_DATE),-1), '
274 (new)	| | 'A.TITLE, '
275 (new)	| | 'A.DEPARTMENT_NUMBER, '
276 (new)	| | 'A.EMPLOYEE_NUMBER) '
277 (new)	| | 'IN '
278 (new)	| | '(SELECT '
279 (new)	| | 'NVL(TO_CHAR(APPOINTMENT_END_DATE),-1), '
280 (new)	| | 'TITLE, '
281 (new)	| | 'DEPARTMENT_NUMBER, '
282 (new)	| | 'EMPLOYEE_NUMBER '
283 (new)	| | 'FROM STAGE_EMPLOYEE_DATA_TRANSFORM '
284 (new)	| | 'MINUS '
285 (new)	| | 'SELECT '

Line	Code
286 (new)	|| 'NVL(TO_CHAR(APPOINTMENT_END_DATE),-1), '
287 (new)	|| 'TITLE, '
288 (new)	|| 'DEPARTMENT_NUMBER, '
289 (new)	|| 'EMPLOYEE_NUMBER '
290 (new)	|| 'FROM DIM_EMPLOYEE)) ';
291 (new)	
292 (new)	EXECUTE IMMEDIATE SQLSTMT;
293 (new)	

The NOT IN statement on the original line 253 is very inefficient, making the job run for a long time. As a result, this statement is rewritten so that it uses the MINUS keyword in its place. Since this is not an Oracle book on the differences between Oracle's handling of MINUS and NOT IN, I will not go into the reason why. The point is that an ETL developer must sometimes consider alternatives in an effort to make a job run more efficiently.

Final Product

Once the updates have been made, the job should still place 55,544 rows of data into the DIM_EMPLOYEE table. The updated job in its entirety is below.

Line	Code
1 (new)	CREATE OR REPLACE PROCEDURE LOAD_EMPLOYEE_DIMENSION
2 (new)	(
3 (new)	DATE_OVERRIDE DATE
4 (new)	)
5 (new)	
6 (new)	AS
7 (new)	
8 (new)	SQLSTMT VARCHAR2(2000),
9 (new)	TBLCOUNT NUMBER := 0;
10 (new)	AS_OF_DATE DATE;
11 (new)	ERR_MSG VARCHAR2(200);
12 (new)	MAX_KEY_EMPLOYEE NUMBER;
13 (new)	NEXT_SEQ_VAL NUMBER;
14 (new)	
15 (new)	BEGIN
16 (new)	--Log the beginning of the job
17 (new)	INSERT INTO ETL_JOB_STATUS
18 (new)	(

Line	Code
19 (new)	ID,
20 (new)	ETL_JOB_NAME,
21 (new)	STATUS_NAME,
22 (new)	STATUS_TIMESTAMP
23 (new)	)
24 (new)	VALUES
25 (new)	(
26 (new)	SEQ_ETL_JOB_STATUS.NEXTVAL,
27 (new)	'LOAD_EMPLOYEE_DIMENSION',
28 (new)	'IN PROGRESS',
29 (new)	SYSTIMESTAMP
30 (new)	);
31 (new)	
32 (new)	COMMIT;
33 (new)	
34 (new)	--Make sure that the sequence that populates the key_employee is set to begin
35 (new)	--at the next integer
36 (new)	SELECT NVL(MAX(KEY_EMPLOYEE), 0) INTO MAX_KEY_EMPLOYEE FROM DIM_EMPLOYEE;
37 (new)	SELECT SEQ_DIM_EMPLOYEE.NEXTVAL INTO NEXT_SEQ_VAL FROM DUAL;
38 (new)	
39 (new)	IF NEXT_SEQ_VAL <> MAX_KEY_EMPLOYEE THEN
40 (new)	SQLSTMT := 'ALTER SEQUENCE SEQ_DIM_EMPLOYEE INCREMENT BY '
41 (new)	|| ((NEXT_SEQ_VAL - MAX_KEY_EMPLOYEE) * -1)
42 (new)	|| ' MINVALUE 0';
43 (new)	EXECUTE IMMEDIATE SQLSTMT;
44 (new)	SELECT SEQ_DIM_EMPLOYEE.NEXTVAL INTO NEXT_SEQ_VAL FROM DUAL;
45 (new)	SQLSTMT := 'ALTER SEQUENCE SEQ_DIM_EMPLOYEE INCREMENT BY 1 MINVALUE 0';
46 (new)	EXECUTE IMMEDIATE SQLSTMT;
47 (new)	END IF;
48 (new)	
49 (new)	--If the table exists, drop it. If not, do nothing. The table will be
50 (new)	--created below.
51 (new)	SELECT COUNT(*) INTO TBLCOUNT

Line	Code
52 (new)	FROM ALL_TABLES
53 (new)	WHERE TABLE_NAME = 'STAGE_EMPLOYEE_DATA'
54 (new)	AND OWNER =
55 (new)	(
56 (new)	SELECT SYS_CONTEXT('USERENV', 'CURRENT_SCHEMA')
57 (new)	FROM DUAL
58 (new)	);
59 (new)	
60 (new)	IF TBLCOUNT > 0 THEN
61 (new)	EXECUTE IMMEDIATE 'DROP TABLE STAGE_EMPLOYEE_DATA';
62 (new)	END IF;
63 (new)	
64 (new)	--If a date was not passed to the procedure, the procedure will pull all
65 (new)	--records that were inserted into (or updated in) the EMPLOYEE table or
66 (new)	--APPOINTMENT table since the date of the last successful refresh date from
67 (new)	--the ETL_JOB_STATUS. The data from the source system is "dumped" into the
68 (new)	--STAGE_EMPLOYEE_DATA table in the staging area.
69 (new)	IF DATE_OVERRIDE IS NULL THEN
70 (new)	SELECT MAX(TRUNC(STATUS_TIMESTAMP)) INTO AS_OF_DATE
71 (new)	FROM ETL_JOB_STATUS
72 (new)	WHERE ETL_JOB_NAME = 'LOAD_EMPLOYEE_DIMENSION'
73 (new)	AND STATUS_NAME = 'SUCCESSFULLY COMPLETED';
74 (new)	ELSE
75 (new)	AS_OF_DATE := DATE_OVERRIDE;
76 (new)	END IF;
77 (new)	
78 (new)	SQLSTMT := 'CREATE TABLE STAGE_EMPLOYEE_DATA '
79 (new)	|| 'AS ('
80 (new)	|| 'SELECT '
81 (new)	|| 'D.ID EMPLOYEE_ID, '
82 (new)	|| 'A.ID APPOINTMENT_ID, '
83 (new)	|| 'D.EMPLOYEE_NUMBER, '
84 (new)	|| 'D.FIRST_NAME, '
85 (new)	|| 'D.LAST_NAME, '
86 (new)	|| 'D.HIGHEST_DEGREE_EARNED, '
87 (new)	|| 'A.APPOINTMENT_BEGIN_DATE, '

Line	Code
88 (new)	|| 'A.APPOINTMENT_END_DATE, '
89 (new)	|| 'B.TITLE_NAME TITLE, '
90 (new)	|| 'C.DEPARTMENT_NAME, '
91 (new)	|| 'C.DEPARTMENT_NUMBER '
92 (new)	|| 'FROM APPOINTMENT A, '
93 (new)	|| 'TITLE B, '
94 (new)	|| 'DEPARTMENT C, '
95 (new)	|| 'EMPLOYEE D '
96 (new)	|| 'WHERE A.DEPARTMENT_ID = C.ID '
97 (new)	|| 'AND A.TITLE_ID = B.ID '
98 (new)	|| 'AND A.EMPLOYEE_ID = D.ID ';
99 (new)	
100 (new)	IF AS_OF_DATE IS NOT NULL THEN
101 (new)	SQLSTMT := SQLSTMT || 'AND (A.INSERT_DATE >= '" || TO_CHAR(AS_OF_DATE,'DD-MON-YYYY') || '" '
102 (new)	|| 'OR A.UPDATE_DATE >= '" || TO_CHAR(AS_OF_DATE,'DD-MON-YYYY') || '" '
103 (new)	|| 'OR D.INSERT_DATE >= '" || TO_CHAR(AS_OF_DATE,'DD-MON-YYYY') || '" '
104 (new)	|| 'OR D.UPDATE_DATE >= '" || TO_CHAR(AS_OF_DATE,'DD-MON-YYYY') || '")';
105 (new)	END IF;
106 (new)	
107 (new)	SQLSTMT := SQLSTMT || ')';
108 (new)	
109 (new)	EXECUTE IMMEDIATE SQLSTMT;
110 (new)	
111 (new)	--The full name field is created for each record. The data is then placed
112 (new)	--into the STAGE_EMPLOYEE_DATA_TRANSFORM table (table is dropped if it exists
113 (new)	--and then created below).
114 (new)	SELECT COUNT(*) INTO TBLCOUNT
115 (new)	FROM ALL_TABLES
116 (new)	WHERE TABLE_NAME = 'STAGE_EMPLOYEE_DATA_TRANSFORM'
117 (new)	AND OWNER =
118 (new)	(
119 (new)	SELECT SYS_CONTEXT('USERENV', 'CURRENT_SCHEMA')
120 (new)	FROM DUAL

Line	Code
121 (new)	);
122 (new)	
123 (new)	IF TBLCOUNT > 0 THEN
124 (new)	EXECUTE IMMEDIATE 'DROP TABLE STAGE_EMPLOYEE_DATA_TRANSFORM';
125 (new)	END IF;
126 (new)	
127 (new)	SQLSTMT := 'CREATE TABLE STAGE_EMPLOYEE_DATA_TRANSFORM '
128 (new)	|| 'AS ('
129 (new)	|| 'SELECT '
130 (new)	|| 'A.EMPLOYEE_ID, '
131 (new)	|| 'A.APPOINTMENT_ID, '
132 (new)	|| 'A.EMPLOYEE_NUMBER, '
133 (new)	|| 'A.FIRST_NAME, '
134 (new)	|| 'A.LAST_NAME, '
135 (new)	|| 'A.FIRST_NAME || " " || A.LAST_NAME FULL_NAME, '
136 (new)	|| 'A.HIGHEST_DEGREE_EARNED, '
137 (new)	|| 'A.APPOINTMENT_BEGIN_DATE, '
138 (new)	|| 'A.APPOINTMENT_END_DATE, '
139 (new)	|| 'A.TITLE, '
140 (new)	|| 'A.DEPARTMENT_NAME, '
141 (new)	|| 'A.DEPARTMENT_NUMBER '
142 (new)	|| 'FROM STAGE_EMPLOYEE_DATA A)';
143 (new)	
144 (new)	EXECUTE IMMEDIATE SQLSTMT;
145 (new)	
146 (new)	--Any records containing data that was updated (not new records) as compared
147 (new)	--to DIM_APPOINTMENT are placed into the STAGE_APPT_DATA_LOAD_UPD
148 (new)	--table (table is dropped if it exists and then created below).
149 (new)	SELECT COUNT(*) INTO TBLCOUNT
150 (new)	FROM ALL_TABLES
151 (new)	WHERE TABLE_NAME = 'STAGE_EMPLOYEE_DATA_LOAD_UPD'
152 (new)	AND OWNER =
153 (new)	(
154 (new)	SELECT SYS_CONTEXT('USERENV', 'CURRENT_SCHEMA')
155 (new)	FROM DUAL

Line	Code
156 (new)	);
157 (new)	
158 (new)	IF TBLCOUNT > 0 THEN
159 (new)	EXECUTE IMMEDIATE 'DROP TABLE STAGE_EMPLOYEE_DATA_LOAD_UPD';
160 (new)	END IF;
161 (new)	
162 (new)	SQLSTMT := 'CREATE TABLE STAGE_EMPLOYEE_DATA_LOAD_UPD '
163 (new)	|| 'AS ('
164 (new)	|| 'SELECT '
165 (new)	|| 'A.EMPLOYEE_ID, '
166 (new)	|| 'A.APPOINTMENT_ID, '
167 (new)	|| 'A.EMPLOYEE_NUMBER, '
166 (new)	|| 'A.FIRST_NAME, '
169 (new)	|| 'A.LAST_NAME, '
170 (new)	|| 'A.FULL_NAME, '
171 (new)	|| 'A.HIGHEST_DEGREE_EARNED, '
172 (new)	|| 'A.APPOINTMENT_BEGIN_DATE, '
173 (new)	|| 'A.APPOINTMENT_END_DATE, '
174 (new)	|| 'A.TITLE, '
175 (new)	|| 'A.DEPARTMENT_NAME, '
176 (new)	|| 'A.DEPARTMENT_NUMBER, '
177 (new)	|| 'B.KEY_EMPLOYEE '
178 (new)	|| 'FROM STAGE_EMPLOYEE_DATA_TRANSFORM A, '
179 (new)	|| 'DIM_EMPLOYEE B '
180 (new)	|| 'WHERE A.APPOINTMENT_BEGIN_DATE = B.APPOINTMENT_BEGIN_DATE '
181 (new)	|| 'AND A.TITLE = B.TITLE '
182 (new)	|| 'AND A.DEPARTMENT_NUMBER = B.DEPARTMENT_NUMBER '
183 (new)	|| 'AND A.EMPLOYEE_NUMBER = B.EMPLOYEE_NUMBER '
184 (new)	|| 'AND (NVL(A.DEPARTMENT_NAME,-1) <> NVL(B.DEPARTMENT_NAME,-1) '
185 (new)	|| 'OR NVL(TO_CHAR(A.APPOINTMENT_END_DATE),-1) <> '
186 (new)	|| 'NVL(TO_CHAR(B.APPOINTMENT_END_DATE),-1) '
187 (new)	|| 'OR NVL(A.FIRST_NAME,-1) <> NVL(B.FIRST_NAME,-1) '
188 (new)	|| 'OR NVL(A.LAST_NAME,-1) <> NVL(B.LAST_NAME,-1) '
189 (new)	|| 'OR NVL(A.FULL_NAME,-1) <> NVL(B.FULL_NAME,-1) '

Line	Code
190 (new)	|| 'OR NVL(A.HIGHEST_DEGREE_EARNED,-1) <> NVL(B.HIGHEST_DEGREE_EARNED,-1) '
190 (new)	|| 'OR NVL(A.EMPLOYEE_ID,-1) <> NVL(B.EMPLOYEE_ID,-1) '
192 (new)	|| 'OR NVL(A.APPOINTMENT_ID,-1) <> NVL(B.APPOINTMENT_ID,-1)) '
193 (new)	|| ') ';
194 (new)	
195 (new)	EXECUTE IMMEDIATE SQLSTMT;
196 (new)	
197 (new)	--Because the STAGE_EMPLOYEE_DATA_LOAD_UPD table is dropped and recreated
198 (new)	--each time, the index that is necessary to make the update statement work
199 (new)	--must be rebuilt each time. An organizational rule of some sort will need
200 (new)	--to make sure that there is no conflict with the name.
201 (new)	SQLSTMT := 'CREATE INDEX INDEX_STAGE_KEY_EMPLOYEE ON '
202 (new)	|| 'STAGE_EMPLOYEE_DATA_LOAD_UPD (KEY_EMPLOYEE)';
203 (new)	EXECUTE IMMEDIATE SQLSTMT;
204 (new)	
205 (new)	SQLSTMT := 'UPDATE DIM_EMPLOYEE A '
206 (new)	|| 'SET (A.APPOINTMENT_END_DATE, '
207 (new)	|| 'A.DEPARTMENT_NAME, '
208 (new)	|| 'A.FIRST_NAME, '
209 (new)	|| 'A.LAST_NAME, '
210 (new)	|| 'A.FULL_NAME, '
211 (new)	|| 'A.HIGHEST_DEGREE_EARNED, '
212 (new)	|| 'A.EMPLOYEE_ID, '
213 (new)	|| 'A.APPOINTMENT_ID) = '
214 (new)	|| '(SELECT B.APPOINTMENT_END_DATE, '
215 (new)	|| 'B.DEPARTMENT_NAME, '
216 (new)	|| 'B.FIRST_NAME, '
217 (new)	|| 'B.LAST_NAME, '
218 (new)	|| 'B.FULL_NAME, '
219 (new)	|| 'B.HIGHEST_DEGREE_EARNED, '
220 (new)	|| 'B.EMPLOYEE_ID, '
221 (new)	|| 'B.APPOINTMENT_ID '
222 (new)	|| 'FROM STAGE_EMPLOYEE_DATA_LOAD_UPD B '
223 (new)	|| 'WHERE A.KEY_EMPLOYEE = B.KEY_EMPLOYEE) '

Line	Code
224 (new)	| | 'WHERE EXISTS '
225 (new)	| | '(SELECT B.APPOINTMENT_END_DATE, '
226 (new)	| | 'B.DEPARTMENT_NAME, '
227 (new)	| | 'B.FIRST_NAME, '
228 (new)	| | 'B.LAST_NAME, '
229 (new)	| | 'B.FULL_NAME, '
230 (new)	| | 'B.HIGHEST_DEGREE_EARNED, B.EMPLOYEE_ID, B.APPOINTMENT_ID '
231 (new)	| | 'FROM STAGE_EMPLOYEE_DATA_LOAD_UPD B '
232 (new)	| | 'WHERE A.KEY_EMPLOYEE = B.KEY_EMPLOYEE) ';
233 (new)	
234 (new)	EXECUTE IMMEDIATE SQLSTMT;
235 (new)	COMMIT;
236 (new)	
237 (new)	--Any records containing new records (not data that was updated) are placed
238 (new)	--into the STAGE_APPT_DATA_LOAD_NEW table (table is dropped if it exists and
239 (new)	--then created below). The KEY_APPOINTMENT is created using the
240 (new)	--SEQ_DIM_APPOINTMENT sequence. This sequence is incremented directly in
241 (new)	--the ETL job (see below) as opposed to using a trigger, so that it will be
242 (new)	--more efficient.
243 (new)	SELECT COUNT(*) INTO TBLCOUNT
244 (new)	FROM ALL_TABLES
245 (new)	WHERE TABLE_NAME = 'STAGE_EMPLOYEE_DATA_LOAD_NEW'
246 (new)	AND OWNER =
247 (new)	(
248 (new)	SELECT SYS_CONTEXT('USERENV', 'CURRENT_SCHEMA')
249 (new)	FROM DUAL
250 (new)	);
251 (new)	
252 (new)	IF TBLCOUNT > 0 THEN
253 (new)	EXECUTE IMMEDIATE 'DROP TABLE STAGE_EMPLOYEE_DATA_LOAD_NEW';
254 (new)	END IF;
255 (new)	
256 (new)	SQLSTMT := 'CREATE TABLE STAGE_EMPLOYEE_DATA_LOAD_NEW '

Line	Code
257 (new)	|| 'AS ('
258 (new)	|| 'SELECT '
259 (new)	|| 'SEQ_DIM_EMPLOYEE.NEXTVAL AS KEY_EMPLOYEE, '
260 (new)	|| 'A.EMPLOYEE_ID, '
261 (new)	|| 'A.APPOINTMENT_ID, '
262 (new)	|| 'A.EMPLOYEE_NUMBER, '
263 (new)	|| 'A.FIRST_NAME, '
264 (new)	|| 'A.LAST_NAME, '
265 (new)	|| 'A.FULL_NAME, '
266 (new)	|| 'A.HIGHEST_DEGREE_EARNED, '
267 (new)	|| 'A.APPOINTMENT_BEGIN_DATE, '
268 (new)	|| 'A.APPOINTMENT_END_DATE, '
269 (new)	|| 'A.TITLE, '
270 (new)	|| 'A.DEPARTMENT_NAME, '
271 (new)	|| 'A.DEPARTMENT_NUMBER '
272 (new)	|| 'FROM STAGE_EMPLOYEE_DATA_TRANSFORM A '
273 (new)	|| 'WHERE (NVL(TO_CHAR(A.APPOINTMENT_END_DATE),-1), '
274 (new)	|| 'A.TITLE, '
275 (new)	|| 'A.DEPARTMENT_NUMBER, '
276 (new)	|| 'A.EMPLOYEE_NUMBER) '
277 (new)	|| 'IN '
278 (new)	|| '(SELECT '
279 (new)	|| 'NVL(TO_CHAR(APPOINTMENT_END_DATE),-1), '
280 (new)	|| 'TITLE, '
281 (new)	|| 'DEPARTMENT_NUMBER, '
282 (new)	|| 'EMPLOYEE_NUMBER '
283 (new)	|| 'FROM STAGE_EMPLOYEE_DATA_TRANSFORM '
284 (new)	|| 'MINUS '
285 (new)	|| 'SELECT '
286 (new)	|| 'NVL(TO_CHAR(APPOINTMENT_END_DATE),-1), '
287 (new)	|| 'TITLE, '
288 (new)	|| 'DEPARTMENT_NUMBER, '
289 (new)	|| 'EMPLOYEE_NUMBER '
290 (new)	|| 'FROM DIM_EMPLOYEE)) ';
291 (new)	
292 (new)	EXECUTE IMMEDIATE SQLSTMT;

Line	Code
293 (new)	
294 (new)	--The new records are added to the DIM_EMPLOYEE table.
295 (new)	SQLSTMT := 'INSERT INTO DIM_EMPLOYEE '
296 (new)	|| '(KEY_EMPLOYEE, '
297 (new)	|| 'EMPLOYEE_ID, '
298 (new)	|| 'APPOINTMENT_ID, '
299 (new)	|| 'EMPLOYEE_NUMBER, '
300 (new)	|| 'FIRST_NAME, '
301 (new)	|| 'LAST_NAME, '
302 (new)	|| 'FULL_NAME, '
303 (new)	|| 'HIGHEST_DEGREE_EARNED, '
304 (new)	|| 'APPOINTMENT_BEGIN_DATE, '
305 (new)	|| 'APPOINTMENT_END_DATE, '
306 (new)	|| 'TITLE, '
307 (new)	|| 'DEPARTMENT_NAME, '
308 (new)	|| 'DEPARTMENT_NUMBER) '
309 (new)	|| 'SELECT A.* '
310 (new)	|| 'FROM STAGE_EMPLOYEE_DATA_LOAD_NEW A';
311 (new)	
312 (new)	EXECUTE IMMEDIATE SQLSTMT;
313 (new)	COMMIT;
314 (new)	
315 (new)	--Log the successful completion of the job.
316 (new)	INSERT INTO ETL_JOB_STATUS
317 (new)	(
318 (new)	ID,
319 (new)	ETL_JOB_NAME,
320 (new)	STATUS_NAME,
321 (new)	STATUS_TIMESTAMP
322 (new)	)
323 (new)	VALUES
324 (new)	(
325 (new)	SEQ_ETL_JOB_STATUS.NEXTVAL,
326 (new)	'LOAD_EMPLOYEE_DIMENSION',
327 (new)	'SUCCESSFULLY COMPLETED',
328 (new)	SYSTIMESTAMP

Line	Code
329 (new)	);
330 (new)	
331 (new)	COMMIT;
332 (new)	
333 (new)	--This is the equivalent of a catch block. Any errors are caught and logged.
334 (new)	EXCEPTION
335 (new)	WHEN OTHERS THEN
336 (new)	ERR_MSG := SUBSTR(SQLERRM, 1, 200);
337 (new)	INSERT INTO ETL_JOB_STATUS
338 (new)	(
339 (new)	ID,
340 (new)	ETL_JOB_NAME,
341 (new)	STATUS_NAME,
342 (new)	ERROR_MESSAGE,
343 (new)	STATUS_TIMESTAMP
344 (new)	)
345 (new)	VALUES
346 (new)	(
347 (new)	SEQ_ETL_JOB_STATUS.NEXTVAL,
348 (new)	'LOAD_EMPLOYEE_DIMENSION',
349 (new)	'ERROR',
350 (new)	ERR_MSG,
351 (new)	SYSTIMESTAMP
352 (new)	);
353 (new)	
354 (new)	COMMIT;
355 (new)	
354 (new)	END;

Verifying the DIM_EMPLOYEE Table

Now that the DIM_EMPLOYEE table has been populated, it is important to verify that the ETL populated that table as designed. The business users will still need to verify that it makes sense from a business perspective (i.e., verify that we interpreted the requirements correctly) but we can give the data a sanity check before passing it off to them. There are several ways of accomplishing this. If you can access the source and the destination using the same query analyzer, then a statement like the one below may be useful. Feel free and edit the SQL statement below or take a different approach. It may be acceptable to identify some sample individuals and limit the results to display only those individuals.

```
SELECT      EMPLOYEE_ID,
            APPOINTMENT_ID,
            EMPLOYEE_NUMBER,
            FIRST_NAME,
            LAST_NAME,
            FULL_NAME,
            HIGHEST_DEGREE_EARNED,
            APPOINTMENT_BEGIN_DATE,
            APPOINTMENT_END_DATE,
            TITLE,
            DEPARTMENT_NAME,
            DEPARTMENT_NUMBER,
            'WAREHOUSE'
FROM        DIM_EMPLOYEE
UNION
SELECT      D.ID,
            A.ID,
            D.EMPLOYEE_NUMBER,
            D.FIRST_NAME,
            D.LAST_NAME,
            D.FIRST_NAME || '' || D.LAST_NAME FULL_NAME,
            D.HIGHEST_DEGREE_EARNED,
            A.APPOINTMENT_BEGIN_DATE,
            A.APPOINTMENT_END_DATE,
            C.TITLE_NAME,
            B.DEPARTMENT_NAME,
            B.DEPARTMENT_NUMBER,
            'SOURCE'
FROM        APPOINTMENT A,
            DEPARTMENT B,
            TITLE C,
            EMPLOYEE D
WHERE       A.EMPLOYEE_ID = D.ID
            AND A.DEPARTMENT_ID = B.ID
            AND A.TITLE_ID = C.ID
ORDER BY    1, 2, 13
```

Populating the FACT_SALARY Fact Table

Next, we will populate the FACT_SALARY table. Remember from chapter five that the goal of an ETL job that populates a fact table is to accomplish the following:

1.) Select all necessary data from the source
   a. Measures
   b. Natural keys of the dimension objects
   c. Degenerate dimension objects

2.) Transform the data as needed
    a. Aggregate measures and group by the appropriate objects
    b. Add foreign keys to dimension tables
3.) Delete any existing rows from the fact table that will be replaced by the new data
4.) Load the fact table

In order to accomplish number one, we need to consider our approach to pulling the data for this fact table. Although the source system provides the date inserted, moving forward with the Based on Timestamp approach may cause some complications along the way. Because this is a fact table, using the Based on Timeframe approach will be best. Refer to the Update Existing Rows and Insert New Rows section in chapter five for more detail.

Only one piece of the setup is needed. The FACT_SALARY table will need to be created so that this job can populate it. Run the following to create the FACT_SALARY table:

```
CREATE TABLE FACT_SALARY
(
    KEY_EMPLOYEE            NUMBER,
    KEY_MONTH               NUMBER,
    KEY_PAY_TYPE            NUMBER,
    AMOUNT                  NUMBER(19,2)
)
```

Now that the infrastructure has been created, we can move forward with actually populating the fact table. We will call the procedure LOAD_SALARY_FACT. Consider this code (not complete) for the preliminary portion of the job. The preliminary portion of the job may be treated as certain housekeeping activities that must occur before it can accomplish any of the four items listed above.

Lines 1 – 19

Line	Code
1	CREATE OR REPLACE PROCEDURE LOAD_SALARY_FACT
2	(
3	BEGIN_MONTH_OVERRIDE NUMBER,
4	BEGIN_YEAR_OVERRIDE NUMBER,
5	END_MONTH_OVERRIDE NUMBER,
6	END_YEAR_OVERRIDE NUMBER,
7	DEFAULT_TIMEPERIOD VARCHAR2
8	)
9	
10	AS
11	
12	SQLSTMT VARCHAR2(3000);

Line	Code
13	TBLCOUNT NUMBER := 0;
14	BEGIN_AS_OF_DATE DATE;
15	END_AS_OF_DATE DATE;
16	DATE_STRING VARCHAR2(10);
17	ERR_MSG VARCHAR2(200);
18	PAY_TYPE_WAGES_KEY NUMBER := -1;
19	

These lines contain the standard beginning of the PL/SQL procedure. The procedure is named, variables are declared, and the job begins. The user may specify the first month and year (BEGIN_MONTH_OVERRIDE and BEGIN_YEAR_OVERRIDE variables) and the last month and year (END_MONTH_OVERRIDE and END_YEAR_OVERRIDE variables) of the timeframe for which the data shall be pulled. A default timeframe (explained later) can be used if the user sets the DEFAULT_TIMEPERIOD variable to a value of 'Y'.

Lines 20 – 38

Line	Code
20	BEGIN
21	--Log the beginning of the job
22	insert into ETL_JOB_STATUS
23	(
24	ID,
25	ETL_JOB_NAME,
26	STATUS_NAME,
27	STATUS_TIMESTAMP
28	)
29	VALUES
30	(
31	SEQ_ETL_JOB_STATUS.NEXTVAL,
32	'LOAD_SALARY_FACT',
33	'IN PROGRESS',
34	SYSTIMESTAMP
35	);
36	
37	COMMIT;
38	

As was done in the earlier procedure, the job is logged in the ETL_JOB_STATUS table as having begun.

Lines 39 – 53

Line	Code
39	--If the table exists, drop it. If not, do nothing. the table will be
40	--created below.
41	SELECT COUNT(*) INTO TBLCOUNT
42	FROM ALL_TABLES
43	WHERE TABLE_NAME = 'STAGE_SALARY_DATA'
44	AND OWNER =
45	(
46	SELECT SYS_CONTEXT('USERENV', 'CURRENT_SCHEMA')
47	FROM DUAL
48	);
49	
50	IF TBLCOUNT > 0 THEN
51	EXECUTE IMMEDIATE 'DROP TABLE STAGE_SALARY_DATA';
52	END IF;
53	

If the first staging table, STAGE_SALARY_DATA, exists it is dropped.

Lines 54 – 105

Line	Code
54	--If the DEFAULT_PERIOD variable is set to 'Y', then the prior month and the
55	--current month are loaded or reloaded into the fact table.
56	--Otherwise, the overrides are used.
57	IF DEFAULT_TIMEPERIOD = 'Y' THEN
58	SELECT TRUNC(TRUNC(SYSDATE,'MM')-1,'MM') INTO BEGIN_AS_OF_DATE FROM DUAL;
59	SELECT LAST_DAY(TRUNC(SYSDATE)) INTO END_AS_OF_DATE FROM DUAL;
60	ELSE
61	--This IF statement is used to place a leading zero before the month number
62	--for those months less than 10
63	IF BEGIN_MONTH_OVERRIDE < 10 THEN

Line	Code
64	BEGIN_AS_OF_DATE := TO_DATE
65	(
66	'0'
67	|| TO_CHAR(BEGIN_MONTH_OVERRIDE)
68	|| '/01/'
69	|| TO_CHAR(BEGIN_YEAR_OVERRIDE),'MM/DD/YYYY'
70	);
71	ELSE
72	BEGIN_AS_OF_DATE := TO_DATE
73	(
74	TO_CHAR(BEGIN_MONTH_OVERRIDE)
75	|| '/01/'
76	|| TO_CHAR(BEGIN_YEAR_OVERRIDE),'MM/DD/YYYY'
77	);
78	END IF;
79	
80	IF END_MONTH_OVERRIDE < 10 THEN
81	END_AS_OF_DATE := LAST_DAY
82	(
83	TO_DATE
84	(
85	'0'
86	|| TO_CHAR(END_MONTH_OVERRIDE)
87	|| '/01/'
88	|| TO_CHAR(END_YEAR_OVERRIDE),'MM/DD/YYYY'
89	)
90	);
91	ELSE
92	END_AS_OF_DATE := LAST_DAY
93	(
94	TO_DATE
95	(
96	TO_CHAR(END_MONTH_OVERRIDE)
97	|| '/01/'
98	||
99	TO_CHAR(END_YEAR_OVERRIDE),'MM/DD/YYYY'

Line	Code
100	)
101	);
102	END IF;
103	
104	END IF;
105	

These lines set the time period for which the data will be loaded. If the DEFAULT_PERIOD variable is set to a value of 'Y', then data that applies to dollars paid in the current month and the previous month will be pulled. The BEGIN_AS_OF_DATE and the END_AS_OF_DATE variables are set to the first day of the previous month and the last day of the current month, respectively.

If the DEFAULT_PERIOD variable is set to 'N', then data that applies to dollars paid in the months provided by the user will be pulled. The BEGIN_AS_OF_DATE and the END_AS_OF_DATE variables are set according to the variables provided by the user.

Extract Data From the Source

This portion of the job extracts data from the source system and places it into the staging area.

Lines 106 – 188

Line	Code
106	--Dump the data into the staging table and transform the PAY_TYPE_NAME into
107	--the values that are used in the DIM_PAY_TYPE table
108	SQLSTMT := 'CREATE TABLE STAGE_SALARY_DATA AS ('
109	|| 'SELECT E.EMPLOYEE_NUMBER, '
110	|| 'C.APPOINTMENT_BEGIN_DATE, '
111	|| 'F.TITLE_NAME, '
112	|| 'G.DEPARTMENT_NUMBER, '
113	|| 'D.PAY_TYPE_NAME, '
114	|| 'CASE WHEN PAY_TYPE_NAME = "Employer Paid - Dental Insurance" '
115	|| 'THEN "Employer Paid Dental Insurance" '
116	|| 'WHEN PAY_TYPE_NAME = "Employee Paid - Dental Insurance" '
117	|| 'THEN "Employee Paid Dental Insurance" '
118	|| 'WHEN PAY_TYPE_NAME = "Employer Paid - Health Insurance" '
119	|| 'THEN "Employer Paid Health Insurance" '
120	|| 'WHEN PAY_TYPE_NAME = "Employee Paid - Health Insurance" '
121	|| 'THEN "Employee Paid Health Insurance" '

Line	Code
122	|| 'WHEN PAY_TYPE_NAME = "Employer Paid - FICA OASDI" '
123	|| 'THEN "Employer Paid FICA OASDI" '
124	|| 'WHEN PAY_TYPE_NAME = "Employee Paid - FICA OASDI" '
125	|| 'THEN "Employee Paid FICA OASDI" '
126	|| 'WHEN PAY_TYPE_NAME = "Employer Paid - FICA Med" '
127	|| 'THEN "Employer Paid FICA MED" '
128	|| 'WHEN PAY_TYPE_NAME = "Employee Paid - FICA Med" '
129	|| 'THEN "Employee Paid FICA MED" '
130	|| 'WHEN PAY_TYPE_NAME = "401K Employee Contribution" '
131	|| 'THEN "Employee Paid 401K Contribution" '
132	|| 'WHEN PAY_TYPE_NAME = "401K Employer Contribution" '
133	|| 'THEN "Employer Paid 401K Contribution" '
134	|| 'WHEN PAY_TYPE_NAME = "Federal Withholding" '
135	|| 'THEN "Federal Withholding" '
136	|| 'ELSE NULL END AS PAY_TYPE_NAME_IN_STAR, '
137	|| 'A.DATE_PAID, '
138	|| 'A.CHECK_NUMBER, '
139	|| 'SUM(B.AMOUNT) AS AMOUNT '
140	|| 'FROM PAYCHECK_HEADER A, '
141	|| 'PAYCHECK_DETAIL B, '
142	|| 'APPOINTMENT C, '
143	|| 'PAY_TYPE D, '
144	|| 'EMPLOYEE E, '
145	|| 'TITLE F, '
146	|| 'DEPARTMENT G '
147	|| 'WHERE B.PAYCHECK_HEADER_ID = A.ID '
148	|| 'AND A.APPOINTMENT_ID = C.ID '
149	|| 'AND B.PAY_TYPE_ID = D.ID '
150	|| 'AND C.EMPLOYEE_ID = E.ID '
151	|| 'AND C.TITLE_ID = F.ID '
152	|| 'AND C.DEPARTMENT_ID = G.ID '
153	|| 'AND A.DATE_PAID BETWEEN '' || TO_CHAR(BEGIN_AS_OF_DATE,'DD-MON-YYYY')
154	|| ''' AND '''

Line	Code
155	|| TO_CHAR(END_AS_OF_DATE,'DD-MON-YYYY') || '" '
156	|| 'GROUP BY E.EMPLOYEE_NUMBER, '
157	|| 'C.APPOINTMENT_BEGIN_DATE, '
158	|| 'F.TITLE_NAME, '
159	|| 'G.DEPARTMENT_NUMBER, '
160	|| 'D.PAY_TYPE_NAME, '
161	|| 'CASE WHEN PAY_TYPE_NAME = "Employer Paid - Dental Insurance" '
162	|| 'THEN "Employer Paid Dental Insurance" '
163	|| 'WHEN PAY_TYPE_NAME = "Employee Paid - Dental Insurance" '
164	|| 'THEN "Employee Paid Dental Insurance" '
165	|| 'WHEN PAY_TYPE_NAME = "Employer Paid - Health Insurance" '
166	|| 'THEN "Employer Paid Health Insurance" '
167	|| 'WHEN PAY_TYPE_NAME = "Employee Paid - Health Insurance" '
168	|| 'THEN "Employee Paid Health Insurance" '
169	|| 'WHEN PAY_TYPE_NAME = "Employer Paid - FICA OASDI" '
170	|| 'THEN "Employer Paid FICA OASDI" '
171	|| 'WHEN PAY_TYPE_NAME = "Employee Paid - FICA OASDI" '
172	|| 'THEN "Employee Paid FICA OASDI" '
173	|| 'WHEN PAY_TYPE_NAME = "Employer Paid - FICA Med" '
174	|| 'THEN "Employer Paid FICA MED" '
175	|| 'WHEN PAY_TYPE_NAME = "Employee Paid - FICA Med" '
176	|| 'THEN "Employee Paid FICA MED" '
177	|| 'WHEN PAY_TYPE_NAME = "401K Employee Contribution" '
178	|| 'THEN "Employee Paid 401K Contribution" '
179	|| 'WHEN PAY_TYPE_NAME = "401K Employer Contribution" '
180	|| 'THEN "Employer Paid 401K Contribution" '
181	|| 'WHEN PAY_TYPE_NAME = "Federal Withholding" '
182	|| 'THEN "Federal Withholding" '
183	|| 'ELSE NULL END, '
184	|| 'A.DATE_PAID, '
185	|| 'A.CHECK_NUMBER) ';
186	
187	EXECUTE IMMEDIATE SQLSTMT;

Line	Code
188	

As described above, this is the extract portion of the job. Remember from chapter five that the first thing that needs to be accomplished is the selection of all necessary data from the source. This includes measures, natural keys of the dimension objects, and degenerate dimension objects. The FACT_SALARY table contains one measure and foreign keys to three dimension tables. Therefore, that measure as well as the natural keys to those three dimension tables needs to be selected from the source. This select statement accomplishes that.

Measure: PAYCHECK_HEADER.AMOUNT (line 139)

Natural Key To DIM_EMPLOYEE:
- EMPLOYEE.EMPLOYEE_NUMBER(line 109)
- APPOINTMENT.APPOINTMENT_BEGIN_DATE (line 110)
- TITLE.TITLE_NAME (line 111)
- DEPARTMENT.DEPARTMENT_NUMBER (line 112)

Natural Key To DIM_MONTH: DATE_PAID (line 137) will be used to derive the month

Natural Key To DIM_PAY_TYPE: PAY_TYPE_NAME and associated case statement (lines 113 – 136)

This select statement is used to create and populate the STAGE_SALARY_DATA table so that, as already discussed, its structure can be easily changed if necessary.

Transform the Data

This portion of the job begins the process of restructuring the data so that it will fit into the fact table.

Lines 189 – 229

Line	Code
189	--If the table exists, drop it. If not, do nothing.
190	--The table will be created below.
191	SELECT COUNT(*) INTO TBLCOUNT
192	FROM ALL_TABLES
193	WHERE TABLE_NAME = 'STAGE_SALARY_DATA_CALC_WAGES'
194	AND OWNER =
195	(
196	SELECT SYS_CONTEXT('USERENV', 'CURRENT_SCHEMA')
197	FROM DUAL
198	);

Line	Code
199	
200	IF TBLCOUNT > 0 THEN
201	EXECUTE IMMEDIATE 'DROP TABLE STAGE_SALARY_DATA_CALC_WAGES';
202	END IF;
203	
204	--The source system stores the gross amount and the detail that is actually
205	--part of the gross total. The detail must be subtracted
206	--from the gross amount to get the net amount. Separating the gross pay from
207	--the amount withheld is done in the table below. The net amount will be
208	--calculated later.
209	SQLSTMT := 'CREATE TABLE STAGE_SALARY_DATA_CALC_WAGES AS ('
210	|| 'SELECT A.CHECK_NUMBER, '
211	|| 'SUM(A.AMOUNT) GROSS_PAY, '
212	|| ' (SELECT SUM(AMOUNT) '
213	|| 'FROM STAGE_SALARY_DATA AA '
214	|| 'WHERE AA.PAY_TYPE_NAME_IN_STAR IN '
215	||'('
216	||'"Federal Withholding", '
217	||'"Employee Paid Health Insurance", '
218	||'"Employee Paid Dental Insurance", '
219	||'"Employee Paid 401K Contribution", '
220	||'"Employee Paid FICA OASDI", '
221	||'"Employee Paid FICA MED" '
222	||')'
223	|| 'AND AA.CHECK_NUMBER = A.CHECK_NUMBER) WITHHELD '
224	|| 'FROM STAGE_SALARY_DATA A '
225	|| 'WHERE A.PAY_TYPE_NAME = "Gross Wages" '
226	|| 'GROUP BY A.CHECK_NUMBER) ';
227	
228	EXECUTE IMMEDIATE SQLSTMT;
229	

In order to place certain dollars into the appropriate buckets (using the DIM_PAY_TYPE dimension) the total amount withheld from each paycheck must be calculated so that the net pay can be calculated later. This SQL statement does that and dynamically creates the STAGE_SALARY_DATA_CALC_WAGES table.

Lines 230 – 271

Line	Code
230	--If the table exists, drop it. If not, do nothing. the table will be created below.
231	SELECT COUNT(*) INTO TBLCOUNT
232	FROM ALL_TABLES
233	WHERE TABLE_NAME = 'STAGE_SALARY_DATA_ADD_KEYS'
234	AND OWNER =
235	(
236	SELECT SYS_CONTEXT('USERENV', 'CURRENT_SCHEMA')
237	FROM DUAL
238	);
239	
240	IF TBLCOUNT > 0 THEN
241	EXECUTE IMMEDIATE 'DROP TABLE STAGE_SALARY_DATA_ADD_KEYS';
242	END IF;
243	
244	SQLSTMT := 'CREATE TABLE STAGE_SALARY_DATA_ADD_KEYS AS ('
245	|| 'SELECT '
246	|| 'NVL((SELECT AA.KEY_EMPLOYEE '
247	|| 'FROM DIM_EMPLOYEE AA '
248	|| 'WHERE AA.EMPLOYEE_NUMBER = A.EMPLOYEE_NUMBER '
249	|| 'AND AA.APPOINTMENT_BEGIN_DATE = A.APPOINTMENT_BEGIN_DATE '
250	|| 'AND AA.TITLE = A.TITLE_NAME '
251	|| 'AND AA.DEPARTMENT_NUMBER = A.DEPARTMENT_NUMBER),-1) KEY_EMPLOYEE, '
252	|| 'NVL((SELECT AA.KEY_MONTH '
253	|| 'FROM DIM_MONTH AA '
254	|| 'WHERE EXTRACT(MONTH FROM A.DATE_PAID) = AA.CALENDAR_MONTH_NUMBER '
255	|| 'AND EXTRACT(YEAR FROM A.DATE_PAID) = AA.CALENDAR_YEAR),-1) KEY_MONTH, '
256	|| 'NVL((SELECT AA.KEY_PAY_TYPE '
257	|| 'FROM DIM_PAY_TYPE AA '
258	|| 'WHERE AA.PAY_CATEGORY_2 = A.PAY_TYPE_NAME_IN_STAR),-1) KEY_PAY_TYPE, '
259	|| 'SUM(A.AMOUNT) AMOUNT '
260	|| 'FROM STAGE_SALARY_DATA A '

Line	Code
261	|| 'WHERE A.PAY_TYPE_NAME <> "Gross Wages" '
262	|| 'GROUP BY A.EMPLOYEE_NUMBER, '
263	|| 'A.DATE_PAID, '
264	|| 'A.PAY_TYPE_NAME_IN_STAR, '
265	|| 'A.TITLE_NAME, '
266	|| 'A.DEPARTMENT_NUMBER, '
267	|| 'A.APPOINTMENT_BEGIN_DATE '
268	|| ')';
269	
270	EXECUTE IMMEDIATE SQLSTMT;
271	

This piece of code drops the STAGE_SALARY_DATA_ADD_KEYS table (if necessary) and then creates it dynamically. The select statement pulls all of the individual components of pay from the STAGE_SALARY_DATA table with the exception of the net pay. The net pay will be calculated and then stored in the next step. This table also joins the outer select statement to the DIM_EMPLOYEE (lines 246 - 251), DIM_MONTH (lines 252 – 255), and DIM_PAY_TYPE (lines 256 – 258) dimensions, via sub-select statements, using the natural keys of each, and places the surrogate key into the STAGE_SALARY_DATA_ADD_KEYS table.

Lines 272 – 302

Line	Code
272	--The insert statement below is calculating the net wages and then adding
273	--the rows with the net wages into the STAGE_SALARY_DATA_ADD_KEYS table.
274	
275	SQLSTMT := 'INSERT INTO STAGE_SALARY_DATA_ADD_KEYS '
276	|| 'SELECT '
277	|| 'NVL((SELECT AA.KEY_EMPLOYEE '
278	|| 'FROM DIM_EMPLOYEE AA '
279	|| 'WHERE AA.EMPLOYEE_NUMBER = A.EMPLOYEE_NUMBER '
280	|| 'AND AA.APPOINTMENT_BEGIN_DATE = A.APPOINTMENT_BEGIN_DATE '
281	|| 'AND AA.TITLE = A.TITLE_NAME '
282	|| 'AND AA.DEPARTMENT_NUMBER = A.DEPARTMENT_NUMBER),-1) KEY_EMPLOYEE, '
283	|| 'NVL((SELECT AA.KEY_MONTH '
284	|| 'FROM DIM_MONTH AA '
285	|| 'WHERE EXTRACT(MONTH FROM A.DATE_PAID) = AA.CALENDAR_MONTH_NUMBER '

Line	Code
286	|| 'AND EXTRACT(YEAR FROM A.DATE_PAID) = AA.CALENDAR_YEAR),-1) KEY_MONTH, '
287	|| 'NVL((SELECT AA.KEY_PAY_TYPE '
288	|| 'FROM DIM_PAY_TYPE AA '
289	|| 'WHERE AA.PAY_CATEGORY_2 = "Wages"),-1) KEY_PAY_TYPE, '
290	|| 'SUM(B.GROSS_PAY - B.WITHHELD) AMOUNT '
291	|| 'FROM STAGE_SALARY_DATA A, '
292	|| 'STAGE_SALARY_DATA_CALC_WAGES B '
293	|| 'WHERE A.CHECK_NUMBER = B.CHECK_NUMBER '
294	|| 'GROUP BY A.EMPLOYEE_NUMBER, '
295	|| 'A.DATE_PAID, '
296	|| 'A.TITLE_NAME, '
297	|| 'A.DEPARTMENT_NUMBER, '
298	|| 'A.APPOINTMENT_BEGIN_DATE ';
299	
300	EXECUTE IMMEDIATE SQLSTMT;
301	COMMIT;
302	

This piece of code accomplishes two general things. First, lines 275 – 289 will join the outer select statement to the DIM_EMPLOYEE (lines 277 - 282), DIM_MONTH (lines 283 – 286), and DIM_PAY_TYPE (lines 287 – 289) dimensions using the natural keys of each, and place the surrogate key into the STAGE_SALARY_DATA_ADD_KEYS table.

Second, line 290 calculates the net pay by subtracting the STAGE_SALARY_DATA_CALC_WAGES.WITHHELD amount from the STAGE_SALARY_DATA_CALC_WAGES.GROSS_PAY amount. This data is inserted into the STAGE_SALARY_DATA_ADD_KEYS table.

Insert New Records

This portion of the job will place the new records into the FACT_SALARY table.

Lines 303 – 319

Line	Code
303	--Updating the existing rows for months in which the amount has changed
304	--(i.e., an additional payroll was processed for that month since the last
305	--load) would be very inefficient. As a result, any existing data pertaining
306	--to the month(s) being pulled into the fact table is completely deleted from
307	--the fact table and reloaded.

Line	Code
308	SQLSTMT := 'DELETE '
309	|| 'FROM FACT_SALARY A '
310	|| 'WHERE A.KEY_MONTH IN ('
311	|| 'SELECT KEY_MONTH '
312	|| 'FROM DIM_MONTH '
313	|| 'WHERE FIRST_DAY BETWEEN '" || TO_CHAR(BEGIN_AS_OF_DATE,'DD-MON-YYYY')
314	|| '" AND '"
315	|| TO_CHAR(END_AS_OF_DATE,'DD-MON-YYYY') || '") ';
316	
317	EXECUTE IMMEDIATE SQLSTMT;
318	COMMIT;
319	

It is certainly possible that rows already exist in the fact table for the time frame for which the job is pulling data. If that is the case, those rows are deleted from the fact table.

Lines 320 – 327

Line	Code
320	--The fact table is loaded
321	
322	SQLSTMT := 'INSERT INTO FACT_SALARY '
323	|| 'SELECT * FROM STAGE_SALARY_DATA_ADD_KEYS ';
324	
325	EXECUTE IMMEDIATE 'INSERT INTO FACT_SALARY SELECT * FROM STAGE_SALARY_DATA_ADD_KEYS';
326	COMMIT;
327	

This statement inserts the rows from the STAGE_SALARY_DATA_ADD_KEYS table into the FACT_SALARY table.

Lines 328 – 345

Line	Code
328	--Log the successful completion of the job.

Line	Code
329	INSERT INTO ETL_JOB_STATUS
330	(
331	ID,
332	ETL_JOB_NAME,
333	STATUS_NAME,
334	STATUS_TIMESTAMP
335	)
336	VALUES
337	(
338	SEQ_ETL_JOB_STATUS.NEXTVAL,
339	'LOAD_SALARY_FACT',
340	'SUCCESSFULLY COMPLETED',
341	SYSTIMESTAMP
342	);
343	
344	COMMIT;
345	

If this step is reached, then the job has been successfully completed. Successfully completed is being defined as a finish free of any errors that keep the procedure from progressing to the end of the job. The data will need to be verified against the source to make sure that the ETL is pulling the data according to the requirements.

Lines 346 – 369

Line	Code
346	--This is the equivalent of a catch block. Any errors are caught and logged.
347	EXCEPTION
348	WHEN OTHERS THEN
349	ERR_MSG := SUBSTR(SQLERRM, 1, 200);
350	INSERT INTO ETL_JOB_STATUS
351	(
352	ID,
353	ETL_JOB_NAME,
354	STATUS_NAME,

Line	Code
355	ERROR_MESSAGE,
356	STATUS_TIMESTAMP
357	)
358	VALUES
359	(
360	SEQ_ETL_JOB_STATUS.NEXTVAL,
361	'LOAD_SALARY_FACT',
362	'ERROR',
363	ERR_MSG,
364	SYSTIMESTAMP
365	);
366	
367	COMMIT;
368	
369	END;

If an exception is thrown earlier in the job, this code will catch that exception, log the job as having an error, and place that error into the ETL_JOB_STATUS table.

Review the ETL Job

This procedure is designed to be executed in the same schema as the source system tables are located. This job should result in 952,730 rows being placed into the FACT_SALARY table, which we will verify shortly. Let us examine a few of the approaches taken with this job:

1.) Running this job multiple times has no negative impact. It will not result in duplicate rows being inserted.
2.) This job may be run for a default time period or for a time period specified by the user.

While the primary key is defined as the combination of the KEY_EMPLOYEE, KEY_MONTH, and KEY_PAY_TYPE (there should be 952,730 unique combinations of these values in this table) that constraint was not created in the database. Placing that constraint into Oracle will cause the insert statement to check to make sure that EACH record is in fact unique, which will possibly slow down the insert. Leaving the constraint out (which we have done) will cause the system to technically allow a duplicate key value to be inserted. As a result, a separate SQL statement may need to be run when the ETL job is finished to ensure that this did not happen. This is a judgment call on the part of the developer.

Verify the ETL Job

When verifying a fact table you are verifying two general things. First, you want to ensure that the measures are being calculated correctly. Second, you want to ensure that the measures are being associated with the correct dimensions. Remember that the source system does not contain any of the data warehouse's surrogate keys. So, when selecting data from the fact table for verification, it is a good idea to aggregate the measures and then group by the natural keys of each of the dimensions.

Verifying the contents of the FACT_SALARY table will be a bit complex due to the placement of dollars into the newly created DIM_PAY_TYPE table. It will probably be easiest to begin by examining one individual. If that looks good, more detail can be added to the select statement(s) used for verification. As with the DIM_EMPLOYEE table, there are several ways of accomplishing this. Something like this may work well.

```
SELECT       C.EMPLOYEE_NUMBER,
             SUM(B.AMOUNT),
             'Source'
FROM         PAYCHECK_HEADER A,
             PAYCHECK_DETAIL B,
             EMPLOYEE C,
             APPOINTMENT D,
             PAY_TYPE E
WHERE        A.ID = B.PAYCHECK_HEADER_ID
             AND A.APPOINTMENT_ID = D.ID
             AND D.EMPLOYEE_ID = C.ID
             AND B.PAY_TYPE_ID = E.ID
             AND C.ID = 37136
             AND E.PAY_TYPE_NAME = 'Gross Wages'
GROUP BY     C.EMPLOYEE_NUMBER
UNION
SELECT       B.EMPLOYEE_NUMBER,
             SUM(A.AMOUNT),
             'Data Warehouse'
FROM         FACT_SALARY A,
             DIM_EMPLOYEE B,
             DIM_PAY_TYPE C,
             DIM_MONTH D
WHERE        A.KEY_EMPLOYEE = B.KEY_EMPLOYEE
             AND A.KEY_PAY_TYPE = C.KEY_PAY_TYPE
             AND A.KEY_MONTH = D.KEY_MONTH
             AND B.EMPLOYEE_ID = 37136
             AND C.COMPONENT_OF_GROSS_PAY = 'Yes'
GROUP BY     B.EMPLOYEE_NUMBER
ORDER BY     1, 3
```

This employee id was chosen since this person has multiple appointments. However, the initial query results (displayed below) cause us to raise a red flag.

EMPLOYEE_NUMBER	SUM(B.AMOUNT)	'SOURCE'
1040763	$1,650,224.60	Source
1040763	$15,835,425.74	Data Warehouse

The star schema contains a higher amount than the source system. So, the ETL job has not been written correctly. This is most easily diagnosed by walking backwards through the process. The staging table that loaded the FACT_SALARY table was the STAGE_SALARY_DATA_ADD_KEYS table. A select statement that allows us to examine data from that table as well as the results are below:

```
SELECT      C.EMPLOYEE_NUMBER,
            SUM(B.AMOUNT),
            'Source'
FROM        PAYCHECK_HEADER A,
            PAYCHECK_DETAIL B,
            EMPLOYEE C,
            APPOINTMENT D,
            PAY_TYPE E
WHERE       A.ID = B.PAYCHECK_HEADER_ID
            AND A.APPOINTMENT_ID = D.ID
            AND D.EMPLOYEE_ID = C.ID
            AND B.PAY_TYPE_ID = E.ID
            AND C.ID = 37136
            AND E.PAY_TYPE_NAME = 'Gross Wages'
GROUP BY    C.EMPLOYEE_NUMBER
UNION
SELECT      B.EMPLOYEE_NUMBER,
            SUM(A.AMOUNT),
            'Data Warehouse'
FROM        STAGE_SALARY_DATA_ADD_KEYS A,
            DIM_EMPLOYEE B,
            DIM_PAY_TYPE C,
            DIM_MONTH D
WHERE       A.KEY_EMPLOYEE = B.KEY_EMPLOYEE
            AND A.KEY_PAY_TYPE = C.KEY_PAY_TYPE
            AND A.KEY_MONTH = D.KEY_MONTH
            AND B.EMPLOYEE_ID = 37136
            AND C.COMPONENT_OF_GROSS_PAY = 'Yes'
GROUP BY    B.EMPLOYEE_NUMBER
ORDER BY    1,3
```

EMPLOYEE_NUMBER	SUM(B.AMOUNT)	'SOURCE'
1040763	$1,650,224.60	Source
1040763	$15,835,425.74	Data Warehouse

The same discrepancy exists at that step. So, we will continue moving backwards through the staging tables. Now, we will examine the first staging table, STAGE_SALARY_DATA.

```
SELECT      C.EMPLOYEE_NUMBER,
            SUM(B.AMOUNT),
            'Source'
```

FROM	PAYCHECK_HEADER A,
	PAYCHECK_DETAIL B,
	EMPLOYEE C,
	APPOINTMENT D,
	PAY_TYPE E
WHERE	A.ID = B.PAYCHECK_HEADER_ID
	AND A.APPOINTMENT_ID = D.ID
	AND D.EMPLOYEE_ID = C.ID
	AND B.PAY_TYPE_ID = E.ID
	AND C.ID = 37136
	AND E.PAY_TYPE_NAME = 'Gross Wages'
GROUP BY	C.EMPLOYEE_NUMBER
UNION	
SELECT	EMPLOYEE_NUMBER,
	SUM(AMOUNT),
	'Data Warehouse'
FROM	STAGE_SALARY_DATA
WHERE	EMPLOYEE_NUMBER = '1040763'
	AND PAY_TYPE_NAME = 'Gross Wages'
GROUP BY	EMPLOYEE_NUMBER

EMPLOYEE_NUMBER	SUM(B.AMOUNT)	'SOURCE'
1040763	$1,650,224.60	Source
1040763	$1,650,224.60	Data Warehouse

So, the data matches at this point, which strongly suggests that something has gone awry in the transformation that occurs in the STAGE_SALARY_DATA_ADD_KEYS table. A close examination of the statement that is populating the STAGE_SALARY_DATA_ADD_KEYS table shows that there is another table involved. The STAGE_SALARY_DATA_CALC_WAGES table is being joined to the STAGE_SALARY_DATA table on line 293 so that the net pay can be inserted into the STAGE_SALARY_DATA_ADD_KEYS table. A close examination of this join helps to reveal the problem. The STAGE_SALARY_DATA table contains multiple rows per CHECK_NUMBER while the STAGE_SALARY_DATA_CALC_WAGES table only contains one row per CHECK_NUMBER. This will need to be addressed before the star is released.

Updates

Unlike the LOAD_EMPLOYEE_DIMENSION job, there are no updated user requirements at this point. There are some opportunities to improve the efficiency and accuracy of this job.

1.) The statement that creates the STAGE_SALARY_DATA_CALC_WAGES table on lines 209 – 226 could be more efficient. Because the join on CHECK_NUMBER is probably slowing that down, this is an instance in which adding an index may help.

2.) The error that was discovered above must be addressed. Selecting one row per check number should solve this problem.

3.)   The efficiency of the code that creates the STAGE_SALARY_DATA_ADD_KEYS table and the code that later inserts data into that table (lines 244 – 271) is running slowly due to the three sub-selects used to populate the keys. Restructuring this so that outer joins are used will help.

In the statement that inserts data into the STAGE_SALARY_DATA_ADD_KEYS table, a lookup is being performed that always returns the DIM_PAY_TYPE.KEY_PAY_TYPE value that corresponds to a PAY_CATEGORY_2 value of 'Wages' (lines 287 – 289). Since we know that we only want to include this foreign key value with these records, it may be more efficient to look it up once.

Enhancements to the Load Salary Fact Job

Update 1

Line (new)	Code
189 (new)	--This index causes the SQL statement below, that creates the
190 (new)	--STAGE_SALARY_DATA_CALC_WAGES table, to run more efficiently
191 (new)	execute immediate 'CREATE INDEX STAGE_SALARY_CHECK_NO ON STAGE_SALARY_DATA(CHECK_NUMBER)';
192 (new)	

Lines 189 – 192 (new)

An index is needed so that the join to the STAGE_SALARY_DATA table via the CHECK_NUMBER will not take so long. These lines create that index. Because the STAGE_SALARY_DATA_CALC_WAGES table is always dropped (if it exists) and recreated by this job, simply adding an index outside of the job will not work. Each time that the table is dropped, the index is dropped as well. So, this is added to the job so that the index is created each time that the job is run. An organizational policy will need to ensure that this is the only index that will be named STAGE_SALARY_CHECK_NO. If a conflict arises, the job will terminate with an error.

Update 2

Line (new)	Code
319 (new)	|| 'FROM '
320 (new)	|| '('
321 (new)	|| 'SELECT DISTINCT EMPLOYEE_NUMBER,'
322 (new)	|| 'APPOINTMENT_BEGIN_DATE,'
323 (new)	|| 'TITLE_NAME,'
324 (new)	|| 'DEPARTMENT_NUMBER,'
325 (new)	|| 'CHECK_NUMBER,'

Line (new)	Code
326 (new)	|| 'DATE_PAID '
327 (new)	|| 'FROM STAGE_SALARY_DATA '
328 (new)	|| ') A, '

Selecting the distinct elements from the STAGE_SALARY_DATA table should prevent the double counting that was noticed earlier.

Update 3

Line (new)	Code
248 (new)	--The last staging table before the data is loaded into the fact table is
249 (new)	--created below. The keys are added via outer joins as opposed
250 (new)	--to separate subselects, since that is MUCH more efficient. A value of -1 is
251 (new)	--used as a foreign key if no value is found. This portion of
252 (new)	--the code only pulls in the withholdings for each check, not the net wages.
253 (new)	SQLSTMT := 'CREATE TABLE STAGE_SALARY_DATA_ADD_KEYS AS ('
254 (new)	|| 'SELECT NVL(B.KEY_EMPLOYEE,-1) KEY_EMPLOYEE, '
255 (new)	|| 'NVL(C.KEY_MONTH,-1) KEY_MONTH, '
256 (new)	|| 'NVL(D.KEY_PAY_TYPE,-1) KEY_PAY_TYPE, '
257 (new)	|| 'SUM(A.AMOUNT) AMOUNT '
258 (new)	|| 'FROM STAGE_SALARY_DATA A, '
259 (new)	|| 'DIM_EMPLOYEE B, '
260 (new)	|| 'DIM_MONTH C, '
261 (new)	|| 'DIM_PAY_TYPE D '
262 (new)	|| 'WHERE A.PAY_TYPE_NAME <> "Gross Wages" '
263 (new)	|| 'AND A.EMPLOYEE_NUMBER = B.EMPLOYEE_NUMBER(+) '
264 (new)	|| 'AND A.APPOINTMENT_BEGIN_DATE = B.APPOINTMENT_BEGIN_DATE(+) '
265 (new)	|| 'AND A.TITLE_NAME = B.TITLE(+) '
266 (new)	|| 'AND A.DEPARTMENT_NUMBER = B.DEPARTMENT_NUMBER(+) '
267 (new)	|| 'AND EXTRACT(MONTH FROM A.DATE_PAID) = C.CALENDAR_MONTH_NUMBER(+) '
268 (new)	|| 'AND EXTRACT(YEAR FROM A.DATE_PAID) = C.CALENDAR_YEAR(+) '
269 (new)	|| 'AND A.PAY_TYPE_NAME_IN_STAR = D.PAY_CATEGORY_2(+) '
270 (new)	|| 'GROUP BY NVL(B.KEY_EMPLOYEE,-1), NVL(C.KEY_MONTH,-1), '

Line (new)	Code
271 (new)	|| 'NVL(D.KEY_PAY_TYPE,-1)) ';
272 (new)	
273 (new)	EXECUTE IMMEDIATE SQLSTMT;
274 (new)	
275 (new)	--The insert statement below is calculating the net wages and then adding the
276 (new)	--rows with the NET WAGES into the STAGE_SALARY_DATA_ADD_KEYS table. the key
277 (new)	--that corresponds to the wages row in the DIM_PAY_TYPE table is inserted with
278 (new)	--EVERY record that is calculated. That is determined ahead of time by this
279 (new)	--SELECT into statement so that a subselect will not have to be used in the
280 (new)	--insert statement. The subselect with the distinct keyword on line 168 must
281 (new)	--be used in order to avoid double counting.
282 (new)	SELECT KEY_PAY_TYPE INTO PAY_TYPE_WAGES_KEY
283 (new)	FROM DIM_PAY_TYPE
284 (new)	WHERE PAY_CATEGORY_2 = 'Wages';
285 (new)	
286 (new)	SQLSTMT := 'INSERT INTO STAGE_SALARY_DATA_ADD_KEYS '
287 (new)	|| 'SELECT NVL(B.KEY_EMPLOYEE,-1) KEY_EMPLOYEE,'
288 (new)	|| 'NVL(C.KEY_MONTH,-1) KEY_MONTH,'
289 (new)	|| PAY_TYPE_WAGES_KEY || ' KEY_PAY_TYPE,'
290 (new)	|| 'SUM(D.GROSS_PAY - D.WITHHELD) '
291 (new)	|| 'FROM '
292 (new)	|| '('
293 (new)	|| 'SELECT DISTINCT EMPLOYEE_NUMBER,'
294 (new)	|| 'APPOINTMENT_BEGIN_DATE,'
295 (new)	|| 'TITLE_NAME,'
296 (new)	|| 'DEPARTMENT_NUMBER,'
297 (new)	|| 'CHECK_NUMBER,'
298 (new)	|| 'DATE_PAID '
299 (new)	|| 'FROM STAGE_SALARY_DATA '
300 (new)	|| ') A,'
301 (new)	|| 'DIM_EMPLOYEE B,'
302 (new)	|| 'DIM_MONTH C,'

Line (new)	Code
303 (new)	|| 'STAGE_SALARY_DATA_CALC_WAGES D '
304 (new)	|| 'WHERE A.EMPLOYEE_NUMBER = B.EMPLOYEE_NUMBER(+) '
305 (new)	|| 'AND A.APPOINTMENT_BEGIN_DATE = B.APPOINTMENT_BEGIN_DATE(+) '
306 (new)	|| 'AND A.TITLE_NAME = B.TITLE(+) '
307 (new)	|| 'AND A.DEPARTMENT_NUMBER = B.DEPARTMENT_NUMBER(+) '
308 (new)	|| 'AND EXTRACT(MONTH FROM A.DATE_PAID) = C.CALENDAR_MONTH_NUMBER(+) '
309 (new)	|| 'AND EXTRACT(YEAR FROM A.DATE_PAID) = C.CALENDAR_YEAR(+) '
310 (new)	|| 'AND A.CHECK_NUMBER = D.CHECK_NUMBER '
311 (new)	|| 'GROUP BY NVL(B.KEY_EMPLOYEE,-1), NVL(C.KEY_MONTH,-1) ';
312 (new)	
313 (new)	EXECUTE IMMEDIATE SQLSTMT;
314 (new)	COMMIT;
315 (new)	

Notice that both SQL statements are no longer using the sub selects to grab the keys (lines 254 – 256 and 287 – 289). The select statement itself is joining to each of the dimensions in order to grab the foreign keys (lines 263 – 269 and 304 – 310). It is important to use outer joins, so that if a record does not have a matching dimension value it will not be excluded.

Update 4

Line	Code
275 (new)	--The insert statement below is calculating the net wages and then adding the
276 (new)	--rows with the NET WAGES into the STAGE_SALARY_DATA_ADD_KEYS table. the key
277 (new)	--that corresponds to the wages row in the DIM_PAY_TYPE table is inserted with
278 (new)	--EVERY record that is calculated. That is determined ahead of time by this
279 (new)	--SELECT into statement so that a subselect will not have to be used in the
280 (new)	--insert statement. The subselect with the distinct keyword on line 168 must
281 (new)	--be used in order to avoid double counting.
282 (new)	SELECT KEY_PAY_TYPE INTO PAY_TYPE_WAGES_KEY
283 (new)	FROM DIM_PAY_TYPE
284 (new)	WHERE PAY_CATEGORY_2 = 'WAGES';
285 (new)	

Line	Code
286 (new)	SQLSTMT := 'INSERT INTO STAGE_SALARY_DATA_ADD_KEYS '
287 (new)	|| 'SELECT NVL(B.KEY_EMPLOYEE,-1) KEY_EMPLOYEE,'
288 (new)	|| 'NVL(C.KEY_MONTH,-1) KEY_MONTH,'
289 (new)	|| PAY_TYPE_WAGES_KEY || ' KEY_PAY_TYPE,'

The surrogate key that corresponds to the row in the DIM_PAY_TYPE table pertaining to 'Wages' is assigned to the PAY_TYPE_WAGES variable once on lines 282 – 284 and then referred to on line 289 so that the select statement will not have to pull that value as each row is selected.

Verify The ETL Job

Now that the ETL has been updated it is time to verify the results again. We can begin with the original SQL statement that we used previously, which only displays gross wages.

```
SELECT      C.EMPLOYEE_NUMBER,
            SUM(B.AMOUNT),
            'Source'
FROM        PAYCHECK_HEADER A,
            PAYCHECK_DETAIL B,
            EMPLOYEE C,
            APPOINTMENT D,
            PAY_TYPE E
WHERE       A.ID = B.PAYCHECK_HEADER_ID
            AND A.APPOINTMENT_ID = D.ID
            AND D.EMPLOYEE_ID = C.ID
            AND B.PAY_TYPE_ID = E.ID
            AND E.PAY_TYPE_NAME = 'Gross Wages'
            AND C.ID = 37136
GROUP BY    C.EMPLOYEE_NUMBER
UNION
SELECT      B.EMPLOYEE_NUMBER,
            SUM(A.AMOUNT),
            'Data Warehouse'
FROM        FACT_SALARY A,
            DIM_EMPLOYEE B,
            DIM_PAY_TYPE C,
            DIM_MONTH D
WHERE       A.KEY_EMPLOYEE = B.KEY_EMPLOYEE
            AND A.KEY_PAY_TYPE = C.KEY_PAY_TYPE
            AND A.KEY_MONTH = D.KEY_MONTH
            AND B.EMPLOYEE_ID = 37136
            AND C.COMPONENT_OF_GROSS_PAY = 'Yes'
GROUP BY    B.EMPLOYEE_NUMBER
```

EMPLOYEE_NUMBER	SUM(B.AMOUNT)	'SOURCE'
1040763	$1,650,224.60	Source
1040763	$1,650,224.60	Data Warehouse

It appears that the dollars are coming over correctly; however, we need to spend some time making sure that they are being applied to the correct dimensions. Consider this example with regards to verifying against the DIM_EMPLOYEE table, again displaying only gross wages:

```
SELECT      C.EMPLOYEE_NUMBER,
            F.DEPARTMENT_NUMBER,
            E.TITLE_NAME,
            D.APPOINTMENT_BEGIN_DATE,
            EXTRACT(YEAR FROM A.DATE_PAID) YEAR,
            EXTRACT(MONTH FROM A.DATE_PAID) MONTH,
            SUM(B.AMOUNT) AMOUNT,
            'Source'
FROM        PAYCHECK_HEADER A,
            PAYCHECK_DETAIL B,
            EMPLOYEE C,
            APPOINTMENT D,
            TITLE E,
            DEPARTMENT F,
            PAY_TYPE G
WHERE       A.ID = B.PAYCHECK_HEADER_ID
            AND A.APPOINTMENT_ID = D.ID
            AND D.EMPLOYEE_ID = C.ID
            AND D.DEPARTMENT_ID = F.ID
            AND D.TITLE_ID = E.ID
            AND B.PAY_TYPE_ID = G.ID
            AND C.ID = 37136
            AND G.PAY_TYPE_NAME = 'Gross Wages'
            AND EXTRACT(YEAR FROM A.DATE_PAID) = 1993
            AND EXTRACT(MONTH FROM A.DATE_PAID) = 1
GROUP BY    C.EMPLOYEE_NUMBER,
            F.DEPARTMENT_NUMBER,
            E.TITLE_NAME,
            D.APPOINTMENT_BEGIN_DATE,
            EXTRACT(YEAR FROM A.DATE_PAID),
            EXTRACT(MONTH FROM A.DATE_PAID),
            'Source'
UNION
SELECT      B.EMPLOYEE_NUMBER,
            B.DEPARTMENT_NUMBER,
            B.TITLE,
            B.APPOINTMENT_BEGIN_DATE,
            D.CALENDAR_YEAR,
            D.CALENDAR_MONTH_NUMBER,
```

```
            SUM(A.AMOUNT),
            'Data Warehouse'
FROM        FACT_SALARY A,
            DIM_EMPLOYEE B,
            DIM_PAY_TYPE C,
            DIM_MONTH D
WHERE       A.KEY_EMPLOYEE = B.KEY_EMPLOYEE
            AND A.KEY_PAY_TYPE = C.KEY_PAY_TYPE
            AND A.KEY_MONTH = D.KEY_MONTH
            AND B.EMPLOYEE_ID = 37136
            AND C.COMPONENT_OF_GROSS_PAY = 'Yes'
            AND D.CALENDAR_YEAR = 1993
            AND D.CALENDAR_MONTH_NUMBER = 1
GROUP BY    B.EMPLOYEE_NUMBER,
            B.DEPARTMENT_NUMBER,
            B.TITLE,
            B.APPOINTMENT_BEGIN_DATE,
            D.CALENDAR_YEAR,
            D.CALENDAR_MONTH_NUMBER
ORDER BY    1,2,3,4,5,6,8
```

EMPLOYEE_ NUMBER	DEPT_ NUMBER	TITLE_ NAME	APPT_ BEGIN_ DATE	YEAR	MONTH	AMOUNT	'SOURCE'
1040763	HR-1268	Human Resources Generalist	20-Dec-92	1993	1	$6,197.19	Data Warehouse
1040763	HR-1268	Human Resources Generalist	20-Dec-92	1993	1	$6,197.19	Source

Based on the results, it appears that the data is being applied to the DIM_EMPLOYEE dimension table correctly. Now, check the DIM_PAY_TYPE table.

```
SELECT      C.EMPLOYEE_NUMBER,
            EXTRACT(YEAR FROM A.DATE_PAID) AS YEAR,
            CASE
            WHEN
                REPLACE(E.PAY_TYPE_NAME, ' - ', ' ') = '401K Employee Contribution'
                    THEN 'Employee Paid 401K Contribution'
            WHEN
                REPLACE(E.PAY_TYPE_NAME, ' - ', ' ') = '401K Employer Contribution'
                THEN 'Employer Paid 401K Contribution'
            ELSE
                REPLACE(E.PAY_TYPE_NAME, ' - ', ' ')
            END AS TYPE,
            SUM(B.AMOUNT) AS AMOUNT,
```

```
                'Source'
FROM            PAYCHECK_HEADER A,
                PAYCHECK_DETAIL B,
                EMPLOYEE C,
                APPOINTMENT D,
                PAY_TYPE E
WHERE           A.ID = B.PAYCHECK_HEADER_ID
                AND A.APPOINTMENT_ID = D.ID
                AND D.EMPLOYEE_ID = C.ID
                AND B.PAY_TYPE_ID = E.ID
                AND C.ID = 37136
                AND EXTRACT(YEAR FROM A.DATE_PAID) = 1993
                AND E.PAY_TYPE_NAME <> 'Gross Wages'
GROUP BY        C.EMPLOYEE_NUMBER,
                EXTRACT(YEAR FROM A.DATE_PAID),
                CASE
                WHEN
                    REPLACE(E.PAY_TYPE_NAME, ' - ', ' ') = '401K Employee Contribution'
                        THEN 'Employee Paid 401K Contribution'
                WHEN
                    REPLACE(E.PAY_TYPE_NAME, ' - ', ' ') = '401K Employer Contribution'
                    THEN 'Employer Paid 401K Contribution'
                ELSE
                    REPLACE(E.PAY_TYPE_NAME, ' - ', ' ')
                END
UNION
SELECT          B.EMPLOYEE_NUMBER,
                D.CALENDAR_YEAR,
                C.PAY_CATEGORY_2,
                SUM(A.AMOUNT),
                'Data Warehouse'
FROM            FACT_SALARY A,
                DIM_EMPLOYEE B,
                DIM_PAY_TYPE C,
                DIM_MONTH D
WHERE           A.KEY_EMPLOYEE = B.KEY_EMPLOYEE
                AND A.KEY_PAY_TYPE = C.KEY_PAY_TYPE
                AND A.KEY_MONTH = D.KEY_MONTH
                AND B.EMPLOYEE_ID = 37136
                AND D.CALENDAR_YEAR = 1993
                AND C.PAY_CATEGORY_2 <> 'Wages'
GROUP BY        B.EMPLOYEE_NUMBER,
                D.CALENDAR_YEAR,
                C.PAY_CATEGORY_2
ORDER BY        1,2,3,5
```

EMPLOYEE_ NUMBER	YEAR	TYPE	AMOUNT	'SOURCE'
1040763	1993	Employee Paid 401K Contribution	$1,353.78	Data Warehouse
1040763	1993	Employee Paid 401K Contribution	$1,353.78	Source
1040763	1993	Employee Paid Dental Insurance	$379.08	Data Warehouse
1040763	1993	Employee Paid Dental Insurance	$379.08	Source
1040763	1993	Employee Paid FICA MED	$773.01	Data Warehouse
1040763	1993	Employee Paid FICA Med	$773.01	Source
1040763	1993	Employee Paid FICA OASDI	$1,943.46	Data Warehouse
1040763	1993	Employee Paid FICA OASDI	$1,943.46	Source
1040763	1993	Employee Paid Health Insurance	$1,804.95	Data Warehouse
1040763	1993	Employee Paid Health Insurance	$1,804.95	Source
1040763	1993	Employer Paid 401K Contribution	$1,353.78	Data Warehouse
1040763	1993	Employer Paid 401K Contribution	$1,353.78	Source
1040763	1993	Employer Paid Dental Insurance	$577.53	Data Warehouse
1040763	1993	Employer Paid Dental Insurance	$577.53	Source
1040763	1993	Employer Paid FICA MED	$773.01	Data Warehouse
1040763	1993	Employer Paid FICA Med	$773.01	Source
1040763	1993	Employer Paid FICA OASDI	$1,943.46	Data Warehouse
1040763	1993	Employer Paid FICA OASDI	$1,943.46	Source
1040763	1993	Employer Paid Health Insurance	$9,596.07	Data Warehouse
1040763	1993	Employer Paid Health Insurance	$9,596.07	Source
1040763	1993	Federal Withholding	$5,935.68	Data Warehouse
1040763	1993	Federal Withholding	$5,935.68	Source

These groupings look good. We have already verified the gross wages grouping in the other select statements; however, we need to verify net pay.

```
SELECT      C.EMPLOYEE_NUMBER,
            EXTRACT(YEAR FROM A.DATE_PAID) YEAR,
            'Source Gross Wages',
            SUM(B.AMOUNT) AMOUNT,
            'Source'
FROM        PAYCHECK_HEADER A,
            PAYCHECK_DETAIL B,
            EMPLOYEE C,
            APPOINTMENT D,
            PAY_TYPE E
WHERE       A.ID = B.PAYCHECK_HEADER_ID
            AND A.APPOINTMENT_ID = D.ID
            AND D.EMPLOYEE_ID = C.ID
```

```
                 AND B.PAY_TYPE_ID = E.ID
                 AND C.ID = 37136
                 AND EXTRACT(YEAR FROM A.DATE_PAID) = 1993
                 AND E.PAY_TYPE_NAME = 'Gross Wages'
GROUP BY         C.EMPLOYEE_NUMBER,
                 EXTRACT(YEAR FROM A.DATE_PAID)
UNION
SELECT           C.EMPLOYEE_NUMBER,
                 EXTRACT(YEAR FROM A.DATE_PAID) YEAR,
                 'Source Withheld',
                 SUM(B.AMOUNT) AMOUNT,
                 'Source'
FROM             PAYCHECK_HEADER A,
                 PAYCHECK_DETAIL B,
                 EMPLOYEE C,
                 APPOINTMENT D,
                 PAY_TYPE E
WHERE            A.ID = B.PAYCHECK_HEADER_ID
                 AND A.APPOINTMENT_ID = D.ID
                 AND D.EMPLOYEE_ID = C.ID
                 AND B.PAY_TYPE_ID = E.ID
                 AND C.ID = 37136
                 AND EXTRACT(YEAR FROM A.DATE_PAID) = 1993
                 AND
                 (
                   E.PAY_TYPE_NAME = 'Federal Withholding'
                   OR
                   E.PAY_TYPE_NAME LIKE '%Employee%'
                 )
GROUP BY         C.EMPLOYEE_NUMBER,
                 EXTRACT(YEAR FROM A.DATE_PAID)
UNION
SELECT           B.EMPLOYEE_NUMBER,
                 D.CALENDAR_YEAR,
                 C.PAY_CATEGORY_1,
                 SUM(A.AMOUNT),
                 'Data Warehouse'
FROM             FACT_SALARY A,
                 DIM_EMPLOYEE B,
                 DIM_PAY_TYPE C,
                 DIM_MONTH D
WHERE            A.KEY_EMPLOYEE = B.KEY_EMPLOYEE
                 AND A.KEY_PAY_TYPE = C.KEY_PAY_TYPE
                 AND A.KEY_MONTH = D.KEY_MONTH
                 AND B.EMPLOYEE_ID = 37136
                 AND D.CALENDAR_YEAR = 1993
                 AND C.PAY_CATEGORY_1 = 'Net Pay'
```

```
GROUP BY    B.EMPLOYEE_NUMBER,
            D.CALENDAR_YEAR,
            C.PAY_CATEGORY_1
ORDER BY 1,2,3,5
```

EMPLOYEE_ NUMBER	YEAR	'SOURCEGROSSWAGES'	AMOUNT	'SOURCE'
1040763	1993	Source Gross Wages	$55,774.71	Source
1040763	1993	Source Withheld	$12,189.96	Source
1040763	1993	Net Pay	$43,584.75	Data Warehouse

Notice that since the net pay is a bit complex to calculate directly out of the source system, we have opted to display the gross wages and the amount withheld on separate lines. Subtracting $12,189.96 from $55,774.71 will result in a net pay of $43,584.75. This matches the data from the star.

We have incorporated the date dimension in several of these select statements already, so we should feel reasonably confident that the data is fine from that perspective. Feel free to edit these select statements if you wish to verify from other perspectives. So, we have verified the data according to each of the dimensions and have found that it matches the star. This suggests that the ETL is working as designed but not that the ETL is designed correctly. At this point in the process, a developer will hand the star to (or run some sample data for) a business user for his verification from a business perspective. Since that is outside of the scope of this book, we will consider this star complete. Once the data has been verified from a business perspective, it will be scheduled to run with a default value of 'Y' in the DEFAULT_TIMEPERIOD parameter. The complete version of the procedure with the updates is below.

Line	Code
1	CREATE OR REPLACE PROCEDURE LOAD_SALARY_FACT
2	(
3	BEGIN_MONTH_OVERRIDE NUMBER,
4	BEGIN_YEAR OVERRIDE NUMBER,
5	END_MONTH_OVERRIDE NUMBER,
6	END_YEAR_OVERRIDE NUMBER,
7	DEFAULT_TIMEPERIOD VARCHAR2
8	)
9	
10	AS
11	
12	SQLSTMT VARCHAR2(3000);
13	TBLCOUNT NUMBER := 0;

Line	Code
14	BEGIN_AS_OF_DATE DATE;
15	END_AS_OF_DATE DATE;
16	DATE_STRING VARCHAR2(10);
17	ERR_MSG VARCHAR2(200);
18	PAY_TYPE_WAGES_KEY NUMBER := -1;
19	
20	BEGIN
21	--Log the beginning of the job
22	INSERT INTO ETL_JOB_STATUS
23	(
24	ID,
25	ETL_JOB_NAME,
26	STATUS_NAME,
27	STATUS_TIMESTAMP
28	)
29	VALUES
30	(
31	SEQ_ETL_JOB_STATUS.NEXTVAL,
32	'LOAD_SALARY_FACT',
33	'IN PROGRESS',
34	SYSTIMESTAMP
35	);
36	
37	COMMIT;
38	
39	--If the table exists, drop it. If not, do nothing. the table will be
40	--created below.
41	SELECT COUNT(*) INTO TBLCOUNT
42	FROM ALL_TABLES
43	WHERE TABLE_NAME = 'STAGE_SALARY_DATA'
44	AND OWNER =
45	(
46	SELECT SYS_CONTEXT('USERENV', 'CURRENT_SCHEMA')

Line	Code
47	FROM DUAL
48	);
49	
50	IF TBLCOUNT > 0 THEN
51	EXECUTE IMMEDIATE 'DROP TABLE STAGE_SALARY_DATA';
52	END IF;
53	
54	--If the DEFAULT_PERIOD variable is set to 'Y', then the prior month and the
55	--current month are loaded or reloaded into the fact table.
56	--Otherwise, the overrides are used.
57	IF DEFAULT_TIMEPERIOD = 'Y' THEN
58	SELECT TRUNC(TRUNC(SYSDATE,'MM')-1,'MM') INTO BEGIN_AS_OF_DATE FROM DUAL;
59	SELECT LAST_DAY(TRUNC(SYSDATE)) INTO END_AS_OF_DATE FROM DUAL;
60	ELSE
61	--This IF statement is used to place a leading zero before the month number
62	--for those months less than 10
63	IF BEGIN_MONTH_OVERRIDE < 10 THEN
64	BEGIN_AS_OF_DATE := TO_DATE
65	(
66	'0'
67	|| TO_CHAR(BEGIN_MONTH_OVERRIDE)
68	|| '/01/'
69	|| TO_CHAR(BEGIN_YEAR_OVERRIDE),'MM/DD/YYYY'
70	);
71	ELSE
72	BEGIN_AS_OF_DATE := TO_DATE
73	(
74	TO_CHAR(BEGIN_MONTH_OVERRIDE)
75	|| '/01/'
76	|| TO_CHAR(BEGIN_YEAR_OVERRIDE),'MM/DD/YYYY'
77	);

Line	Code
78	END IF;
79	
80	IF END_MONTH_OVERRIDE < 10 THEN
81	END_AS_OF_DATE := LAST_DAY
82	(
83	TO_DATE
84	(
85	'0'
86	|| TO_CHAR(END_MONTH_OVERRIDE)
87	|| '/01/'
88	|| TO_CHAR(END_YEAR_OVERRIDE),'MM/DD/YYYY'
89	)
90	);
91	ELSE
92	END_AS_OF_DATE := LAST_DAY
93	(
94	TO_DATE
95	(
96	TO_CHAR(END_MONTH_OVERRIDE)
97	|| '/01/'
98	||
99	TO_CHAR(END_YEAR_OVERRIDE),'MM/DD/YYYY'
100	)
101	);
102	end if;
103	
104	END IF;
105	
106	--Dump the data into the staging table and transform the PAY_TYPE_NAME into
107	--the values that are used in the DIM_PAY_TYPE table
108	SQLSTMT := 'CREATE TABLE STAGE_SALARY_DATA AS ('
109	|| 'SELECT E.EMPLOYEE_NUMBER, '
110	|| 'C.APPOINTMENT_BEGIN_DATE, '

Line	Code
111	|| 'F.TITLE_NAME, '
112	|| 'G.DEPARTMENT_NUMBER, '
113	|| 'D.PAY_TYPE_NAME, '
114	|| 'CASE WHEN PAY_TYPE_NAME = "Employer Paid - Dental Insurance" '
115	|| 'THEN "Employer Paid Dental Insurance" '
116	|| 'WHEN PAY_TYPE_NAME = "Employee Paid - Dental Insurance" '
117	|| 'THEN "Employee Paid Dental Insurance" '
118	|| 'WHEN PAY_TYPE_NAME = "Employer Paid - Health Insurance" '
119	|| 'THEN "Employer Paid Health Insurance" '
120	|| 'WHEN PAY_TYPE_NAME = "Employee Paid - Health Insurance" '
121	|| 'THEN "Employee Paid Health Insurance" '
122	|| 'WHEN PAY_TYPE_NAME = "Employer Paid - FICA OASDI" '
123	|| 'THEN "Employer Paid FICA OASDI" '
124	|| 'WHEN PAY_TYPE_NAME = "Employee Paid - FICA OASDI" '
125	|| 'THEN "Employee Paid FICA OASDI" '
126	|| 'WHEN PAY_TYPE_NAME = "Employer Paid - FICA Med" '
127	|| 'THEN "Employer Paid FICA MED" '
128	|| 'WHEN PAY_TYPE_NAME = "Employee Paid - FICA Med" '
129	|| 'THEN "Employee Paid FICA MED" '
130	|| 'WHEN PAY_TYPE_NAME = "401K Employee Contribution" '
131	|| 'THEN "Employee Paid 401K Contribution" '
132	|| 'WHEN PAY_TYPE_NAME = "401K Employer Contribution" '
133	|| 'THEN "Employer Paid 401K Contribution" '
134	|| 'WHEN PAY_TYPE_NAME = "Federal Withholding" '
135	|| 'THEN "Federal Withholding" '
136	|| 'ELSE NULL END AS PAY_TYPE_NAME_IN_STAR, '
137	|| 'A.DATE_PAID, '
138	|| 'A.CHECK_NUMBER, '
139	|| 'SUM(B.AMOUNT) AS AMOUNT '
140	|| 'FROM PAYCHECK_HEADER A, '
141	|| 'PAYCHECK_DETAIL B, '
142	|| 'APPOINTMENT C, '
143	|| 'PAY_TYPE D, '

Line	Code
144	|| 'EMPLOYEE E, '
145	|| 'TITLE F, '
146	|| 'DEPARTMENT G '
147	|| 'WHERE B.PAYCHECK_HEADER_ID = A.ID '
148	|| 'AND A.APPOINTMENT_ID = C.ID '
149	|| 'AND B.PAY_TYPE_ID = D.ID '
150	|| 'AND C.EMPLOYEE_ID = E.ID '
151	|| 'AND C.TITLE_ID = F.ID '
152	|| 'AND C.DEPARTMENT_ID = G.ID '
153	|| 'AND A.DATE_PAID BETWEEN '" || TO_CHAR(BEGIN_AS_OF_DATE,'DD-MON-YYYY')
154	|| '" AND '"
155	|| TO_CHAR(END_AS_OF_DATE,'DD-MON-YYYY') || '" '
156	|| 'GROUP BY E.EMPLOYEE_NUMBER, '
157	|| 'C.APPOINTMENT_BEGIN_DATE, '
158	|| 'F.TITLE_NAME, '
159	|| 'G.DEPARTMENT_NUMBER, '
160	|| 'D.PAY_TYPE_NAME, '
161	|| 'CASE WHEN PAY_TYPE_NAME = "Employer Paid - Dental Insurance" '
162	|| 'THEN "Employer Paid Dental Insurance" '
163	|| 'WHEN PAY_TYPE_NAME = "Employee Paid - Dental Insurance" '
164	|| 'THEN "Employee Paid Dental Insurance" '
165	|| 'WHEN PAY_TYPE_NAME = "Employer Paid - Health Insurance" '
166	|| 'THEN "Employer Paid Health Insurance" '
167	|| 'WHEN PAY_TYPE_NAME = "Employee Paid - Health Insurance" '
168	|| 'THEN "Employee Paid Health Insurance" '
169	|| 'WHEN PAY_TYPE_NAME = "Employer Paid - FICA OASDI" '
170	|| 'THEN "Employer Paid FICA OASDI" '
171	|| 'WHEN PAY_TYPE_NAME = "Employee Paid - FICA OASDI" '
172	|| 'THEN "Employee Paid FICA OASDI" '
173	|| 'WHEN PAY_TYPE_NAME = "Employer Paid - FICA Med" '
174	|| 'THEN "Employer Paid FICA MED" '
175	|| 'WHEN PAY_TYPE_NAME = "Employee Paid - FICA Med" '
176	|| 'THEN "Employee Paid FICA MED" '

Line	Code
177	|| 'WHEN PAY_TYPE_NAME = "401K Employee Contribution" '
178	|| 'THEN "Employee Paid 401K Contribution" '
179	|| 'WHEN PAY_TYPE_NAME = "401K Employer Contribution" '
180	|| 'THEN "Employer Paid 401K Contribution" '
181	|| 'WHEN PAY_TYPE_NAME = "Federal Withholding" '
182	|| 'THEN "Federal Withholding" '
183	|| 'ELSE NULL END, '
184	|| 'A.DATE_PAID, '
185	|| 'A.CHECK_NUMBER) ';
186	
187	EXECUTE IMMEDIATE SQLSTMT;
188	
189 (new)	--This index causes the SQL statement below, that creates the
190 (new)	--STAGE_SALARY_DATA_CALC_WAGES table, to run more efficiently
191 (new)	EXECUTE IMMEDIATE 'CREATE INDEX STAGE_SALARY_CHECK_NO ON STAGE_SALARY_DATA(CHECK_NUMBER)';
192 (new)	
193 (new)	--If the table exists, drop it. If not, do nothing.
194 (new)	--The table will be created below.
195 (new)	SELECT COUNT(*) INTO TBLCOUNT
196 (new)	FROM ALL_TABLES
197 (new)	WHERE TABLE_NAME = 'STAGE_SALARY_DATA_CALC_WAGES'
198 (new)	AND OWNER =
199 (new)	(
200 (new)	SELECT SYS_CONTEXT('USERENV', 'CURRENT_SCHEMA')
201 (new)	FROM DUAL
202 (new)	);
203 (new)	
204 (new)	IF TBLCOUNT > 0 THEN
205 (new)	EXECUTE IMMEDIATE 'DROP TABLE STAGE_SALARY_DATA_CALC_WAGES';
206 (new)	END IF;
207 (new)	
208 (new)	--The source system stores the gross amount and the detail that is actually

Line	Code
209 (new)	--part of the gross total. The detail must be subtracted
210 (new)	--from the gross amount to get the net amount. Separating the gross pay from
211 (new)	--the amount withheld is done in the table below. The net amount will be
212 (new)	--calculated later.
213 (new)	SQLSTMT := 'CREATE TABLE STAGE_SALARY_DATA_CALC_WAGES AS ('
214 (new)	|| 'SELECT A.CHECK_NUMBER, '
215 (new)	|| 'SUM(A.AMOUNT) GROSS_PAY, '
216 (new)	|| ' (SELECT SUM(AMOUNT) '
217 (new)	|| 'FROM STAGE_SALARY_DATA AA '
218 (new)	|| 'WHERE AA.PAY_TYPE_NAME_IN_STAR IN '
219 (new)	||'('
220 (new)	||'"Federal Withholding", '
221 (new)	||'"Employee Paid Health Insurance", '
222 (new)	||'"Employee Paid Dental Insurance", '
223 (new)	||'"Employee Paid 401K Contribution", '
224 (new)	||'"Employee Paid FICA OASDI", '
225 (new)	||'"Employee Paid FICA MED" '
226 (new)	||')'
227 (new)	|| 'AND AA.CHECK_NUMBER = A.CHECK_NUMBER) WITHHELD '
228 (new)	|| 'FROM STAGE_SALARY_DATA A '
229 (new)	|| 'WHERE A.PAY_TYPE_NAME = "Gross Wages" '
230 (new)	|| 'GROUP BY A.CHECK_NUMBER) ';
231 (new)	
232 (new)	EXECUTE IMMEDIATE SQLSTMT;
233 (new)	
234 (new)	--If the table exists, drop it. If not, do nothing. the table will be created below.
235 (new)	SELECT COUNT(*) INTO TBLCOUNT
236 (new)	FROM ALL_TABLES
237 (new)	WHERE TABLE_NAME = 'STAGE_SALARY_DATA_ADD_KEYS'
238 (new)	AND OWNER =
239 (new)	(
240 (new)	SELECT SYS_CONTEXT('USERENV', 'CURRENT_SCHEMA')
241 (new)	FROM DUAL

Line	Code
242 (new)	);
243 (new)	
244 (new)	IF TBLCOUNT > 0 THEN
245 (new)	EXECUTE IMMEDIATE 'DROP TABLE STAGE_SALARY_DATA_ADD_KEYS';
246 (new)	END IF;
247 (new)	
248 (new)	--The last staging table before the data is loaded into the fact table is
249 (new)	--created below. The keys are added via outer joins as opposed
250 (new)	--to separate subselects, since that is MUCH more efficient. A value of -1 is
251 (new)	--used as a foreign key if no value is found. This portion of
252 (new)	--the code only pulls in the withholdings for each check, not the net wages.
253 (new)	SQLSTMT := 'CREATE TABLE STAGE_SALARY_DATA_ADD_KEYS AS ('
254 (new)	|| 'SELECT NVL(B.KEY_EMPLOYEE,-1) KEY_EMPLOYEE, '
255 (new)	|| 'NVL(C.KEY_MONTH,-1) KEY_MONTH, '
256 (new)	|| 'NVL(D.KEY_PAY_TYPE,-1) KEY_PAY_TYPE, '
257 (new)	|| 'SUM(A.AMOUNT) AMOUNT '
258 (new)	|| 'FROM STAGE_SALARY_DATA A, '
259 (new)	|| 'DIM_EMPLOYEE B, '
260 (new)	|| 'DIM_MONTH C, '
261 (new)	|| 'DIM_PAY_TYPE D '
262 (new)	|| 'WHERE A.PAY_TYPE_NAME <> "Gross Wages" '
263 (new)	|| 'AND A.EMPLOYEE_NUMBER = B.EMPLOYEE_NUMBER(+) '
264 (new)	|| 'AND A.APPOINTMENT_BEGIN_DATE = B.APPOINTMENT_BEGIN_DATE(+) '
265 (new)	|| 'AND A.TITLE_NAME = B.TITLE(+) '
266 (new)	|| 'AND A.DEPARTMENT_NUMBER = B.DEPARTMENT_NUMBER(+) '
267 (new)	|| 'AND EXTRACT(MONTH FROM A.DATE_PAID) = C.CALENDAR_MONTH_NUMBER(+) '
268 (new)	|| 'AND EXTRACT(YEAR FROM A.DATE_PAID) = C.CALENDAR_YEAR(+) '
269 (new)	|| 'AND A.PAY_TYPE_NAME_IN_STAR = D.PAY_CATEGORY_2(+) '
270 (new)	|| 'GROUP BY NVL(B.KEY_EMPLOYEE,-1), NVL(C.KEY_MONTH,-1), '
271 (new)	|| 'NVL(D.KEY_PAY_TYPE,-1) ';
272 (new)	

Line	Code
273 (new)	EXECUTE IMMEDIATE SQLSTMT;
274 (new)	
275 (new)	--The insert statement below is calculating the net wages and then adding the
276 (new)	--rows with the NET WAGES into the STAGE_SALARY_DATA_ADD_KEYS table. the key
277 (new)	--that corresponds to the wages row in the DIM_PAY_TYPE table is inserted with
278 (new)	--EVERY record that is calculated. That is determined ahead of time by this
279 (new)	--SELECT into statement so that a subselect will not have to be used in the
280 (new)	--insert statement. The subselect with the distinct keyword on line 168 must
281 (new)	--be used in order to avoid double counting.
282 (new)	SELECT KEY_PAY_TYPE INTO PAY_TYPE_WAGES_KEY
283 (new)	FROM DIM_PAY_TYPE
284 (new)	WHERE PAY_CATEGORY_2 = 'Wages';
285 (new)	
286 (new)	SQLSTMT := 'INSERT INTO STAGE_SALARY_DATA_ADD_KEYS '
287 (new)	|| 'SELECT NVL(B.KEY_EMPLOYEE,-1) KEY_EMPLOYEE, '
288 (new)	|| 'NVL(C.KEY_MONTH,-1) KEY_MONTH, '
289 (new)	|| PAY_TYPE_WAGES_KEY || ' KEY_PAY_TYPE, '
290 (new)	|| 'SUM(D.GROSS_PAY - D.WITHHELD) '
291 (new)	|| 'FROM '
292 (new)	|| '('
293 (new)	|| 'SELECT DISTINCT EMPLOYEE_NUMBER, '
294 (new)	|| 'APPOINTMENT_BEGIN_DATE, '
295 (new)	|| 'TITLE_NAME, '
296 (new)	|| 'DEPARTMENT_NUMBER, '
297 (new)	|| 'CHECK_NUMBER, '
298 (new)	|| 'DATE_PAID '
299 (new)	|| 'FROM STAGE_SALARY_DATA '
300 (new)	|| ') A, '
301 (new)	|| 'DIM_EMPLOYEE B, '
302 (new)	|| 'DIM_MONTH C, '
303 (new)	|| 'STAGE_SALARY_DATA_CALC_WAGES D '
304 (new)	|| 'WHERE A.EMPLOYEE_NUMBER = B.EMPLOYEE_NUMBER(+) '

Line	Code
305 (new)	|| 'AND A.APPOINTMENT_BEGIN_DATE = B.APPOINTMENT_BEGIN_DATE(+) '
306 (new)	|| 'AND A.TITLE_NAME = B.TITLE(+) '
307 (new)	|| 'AND A.DEPARTMENT_NUMBER = B.DEPARTMENT_NUMBER(+) '
308 (new)	|| 'AND EXTRACT(MONTH FROM A.DATE_PAID) = C.CALENDAR_MONTH_NUMBER(+) '
309 (new)	|| 'AND EXTRACT(YEAR FROM A.DATE_PAID) = C.CALENDAR_YEAR(+) '
310 (new)	|| 'AND A.CHECK_NUMBER = D.CHECK_NUMBER '
311 (new)	|| 'GROUP BY NVL(B.KEY_EMPLOYEE,-1), NVL(C.KEY_MONTH,-1) ';
312 (new)	
313 (new)	EXECUTE IMMEDIATE SQLSTMT;
314 (new)	COMMIT;
315 (new)	
316 (new)	--Updating the existing rows for months in which the amount has changed
317 (new)	--(i.e., an additional payroll was processed for that month since the last
318 (new)	--load) would be very inefficient. As a result, any existing data pertaining
319 (new)	--to the month(s) being pulled into the fact table is completely deleted from
320 (new)	--the fact table and reloaded.
321 (new)	SQLSTMT := 'DELETE '
322 (new)	|| 'FROM FACT_SALARY A '
323 (new)	|| 'WHERE A.KEY_MONTH IN ('
324 (new)	|| 'SELECT KEY_MONTH '
325 (new)	|| 'FROM DIM_MONTH '
326 (new)	|| 'WHERE FIRST_DAY BETWEEN '" || TO_CHAR(BEGIN_AS_OF_DATE,'DD-MON-YYYY')
327 (new)	|| '" AND '"
328 (new)	|| TO_CHAR(END_AS_OF_DATE,'DD-MON-YYYY') || '") ';
329 (new)	
330 (new)	EXECUTE IMMEDIATE SQLSTMT;
331 (new)	COMMIT;
332 (new)	
333 (new)	--The fact table is loaded
334 (new)	
335 (new)	EXECUTE IMMEDIATE 'INSERT INTO FACT_SALARY SELECT * FROM STAGE_SALARY_DATA_ADD_KEYS';

Line	Code
336 (new)	
337 (new)	COMMIT;
338 (new)	
339 (new)	--Log the successful completion of the job.
340 (new)	INSERT INTO ETL_JOB_STATUS
341 (new)	(
342 (new)	ID,
343 (new)	ETL_JOB_NAME,
344 (new)	STATUS_NAME,
345 (new)	STATUS_TIMESTAMP
346 (new)	)
347 (new)	VALUES
348 (new)	(
349 (new)	SEQ_ETL_JOB_STATUS.NEXTVAL,
350 (new)	'LOAD_SALARY_FACT',
351 (new)	'SUCCESSFULLY COMPLETED',
352 (new)	SYSTIMESTAMP
353 (new)	);
354 (new)	
355 (new)	COMMIT;
356 (new)	
357 (new)	--This is the equivalent of a catch block. Any errors are caught and logged.
358 (new)	EXCEPTION
359 (new)	WHEN OTHERS THEN
360 (new)	ERR_MSG := SUBSTR(SQLERRM, 1, 200);
361 (new)	INSERT INTO ETL_JOB_STATUS
362 (new)	(
363 (new)	ID,
364 (new)	ETL_JOB_NAME,
365 (new)	STATUS_NAME,
366 (new)	ERROR_MESSAGE,
367 (new)	STATUS_TIMESTAMP
368 (new)	)

Line	Code
369 (new)	VALUES
370 (new)	(
371 (new)	SEQ_ETL_JOB_STATUS.NEXTVAL,
372 (new)	'LOAD_SALARY_FACT',
373 (new)	'ERROR',
374 (new)	ERR_MSG,
375 (new)	SYSTIMESTAMP
376 (new)	);
377 (new)	
378 (new)	COMMIT;
379 (new)	
380 (new)	END;

7
SALARY DATA DAILY

Updated Requirements

In the previous chapter we completed a star schema that allows the user to analyze salary data at a monthly level. Now suppose that the users have requested to see this data at a daily level, based on date paid. The business process has not changed, but the analytical requirements provided by the users have. Since we have already completed the other star schema at a monthly grain, a couple of options exist:

1.)   We can edit the existing fact table so that it changes granularity from a monthly grain to a daily grain

2.)   We can create a brand new fact table to contain data at a daily grain, which will coexist with the original

While neither option is right or wrong, consider the fact that although this new requirement allows the users to analyze data at a more granular level, high-level analysis will not go away. Some people will still want to only see data at a monthly level or higher. If those analysts are using the new fact table, their queries will probably be less efficient than they would be using the monthly star. As a result, we will go with option two and create an additional fact table which will coexist with the original.

Also, this design will allow the analyst to see the data by individual paycheck. As a result, we can include the paycheck number in this fact table. Based on these requirements, this is the table design of this star schema that our ETL will need to populate.

Figure 7-1

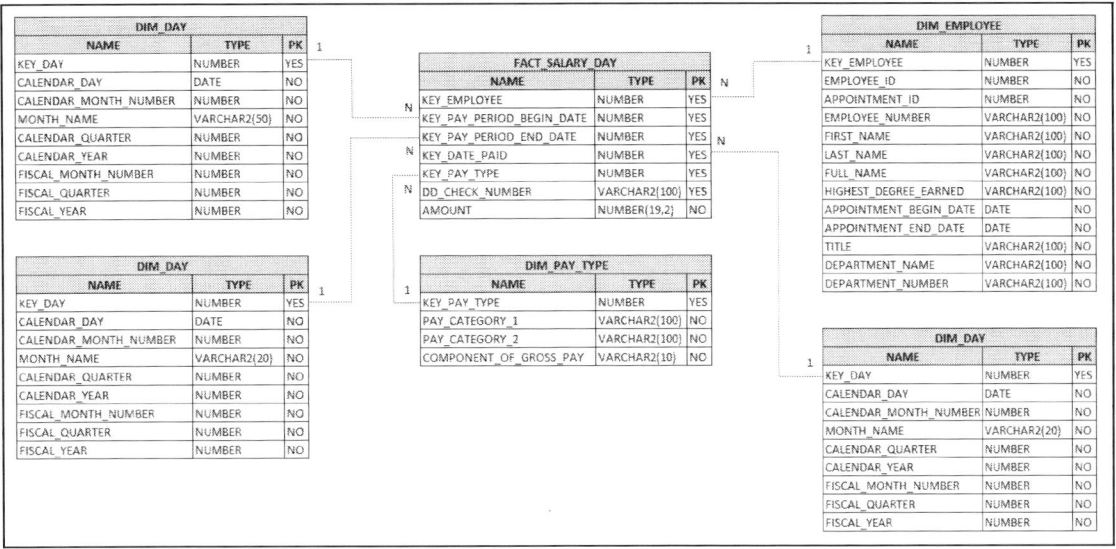

DIM_DAY: This is a standard type zero date dimension table at the daily level. This dimension has no source system and will be populated by the ETL developer.

FACT_SALARY_DAY: This is a basic fact table that allows the user to analyze salary dollars by date paid, pay period begin date, pay period end date, pay type, employee, and check number. It is a more detailed version of the FACT_SALARY table. The data warehouse architect has decided to add the date paid, the pay period begin date, the pay period end date, and the check number to the star since all of these elements exist at the same grain as the date paid. The FACT_SALARY_DAY.AMOUNT value will come from the PAYCHECK_DETAIL.AMOUNT column. The five key values will refer to their associated dimension tables. The DD_CHECK_NUMBER field will be included as a degenerate dimension, with the source being the PAYCHECK_DETAIL.CHECK_NUMBER column. Because the KEY_PAY_PERIOD BEGIN_DATE, KEY_PAY_PERIOD_END_DATE, and KEY_DATE_PAID columns all refer to a particular day, they all "point" to the same D_DAY dimension table. If a SQL statement that is written to analyze this star must include all three of these dates, then the same table will need to be included multiple times in the SQL statement and aliased.

Strategy for ETL

This salary data star contains one fact table and three dimension tables, with one of the dimension tables being referenced three times. Because the addition of new rows into the fact table will require references to their respective dimension tables, the dimension tables must be created and updated first. While it is possible to populate the three dimension tables and the fact table as one PL/SQL procedure, it is probably smarter to write a separate procedure for each table. If a dimension is a conformed dimension (referred to by multiple fact tables) the code to populate it can be called by other procedures.

Because the FACT_SALARY_DAY and the FACT_SALARY tables come from the same source, it is possible for the aggregated version to be populated by the one with the more granular data. In other words, the procedure to load the FACT_SALARY_DAY can also be used to load the FACT_SALARY table. Data will be pulled from the source system to load FACT_SALARY_DAY. Once that is done, the data from FACT_SALARY_DAY will be aggregated to a monthly level and then placed into the FACT_SALARY table. As a result, the original LOAD_SALARY_FACT job that we created previously can be "retired."

Populating the FACT_SALARY_DAY Table

It is now time to populate the FACT_SALARY_DAY table. This task will be a little different than writing an ETL job from scratch for a couple of reasons. First, as already discussed, this job will be used to replace the LOAD_SALARY_FACT job that we already created. As a result, all of that code will be incorporated into this job and slightly edited. Second, the last step will populate two fact tables, the FACT_SALARY table and the FACT_SALARY_DAY table. Remember from chapter five that the goal of an ETL job that populates a fact table is to accomplish the following.

1.) Select all necessary data from the source
    a. Measures
    b. Natural keys of the dimension objects
    c. Degenerate dimension objects
2.) Transform the data as needed
    a. Aggregate measures and group by the appropriate objects
    b. Add foreign keys to dimension tables
3.) Delete any existing rows from the fact table that will be replaced by the new data
4.) Load the fact table

Using the Based on Timeframe approach will be best. Refer to the Update Existing Rows and Insert New Rows section in chapter five for more detail regarding this approach.

Only one piece of the setup is needed. The FACT_SALARY_DAY table will need to be created so that this job can populate it. Run the following to create the FACT_SALARY_DAY table:

```
CREATE TABLE FACT_SALARY_DAY
  (
    KEY_EMPLOYEE                 NUMBER,
    KEY_PAY_PERIOD_BEGIN_DATE    NUMBER,
    KEY_PAY_PERIOD_END_DATE      NUMBER,
    KEY_DATE_PAID                NUMBER,
    KEY_PAY_TYPE                 NUMBER,
    DD_CHECK_NUMBER              VARCHAR2(100),
    AMOUNT                       NUMBER(19,2)
  )
```

The infrastructure has been created, so now it is time to populate the new fact table as well as the original. Let us examine this code from the beginning. Notice that this code is almost identical to the first 104 lines of the LOAD_SALARY_FACT procedure.

Lines 1 – 19

Line	Code
1	CREATE OR REPLACE PROCEDURE LOAD_SALARY_FACT_TABLES
2	(
3	BEGIN_MONTH_OVERRIDE NUMBER,
4	BEGIN_YEAR_OVERRIDE NUMBER,
5	END_MONTH_OVERRIDE NUMBER,
6	END_YEAR_OVERRIDE NUMBER,
7	DEFAULT_TIMEPERIOD VARCHAR2
8	)
9	
10	AS
11	
12	SQLSTMT VARCHAR2(3000);
13	TBLCOUNT NUMBER := 0;
14	BEGIN_AS_OF_DATE DATE;
15	END_AS_OF_DATE DATE;
16	DATE_STRING VARCHAR(10);
17	ERR_MSG VARCHAR2(200);
18	PAY_TYPE_WAGES_KEY NUMBER := -1;
19	

These lines contain the standard beginning of the PL/SQL procedure. The procedure is named, variables are declared, and the job begins. The user may specify the first month and year (BEGIN_MONTH_OVERRIDE and BEGIN_YEAR_OVERRIDE variables) and the last month and year (END_MONTH_OVERRIDE and END_YEAR_OVERRIDE variables) of the timeframe for which the data shall be pulled. A default timeframe (explained later) can be used if the user sets the DEFAULT_TIMEPERIOD variable to a value of 'Y'.

Lines 20 – 38

Line	Code
20	BEGIN
21	--Log the beginning of the job
22	INSERT INTO ETL_JOB_STATUS
23	(
24	ID,

Line	Code
25	ETL_JOB_NAME,
26	STATUS_NAME,
27	STATUS_TIMESTAMP
28	)
29	VALUES
30	(
31	SEQ_ETL_JOB_STATUS.NEXTVAL,
32	'LOAD_SALARY_FACT_TABLES',
33	'IN PROGRESS',
34	SYSTIMESTAMP
35	);
36	
37	COMMIT;
38	

The job is logged in the ETL_JOB_STATUS table as having begun.

Lines 39 – 52

Line	Code
39	--If the table exists, drop it. If not, do nothing. The table will be created below.
40	SELECT COUNT(*) INTO TBLCOUNT
41	FROM ALL_TABLES
42	WHERE TABLE_NAME = 'STAGE_SALARY_DATA'
43	AND OWNER =
44	(
45	SELECT SYS_CONTEXT('USERENV', 'CURRENT_SCHEMA')
46	FROM DUAL
47	);
48	
49	IF TBLCOUNT > 0 THEN
50	EXECUTE IMMEDIATE 'DROP TABLE STAGE_SALARY_DATA';
51	END IF;
52	

If the first staging table, STAGE_SALARY_DATA, exists it is dropped.

Lines 53 – 101

Line	Code
53	--If the DEFAULT_PERIOD variable is set to 'Y', then the prior month and the current month are loaded or reloaded into the fact table.
54	--Otherwise, the overrides are used.
55	IF DEFAULT_TIMEPERIOD = 'Y' THEN
56	SELECT TRUNC(TRUNC(SYSDATE,'MM')-1,'MM') INTO BEGIN_AS_OF_DATE FROM DUAL;
57	SELECT LAST_DAY(TRUNC(SYSDATE)) INTO END_AS_OF_DATE FROM DUAL;
58	ELSE
59	--This IF statement is used to place a leading zero before the month number for those months less than 10
60	IF BEGIN_MONTH_OVERRIDE < 10 THEN
61	BEGIN_AS_OF_DATE := TO_DATE
62	(
63	'0'
64	|| TO_CHAR(BEGIN_MONTH_OVERRIDE)
65	|| '/01/'
66	|| TO_CHAR(BEGIN_YEAR_OVERRIDE),'MM/DD/YYYY'
67	);
68	ELSE
69	BEGIN_AS_OF_DATE := TO_DATE
70	(
71	TO_CHAR(BEGIN_MONTH_OVERRIDE)
72	|| '/01/'
73	|| TO_CHAR(BEGIN_YEAR_OVERRIDE),'MM/DD/YYYY'
74	);
75	END IF;
76	
77	IF END_MONTH_OVERRIDE < 10 THEN
78	END_AS_OF_DATE := LAST_DAY
79	(
80	TO_DATE

Line	Code
81	(
82	'0'
83	|| TO_CHAR(END_MONTH_OVERRIDE)
84	|| '/01/'
85	|| TO_CHAR(END_YEAR_OVERRIDE),'MM/DD/YYYY'
86	)
87	);
88	ELSE
89	END_AS_OF_DATE := LAST_DAY
90	(
91	TO_DATE
92	(
93	TO_CHAR(END_MONTH_OVERRIDE)
94	|| '/01/'
95	|| TO_CHAR(END_YEAR_OVERRIDE),'MM/DD/YYYY'
96	)
97	);
98	END IF;
99	
100	END IF;
101	

These lines set the time period for which the data will be loaded. If the DEFAULT_PERIOD variable is set to a value of 'Y', then data that applies to dollars paid in the current month and the previous month will be pulled. The BEGIN_AS_OF_DATE and the END_AS_OF_DATE variables are set to the first day of the previous month and the last day of the current month, respectively.

If the DEFAULT_PERIOD variable is set to 'N', then data that applies to dollars paid in the months provided by the user will be pulled. The BEGIN_AS_OF_DATE and the END_AS_OF_DATE variables are set according to the variables provided by the user.

Extract Data From the Source
This portion of the job extracts data from the source system and places it into the staging area.

Lines 102 – 188

Line	Code
102	--Dump the data into the staging table and transform the PAY_TYPE_NAME into the values that are used in the DIM_PAY_TYPE table
103	SQLSTMT := 'CREATE TABLE STAGE_SALARY_DATA AS ('
104	|| 'SELECT E.EMPLOYEE_NUMBER,'
105	|| 'C.APPOINTMENT_BEGIN_DATE,'
106	|| 'F.TITLE_NAME,'
107	|| 'G.DEPARTMENT_NUMBER,'
108	|| 'D.PAY_TYPE_NAME,'
109	|| 'CASE WHEN PAY_TYPE_NAME = "Employer Paid - Dental Insurance"'
110	|| 'THEN "Employer Paid Dental Insurance"'
111	|| 'WHEN PAY_TYPE_NAME = "Employee Paid - Dental Insurance"'
112	|| 'THEN "Employee Paid Dental Insurance"'
113	|| 'WHEN PAY_TYPE_NAME = "Employer Paid - Health Insurance"'
114	|| 'THEN "Employer Paid Health Insurance"'
115	|| 'WHEN PAY_TYPE_NAME = "Employee Paid - Health Insurance"'
116	|| 'THEN "Employee Paid Health Insurance"'
117	|| 'WHEN PAY_TYPE_NAME = "Employer Paid - FICA OASDI"'
118	|| 'THEN "Employer Paid FICA OASDI"'
119	|| 'WHEN PAY_TYPE_NAME = "Employee Paid - FICA OASDI"'
120	|| 'THEN "Employee Paid FICA OASDI"'
121	|| 'WHEN PAY_TYPE_NAME = "Employer Paid - FICA Med"'
122	|| 'THEN "Employer Paid FICA MED"'
123	|| 'WHEN PAY_TYPE_NAME = "Employee Paid - FICA Med"'
124	|| 'THEN "Employee Paid FICA MED"'
125	|| 'WHEN PAY_TYPE_NAME = "401K Employee Contribution"'
126	|| 'THEN "Employee Paid 401K Contribution"'
127	|| 'WHEN PAY_TYPE_NAME = "401K Employer Contribution"'
128	|| 'THEN "Employer Paid 401K Contribution"'
129	|| 'WHEN PAY_TYPE_NAME = "Federal Withholding"'
130	|| 'THEN "Federal Withholding"'
131	|| 'ELSE NULL END AS PAY_TYPE_NAME_IN_STAR,'
132	|| 'A.DATE_PAID,'

Line	Code
133	|| 'A.PAY_PERIOD_BEGIN_DATE, '
134	|| 'A.PAY_PERIOD_END_DATE, '
135	|| 'A.CHECK_NUMBER, '
136	|| 'SUM(B.AMOUNT) AS AMOUNT '
137	|| 'FROM PAYCHECK_HEADER A, '
138	|| 'PAYCHECK_DETAIL B, '
139	|| 'APPOINTMENT C, '
140	|| 'PAY_TYPE D, '
141	|| 'EMPLOYEE E, '
142	|| 'TITLE F, '
143	|| 'DEPARTMENT G '
144	|| 'WHERE B.PAYCHECK_HEADER_ID = A.ID '
145	|| 'AND A.APPOINTMENT_ID = C.ID '
146	|| 'AND B.PAY_TYPE_ID = D.ID '
147	|| 'AND C.EMPLOYEE_ID = E.ID '
148	|| 'AND C.TITLE_ID = F.ID '
149	|| 'AND C.DEPARTMENT_ID = G.ID '
150	|| 'AND A.DATE_PAID BETWEEN '''
151	|| TO_CHAR(BEGIN_AS_OF_DATE,'DD-MON-YYYY')
152	|| ''' AND '''
153	|| TO_CHAR(END_AS_OF_DATE,'DD-MON-YYYY') || ''' '
154	|| 'GROUP BY E.EMPLOYEE_NUMBER, '
155	|| 'C.APPOINTMENT_BEGIN_DATE, '
156	|| 'F.TITLE_NAME, '
157	|| 'G.DEPARTMENT_NUMBER, '
158	|| 'D.PAY_TYPE_NAME, '
159	|| 'CASE WHEN PAY_TYPE_NAME = "Employer Paid - Dental Insurance" '
160	|| 'THEN "Employer Paid Dental Insurance" '
161	|| 'WHEN PAY_TYPE_NAME = "Employee Paid - Dental Insurance" '
162	|| 'THEN "Employee Paid Dental Insurance" '
163	|| 'WHEN PAY_TYPE_NAME = "Employer Paid - Health Insurance" '
164	|| 'THEN "Employer Paid Health Insurance" '
165	|| 'WHEN PAY_TYPE_NAME = "Employee Paid - Health Insurance" '

Line	Code
166	|| 'THEN "Employee Paid Health Insurance" '
167	|| 'WHEN PAY_TYPE_NAME = "Employer Paid - FICA OASDI" '
168	|| 'THEN "Employer Paid FICA OASDI" '
169	|| 'WHEN PAY_TYPE_NAME = "Employee Paid - FICA OASDI" '
170	|| 'THEN "Employee Paid FICA OASDI" '
171	|| 'WHEN PAY_TYPE_NAME = "Employer Paid - FICA Med" '
172	|| 'THEN "Employer Paid FICA MED" '
173	|| 'WHEN PAY_TYPE_NAME = "Employee Paid - FICA Med" '
174	|| 'THEN "Employee Paid FICA MED" '
175	|| 'WHEN PAY_TYPE_NAME = "401K Employee Contribution" '
176	|| 'THEN "Employee Paid 401K Contribution" '
177	|| 'WHEN PAY_TYPE_NAME = "401K Employer Contribution" '
178	|| 'THEN "Employer Paid 401K Contribution" '
179	|| 'WHEN PAY_TYPE_NAME = "Federal Withholding" '
180	|| 'THEN "Federal Withholding" '
181	|| 'ELSE NULL END, '
182	|| 'A.DATE_PAID, '
183	|| 'A.PAY_PERIOD_BEGIN_DATE, '
184	|| 'A.PAY_PERIOD_END_DATE, '
185	|| 'A.CHECK_NUMBER) ';
186	
187	EXECUTE IMMEDIATE SQLSTMT;
188	

Remember from chapter five that the first thing that needs to be accomplished during the extract portion of the job is the selection of all necessary data from the source. This includes measures, natural keys of the dimension objects, and degenerate dimension objects. The FACT_SALARY table contains one measure and foreign keys to three dimension tables. The FACT_SALARY_DAY table contains one measure, foreign keys to five dimension tables, and one degenerate dimension. The SQL within these lines are used to create and populate the STAGE_SALARY_DATA table with this data.

Measure: PAYCHECK_HEADER.AMOUNT (line 136)

Natural Key To DIM_EMPLOYEE:
- EMPLOYEE.EMPLOYEE_NUMBER(line 104)
- APPOINTMENT.APPOINTMENT_BEGIN_DATE (line 105)

- TITLE.TITLE_NAME (line 106)
- DEPARTMENT.DEPARTMENT_NUMBER (line 107)

Natural Key To DIM_MONTH: PAYCHECK_HEADER.DATE_PAID (line 132) will be used to derive the month

Natural Key To DIM_DAY (three separate references to the dimension):
- PAYCHECK_HEADER.DATE_PAID (line 132),
- PAYCHECK_HEADER.PAY_PERIOD_BEGIN_DATE (line 133)
- PAYCHECK_HEADER.PAY_PERIOD_END_DATE (line 134)

Natural Key To DIM_PAY_TYPE: PAYCHECK_DETAIL.PAY_TYPE_NAME and associated case statement (lines 108 – 131)

Degenerate Dimension: PAYCHECK_HEADER.CHECK_NUMBER (line 135)

Lines 189 – 192

Line	Code
189	--This index causes the SQL statement below, that creates the STAGE_SALARY_DATA_CALC_WAGES table, to run more efficiently
190	SQLSTMT := 'CREATE INDEX STAGE_SALARY_CHECK_NO ON STAGE_SALARY_DATA(CHECK_NUMBER)';
191	EXECUTE IMMEDIATE SQLSTMT;
192	

We learned from the LOAD_SALARY_FACT job that an index is needed on the STAGE_SALARY_DATA table in order to increase efficiency. These lines add that index.

Transform the Data
This portion of the job begins to transform the data so that it will fit into the fact tables.

Lines 193 – 206

Line	Code
193	--If the table exists, drop it. If not, do nothing. The table will be created below.
194	SELECT COUNT(*) INTO TBLCOUNT
195	FROM ALL_TABLES
196	WHERE TABLE_NAME = 'STAGE_SALARY_DATA_CALC_WAGES'
197	AND OWNER =
198	(
199	SELECT SYS_CONTEXT('USERENV', 'CURRENT_SCHEMA')

Line	Code
200	FROM DUAL
201	);
202	
203	IF TBLCOUNT > 0 THEN
204	EXECUTE IMMEDIATE 'DROP TABLE STAGE_SALARY_DATA_CALC_WAGES';
205	END IF;
206	

If the STAGE_SALARY_DATA_CALC_WAGES table already exists, drop it.

Lines 207 – 232

Line	Code
207	--The source system stores the gross amount and the detail that is actually
208	--part of the gross total. The detail must be subtracted from the gross
209	--amount to get the net amount. Separating the gross pay from the amount
210	--withheld is done in the table below. The net amount will be calculated
211	--later.
212	SQLSTMT := 'CREATE TABLE STAGE_SALARY_DATA_CALC_WAGES AS ('
213	|| 'SELECT A.CHECK_NUMBER,'
214	|| 'SUM(A.AMOUNT) GROSS_PAY,'
215	|| ' (SELECT SUM(AMOUNT) '
216	|| 'FROM STAGE_SALARY_DATA AA '
217	|| 'WHERE AA.PAY_TYPE_NAME_IN_STAR IN '
218	|| '(
219	|| '"Federal Withholding", '
220	|| '"Employee Paid Health Insurance", '
221	|| '"Employee Paid Dental Insurance", '
222	|| '"Employee Paid 401K Contribution", '
223	|| '"Employee Paid FICA OASDI", '
224	|| '"Employee Paid FICA MED"'
225	||')'
226	|| 'AND AA.CHECK_NUMBER = A.CHECK_NUMBER) WITHHELD '
227	|| 'FROM STAGE_SALARY_DATA A '

Line	Code
228	|| 'WHERE A.PAY_TYPE_NAME = "Gross Wages" '
229	|| 'GROUP BY A.CHECK_NUMBER) ';
230	
231	EXECUTE IMMEDIATE SQLSTMT;
232	

In order to place certain dollars into the appropriate buckets (using the DIM_PAY_TYPE dimension) the total amount withheld from each paycheck must be calculated so that the net pay can be calculated later.

Lines 233 – 246

Line	Code
233	--If the table exists, drop it. If not, do nothing. The table will be created below.
234	SELECT COUNT(*) INTO TBLCOUNT
235	FROM ALL_TABLES
236	WHERE TABLE_NAME = 'STAGE_SALARY_DATA_ADD_KEYS'
237	AND OWNER =
238	(
239	SELECT SYS_CONTEXT('USERENV', 'CURRENT_SCHEMA')
240	FROM DUAL
241	);
242	
243	IF TBLCOUNT > 0 THEN
244	EXECUTE IMMEDIATE 'DROP TABLE STAGE_SALARY_DATA_ADD_KEYS';
245	END IF;
246	

If the STAGE_SALARY_DATA_ADD_KEYS table exists, drop it.

Lines 247 – 280

Line	Code
247	--The last staging table before the data is loaded into the fact table is
248	--created below. The keys are added via outer joins as opposed to separate
249	--subselects, since that is MUCH more efficient. A value of -1 is used as a

Line	Code
250	--foreign key if no value is found. This portion of the code only pulls in
251	--the withholdings for each check, not the net wages.
252	SQLSTMT := 'CREATE TABLE STAGE_SALARY_DATA_ADD_KEYS AS ('
253	|| 'SELECT NVL(B.KEY_EMPLOYEE,-1) KEY_EMPLOYEE, '
254	|| 'NVL(D.KEY_DAY,-1) KEY_PAY_PERIOD_BEGIN_DATE, '
255	|| 'NVL(E.KEY_DAY,-1) KEY_PAY_PERIOD_END_DATE, '
256	|| 'NVL(C.KEY_DAY,-1) KEY_DATE_PAID, '
257	|| 'NVL(F.KEY_PAY_TYPE,-1) KEY_PAY_TYPE, '
258	|| 'A.CHECK_NUMBER DD_CHECK_NUMBER, '
259	|| 'SUM(A.AMOUNT) AMOUNT '
260	|| 'FROM STAGE_SALARY_DATA A, '
261	|| 'DIM_EMPLOYEE B, '
262	|| 'DIM_DAY C, '
263	|| 'DIM_DAY D, '
264	|| 'DIM_DAY E, '
265	|| 'DIM_PAY_TYPE F '
266	|| 'WHERE A.PAY_TYPE_NAME <> "Gross Wages" '
267	|| 'AND A.EMPLOYEE_NUMBER = B.EMPLOYEE_NUMBER(+) '
268	|| 'AND A.APPOINTMENT_BEGIN_DATE = B.APPOINTMENT_BEGIN_DATE(+) '
269	|| 'AND A.TITLE_NAME = B.TITLE(+) '
270	|| 'AND A.DEPARTMENT_NUMBER = B.DEPARTMENT_NUMBER(+) '
271	|| 'AND A.DATE_PAID = C.CALENDAR_DAY(+) '
272	|| 'AND A.PAY_PERIOD_BEGIN_DATE = D.CALENDAR_DAY(+) '
273	|| 'AND A.PAY_PERIOD_END_DATE = E.CALENDAR_DAY(+) '
274	|| 'AND A.PAY_TYPE_NAME_IN_STAR = F.PAY_CATEGORY_2(+) '
275	|| 'GROUP BY NVL(B.KEY_EMPLOYEE,-1), NVL(C.KEY_DAY,-1), NVL(D.KEY_DAY,-1), '
276	|| 'NVL(E.KEY_DAY,-1), NVL(F.KEY_PAY_TYPE,-1), A.CHECK_NUMBER '
277	|| ')';
278	
279	EXECUTE IMMEDIATE SQLSTMT;
280	

The select statement pulls all of the individual components of pay from the STAGE_SALARY_DATA table with the exception of the net pay. The net pay will be calculated and then stored in the next step. This select statement also selects the KEY_EMPLOYEE from the DIM_EMPLOYEE table (line 253), the KEY_DAY from the DIM_DAY table (lines 254 – 256), and the KEY_PAY_TYPE from the DIM_PAY_TYPE table (line 257). The CHECK_NUMBER (degenerate dimension) is included as well (line 258). The STAGE_SALARY_DATA table is joined to each of the associated dimension tables based on the natural key of each dimension. Outer joins are used so that if a dimension value is not found the row will still be included, with a value of -1 being stored as the surrogate key value.

Lines 281 – 291

Line	Code
281	--The insert statement below is calculating the net wages and then adding the
282	--rows with the net wages into the STAGE_SALARY_DATA_ADD_KEYS table. The key
283	--that corresponds to the wages row in the DIM_PAY_TYPE table is inserted
284	--with EVERY record that is calculated. That is determined ahead of time by
285	--this SELECT INTO statement so that a subselect will not have to be used in
286	--the INSERT statement. The distinct keyword MUST be used in the sum in
287	--order to avoid double counting.
288	SELECT KEY_PAY_TYPE INTO PAY_TYPE_WAGES_KEY
289	FROM DIM_PAY_TYPE
290	WHERE PAY_CATEGORY_2 = 'Wages';
291	

The KEY_PAY_TYPE associated with net pay is stored in the PAY_TYPE_WAGES_KEY variable so that it is only retrieved once, instead of being retrieved for EACH row in the select statement.

Lines 292 – 330

Line	Code
292	SQLSTMT := 'INSERT INTO STAGE_SALARY_DATA_ADD_KEYS '
293	|| 'SELECT NVL(B.KEY_EMPLOYEE,-1),'
294	|| 'NVL(D.KEY_DAY,-1),'
295	|| 'NVL(E.KEY_DAY,-1),'
296	|| 'NVL(C.KEY_DAY,-1),'
297	|| PAY_TYPE_WAGES_KEY || ','
298	|| 'A.CHECK_NUMBER,'

Line	Code
299	| | 'SUM(F.GROSS_PAY - F.WITHHELD) '
300	| | 'FROM '
301	| | '(
302	| | 'SELECT DISTINCT EMPLOYEE_NUMBER, '
303	| | 'APPOINTMENT_BEGIN_DATE, '
304	| | 'TITLE_NAME, '
305	| | 'DEPARTMENT_NUMBER, '
306	| | 'CHECK_NUMBER, '
307	| | 'DATE_PAID, '
308	| | 'PAY_PERIOD_BEGIN_DATE, '
309	| | 'PAY_PERIOD_END_DATE '
310	| | 'FROM STAGE_SALARY_DATA '
311	| | ') A, '
312	| | 'DIM_EMPLOYEE B, '
313	| | 'DIM_DAY C, '
314	| | 'DIM_DAY D, '
315	| | 'DIM_DAY E, '
316	| | 'STAGE_SALARY_DATA_CALC_WAGES F '
317	| | 'WHERE A.EMPLOYEE_NUMBER = B.EMPLOYEE_NUMBER(+) '
318	| | 'AND A.APPOINTMENT_BEGIN_DATE = B.APPOINTMENT_BEGIN_DATE(+) '
319	| | 'AND A.TITLE_NAME = B.TITLE(+) '
320	| | 'AND A.DEPARTMENT_NUMBER = B.DEPARTMENT_NUMBER(+) '
321	| | 'AND A.DATE_PAID = C.CALENDAR_DAY(+) '
322	| | 'AND A.PAY_PERIOD_BEGIN_DATE = D.CALENDAR_DAY(+) '
323	| | 'AND A.PAY_PERIOD_END_DATE = E.CALENDAR_DAY(+) '
324	| | 'AND A.CHECK_NUMBER = F.CHECK_NUMBER '
325	| | 'GROUP BY NVL(B.KEY_EMPLOYEE,-1), NVL(C.KEY_DAY,-1), NVL(D.KEY_DAY,-1), '
326	| | 'NVL(E.KEY_DAY,-1), A.CHECK_NUMBER ';
327	
328	EXECUTE IMMEDIATE SQLSTMT;
329	COMMIT;
330	

This select statement (within an insert statement) is used to place the net pay into the STAGE_SALARY_DATA_ADD_KEYS table. The net pay is calculated on line 299. Remember from the LOAD_SALARY_FACT job that a select distinct sub query was needed to avoid double-counting. This applies to this job as well and exists on line 302.

Insert New Records

This portion of the job will place the new records into the FACT_SALARY_DAY and the FACT_SALARY tables.

Lines 331 – 349

Line	Code
331	--Updating the existing rows for months in which the amount has changed
332	--(i.e., an additional payroll was processed for that month since the last
333	--load) would be very inefficient. As a result, any existing data pertaining
334	--to the month(s) being pulled into the fact table is completely deleted from
335	--the fact table and reloaded.
336	SQLSTMT := 'DELETE '
337	|| 'FROM FACT_SALARY_DAY A '
338	|| 'WHERE A.KEY_DATE_PAID IN ('
339	|| 'SELECT KEY_DAY '
340	|| 'FROM DIM_DAY '
341	|| 'WHERE CALENDAR_DAY BETWEEN '''
342	|| TO_CHAR(BEGIN_AS_OF_DATE,'DD-MON-YYYY')
343	|| ''' AND '''
344	|| TO_CHAR(END_AS_OF_DATE,'DD-MON-YYYY')
345	|| ''') ';
346	
347	EXECUTE IMMEDIATE SQLSTMT;
348	COMMIT;
349	

It is possible that rows already exist in the fact table for the time frame for which the job is pulling data. If that is the case, those rows are deleted from the fact table.

Lines 350 – 356

Line	Code
350	--The fact table is loaded
351	SQLSTMT := 'INSERT INTO FACT_SALARY_DAY '
352	|| 'SELECT * FROM STAGE_SALARY_DATA_ADD_KEYS ';
353	
354	EXECUTE IMMEDIATE SQLSTMT;
355	COMMIT;
356	

This statement inserts the rows from the STAGE_SALARY_DATA_ADD_KEYS table into the FACT_SALARY_DAY table.

Insert Into FACT_SALARY

Since the FACT_SALARY and the FACT_SALARY_DAY tables contain the same data but at different levels of granularity, the more detailed (FACT_SALARY_DAY) can be used to populate the more aggregated (FACT_SALARY).

Lines 357 – 370

Line	Code
357	SQLSTMT := 'DELETE '
358	|| 'FROM FACT_SALARY A '
359	|| 'WHERE A.KEY_MONTH IN ('
360	|| 'SELECT KEY_MONTH '
361	|| 'FROM DIM_MONTH '
362	|| 'WHERE FIRST_DAY BETWEEN ''
363	|| TO_CHAR(BEGIN_AS_OF_DATE,'DD-MON-YYYY')
364	|| ''' AND '''
365	|| TO_CHAR(END_AS_OF_DATE,'DD-MON-YYYY')
366	|| '') ';
367	
368	EXECUTE IMMEDIATE SQLSTMT;
369	COMMIT;
370	

It is possible that rows already exist in the LOAD_SALARY_FACT table for the time frame for which the job is pulling data. If that is the case, those rows are deleted from the fact table.

Lines 371 – 386

Line	Code
371	--The fact table is loaded
372	SQLSTMT := 'INSERT INTO FACT_SALARY '
373	|| 'SELECT A.KEY_EMPLOYEE, '
374	|| 'NVL(B.KEY_MONTH,-1), '
375	|| 'A.KEY_PAY_TYPE, '
376	|| 'SUM(A.AMOUNT) '
377	|| 'FROM STAGE_SALARY_DATA_ADD_KEYS A, '
378	|| 'DIM_MONTH B, '
379	|| 'DIM_DAY C '
380	|| 'WHERE A.KEY_DATE_PAID = C.KEY_DAY '
381	|| 'AND C.CALENDAR_DAY BETWEEN B.FIRST_DAY AND B.LAST_DAY '
382	|| 'GROUP BY A.KEY_EMPLOYEE, B.KEY_MONTH, A.KEY_PAY_TYPE ';
383	
384	EXECUTE IMMEDIATE SQLSTMT;
385	COMMIT;
386	

The daily salary data from the LOAD_SALARY_FACT_DAY table is aggregated to a monthly level and then placed into the LOAD_SALARY_FACT table.

Lines 387 – 404

Line	Code
387	--Log the successful completion of the job.
388	INSERT INTO ETL_JOB_STATUS
389	(
390	ID,
391	ETL_JOB_NAME,
392	STATUS_NAME,
393	STATUS_TIMESTAMP
394	)
395	VALUES

Line	Code
396	(
397	SEQ_ETL_JOB_STATUS.NEXTVAL,
398	'LOAD_SALARY_FACT_TABLES',
399	'SUCCESSFULLY COMPLETED',
400	SYSTIMESTAMP
401	);
402	
403	COMMIT;
404	

If this step is reached, then the job has been successfully completed. Successfully completed is being defined as a finish free of any errors that prevent the procedure from progressing to the end of the job. The data will need to be verified against the source to make sure that the ETL is pulling the data according to the requirements.

Lines 405 – 428

Line	Code
405	--This is the equivalent of a catch block. Any errors are caught and logged.
406	EXCEPTION
407	WHEN OTHERS THEN
408	ERR_MSG := SUBSTR(SQLERRM, 1, 200);
409	INSERT INTO ETL_JOB_STATUS
410	(
411	ID,
412	ETL_JOB_NAME,
413	STATUS_NAME,
414	ERROR_MESSAGE,
415	STATUS_TIMESTAMP
416	)
417	VALUES
418	(
419	SEQ_ETL_JOB_STATUS.NEXTVAL,
420	'LOAD_SALARY_FACT_TABLES',
421	'ERROR',
422	ERR_MSG,
423	SYSTIMESTAMP

Line	Code
424	);
425	
426	COMMIT;
427	
428	END;

If an exception is thrown earlier in the job, this code will catch that exception, log the job as having an error, and place that error into the ETL_JOB_STATUS table.

Review the ETL Job

This procedure is designed to be executed in the same schema as the source system tables are located. This job should result in 1,314,908 rows being placed into the FACT_SALARY_DAY table, which we will verify shortly. Let us examine a few of the approaches taken with this job:

1.) Running this job multiple times has no negative impact. It will not result in a duplication of rows.
2.) This job may be run for a default time period or for a time period specified by the user.
3.) While the primary key is defined as the combination of the KEY_EMPLOYEE, KEY_PAY_PERIOD_BEGIN_DATE, KEY_PAY_PERIOD_END_DATE, KEY_DATE_PAID, KEY_PAY_TYPE, and DD_CHECK_NUMBER (there should be 1,314,908 unique combinations of these values in this table) that constraint was not created in the database. In other words, the system will not stop a situation in which a duplicate is mistakenly inserted. As a result, a separate SQL statement may need to be run when the ETL job is finished to ensure that this did not happen. Enforcing such a constraint at the database level may slow down the insert. To include or not include this constraint at the database level is a judgment call on the part of the developer.

Verify the ETL Job

Remember from the LOAD_SALARY_FACT job that verifying the data within a fact table involves verifying that the measures have been aggregated correctly as well as verifying that the data has been associated with the appropriate dimensions. Aggregating the measures and grouping them by the natural keys of the dimension objects is a good strategy.

Similar to the LOAD_SALARY_FACT job, verifying the contents of the FACT_SALARY_DAY table will be a bit complex due to the placement of dollars into the newly created DIM_PAY_TYPE table. We will begin with a simple example.

```
SELECT      C.EMPLOYEE_NUMBER,
            SUM(B.AMOUNT),
            'Source'
FROM        PAYCHECK_HEADER A,
            PAYCHECK_DETAIL B,
            EMPLOYEE C,
            APPOINTMENT D,
            PAY_TYPE E
```

```
WHERE        A.ID = B.PAYCHECK_HEADER_ID
             AND A.APPOINTMENT_ID = D.ID
             AND D.EMPLOYEE_ID = C.ID
             AND B.PAY_TYPE_ID = E.ID
             AND C.ID = 37136
             AND E.PAY_TYPE_NAME = 'Gross Wages'
GROUP BY     C.EMPLOYEE_NUMBER
UNION
SELECT       B.EMPLOYEE_NUMBER,
             SUM(A.AMOUNT),
             'Data Warehouse'
FROM         FACT_SALARY_DAY A,
             DIM_EMPLOYEE B,
             DIM_PAY_TYPE C,
             DIM_DAY D,
             DIM_DAY E,
             DIM_DAY F
WHERE        A.KEY_EMPLOYEE = B.KEY_EMPLOYEE
             AND A.KEY_PAY_TYPE = C.KEY_PAY_TYPE
             AND A.KEY_DATE_PAID = D.KEY_DAY
             AND A.KEY_PAY_PERIOD_BEGIN_DATE = E.KEY_DAY
             AND A.KEY_PAY_PERIOD_END_DATE = F.KEY_DAY
             AND B.EMPLOYEE_ID = 37136
             AND C.COMPONENT_OF_GROSS_PAY = 'Yes'
GROUP BY     B.EMPLOYEE_NUMBER
ORDER BY     1,3
```

EMPLOYEE_NUMBER	SUM(B.AMOUNT)	'SOURCE'
1040763	$1,650,224.60	Source
1040763	$1,650,224.60	Data Warehouse

The data appears to be populating correctly. One positive thing about this approach is that the errors were identified when writing the LOAD_SALARY_FACT job. However, we still need to go through the verification process. Consider this as a way to verify the DIM_EMPLOYEE dimension.

```
SELECT       C.EMPLOYEE_NUMBER,
             F.DEPARTMENT_NUMBER,
             G.TITLE_NAME,
             D.APPOINTMENT_BEGIN_DATE,
             A.DATE_PAID,
             SUM(B.AMOUNT) AMOUNT,
             'Source'
FROM         PAYCHECK_HEADER A,
             PAYCHECK_DETAIL B,
             EMPLOYEE C,
             APPOINTMENT D,
```

```
                PAY_TYPE E,
                DEPARTMENT F,
                TITLE G
WHERE           A.ID = B.PAYCHECK_HEADER_ID
                AND A.APPOINTMENT_ID = D.ID
                AND D.EMPLOYEE_ID = C.ID
                AND B.PAY_TYPE_ID = E.ID
                AND D.DEPARTMENT_ID = F.ID
                AND D.TITLE_ID = G.ID
                AND C.ID = 37136
                AND E.PAY_TYPE_NAME = 'Gross Wages'
                AND EXTRACT(YEAR FROM A.DATE_PAID) = 1993
                AND EXTRACT(MONTH FROM A.DATE_PAID) = 1
GROUP BY        C.EMPLOYEE_NUMBER,
                F.DEPARTMENT_NUMBER,
                G.TITLE_NAME,
                D.APPOINTMENT_BEGIN_DATE,
                A.DATE_PAID
UNION
SELECT          B.EMPLOYEE_NUMBER,
                B.DEPARTMENT_NUMBER,
                B.TITLE,
                B.APPOINTMENT_BEGIN_DATE,
                D.CALENDAR_DAY,
                SUM(A.AMOUNT),
                'Data Warehouse'
FROM            FACT_SALARY_DAY A,
                DIM_EMPLOYEE B,
                DIM_PAY_TYPE C,
                DIM_DAY D,
                DIM_DAY E,
                DIM_DAY F
WHERE           A.KEY_EMPLOYEE = B.KEY_EMPLOYEE
                AND A.KEY_PAY_TYPE = C.KEY_PAY_TYPE
                AND A.KEY_DATE_PAID = D.KEY_DAY
                AND A.KEY_PAY_PERIOD_BEGIN_DATE = E.KEY_DAY
                AND A.KEY_PAY_PERIOD_END_DATE = F.KEY_DAY
                AND B.EMPLOYEE_ID = 37136
                AND C.COMPONENT_OF_GROSS_PAY = 'Yes'
                AND D.CALENDAR_YEAR = 1993
                AND D.CALENDAR_MONTH_NUMBER = 1
GROUP BY        B.EMPLOYEE_NUMBER,
                B.DEPARTMENT_NUMBER,
                B.TITLE,
                B.APPOINTMENT_BEGIN_DATE,
                D.CALENDAR_DAY
ORDER BY        1,2,3,4,5,7
```

EMPLOYEE_ NUMBER	DEPARTMENT_ NUMBER	TITLE_NAME	APPT_BEGIN_ DATE	DATE_PAID	AMOUNT	'SOURCE'
1040763	HR-1268	Human Resources Generalist	20-Dec-92	1-Jan-93	$2,065.73	Data Wareho use
1040763	HR-1268	Human Resources Generalist	20-Dec-92	1-Jan-93	$2,065.73	Source
1040763	HR-1268	Human Resources Generalist	20-Dec-92	15-Jan-93	$2,065.73	Data Wareho use
1040763	HR-1268	Human Resources Generalist	20-Dec-92	15-Jan-93	$2,065.73	Source
1040763	HR-1268	Human Resources Generalist	20-Dec-92	29-Jan-93	$2,065.73	Data Wareho use
1040763	HR-1268	Human Resources Generalist	20-Dec-92	29-Jan-93	$2,065.73	Source

Based on the results, it appears that the data is being applied to the DIM_EMPLOYEE dimension table correctly. Now, check the DIM_PAY_TYPE table.

```
SELECT        C.EMPLOYEE_NUMBER,
              A.DATE_PAID,
              CASE
              WHEN REPLACE(E.PAY_TYPE_NAME, ' - ', ' ') = '401K Employee
Contribution'
              THEN 'Employee Paid 401K Contribution'
              WHEN REPLACE(E.PAY_TYPE_NAME, ' - ', ' ') = '401K Employer
Contribution'
              THEN 'Employer Paid 401K Contribution'
              ELSE REPLACE(E.PAY_TYPE_NAME, ' - ', ' ')
              END AS TYPE,
              SUM(B.AMOUNT) AS AMOUNT,
              'Source'
FROM          PAYCHECK_HEADER A,
              PAYCHECK_DETAIL B,
              EMPLOYEE C,
              APPOINTMENT D,
              PAY_TYPE E
WHERE         A.ID = B.PAYCHECK_HEADER_ID
              AND A.APPOINTMENT_ID = D.ID
              AND D.EMPLOYEE_ID = C.ID
              AND B.PAY_TYPE_ID = E.ID
```

```
                AND C.ID = 37136
                AND EXTRACT(YEAR FROM A.DATE_PAID) = 1993
                AND EXTRACT(MONTH FROM A.DATE_PAID) = 1
                AND E.PAY_TYPE_NAME <> 'Gross Wages'
GROUP BY        C.EMPLOYEE_NUMBER,
                A.DATE_PAID,
                CASE
                WHEN REPLACE(E.PAY_TYPE_NAME, ' - ', ' ') = '401K Employee
Contribution'
                THEN 'Employee Paid 401K Contribution'
                WHEN REPLACE(E.PAY_TYPE_NAME, ' - ', ' ') = '401K Employer
Contribution'
                THEN 'Employer Paid 401K Contribution'
                ELSE REPLACE(E.PAY_TYPE_NAME, ' - ', ' ')
                END
UNION
SELECT          B.EMPLOYEE_NUMBER,
                D.CALENDAR_DAY,
                C.PAY_CATEGORY_2,
                SUM(A.AMOUNT),
                'Data Warehouse'
FROM            FACT_SALARY_DAY A,
                DIM_EMPLOYEE B,
                DIM_PAY_TYPE C,
                DIM_DAY D,
                DIM_DAY E,
                DIM_DAY F
WHERE           A.KEY_EMPLOYEE = B.KEY_EMPLOYEE
                AND A.KEY_PAY_TYPE = C.KEY_PAY_TYPE
                AND A.KEY_DATE_PAID = D.KEY_DAY
                AND A.KEY_PAY_PERIOD_BEGIN_DATE = E.KEY_DAY
                AND A.KEY_PAY_PERIOD_END_DATE = F.KEY_DAY
                AND B.EMPLOYEE_ID = 37136
                AND D.CALENDAR_YEAR = 1993
                AND D.CALENDAR_MONTH_NUMBER = 1
                AND C.PAY_CATEGORY_2 <> 'Wages'
GROUP BY        B.EMPLOYEE_NUMBER,
                D.CALENDAR_DAY,
                C.PAY_CATEGORY_2
ORDER BY        1,2,3,5
```

EMPLOYEE_ NUMBER	DATE_PAID	TYPE	AMOUNT	'SOURCE'
1040763	1-Jan-93	Employee Paid 401K Contribution	$50.14	Data Warehouse

128

EMPLOYEE_ NUMBER	DATE_PAID	TYPE	AMOUNT	'SOURCE'
1040763	1-Jan-93	Employee Paid 401K Contribution	$50.14	Source
1040763	1-Jan-93	Employee Paid Dental Insurance	$14.04	Data Warehouse
1040763	1-Jan-93	Employee Paid Dental Insurance	$14.04	Source
1040763	1-Jan-93	Employee Paid FICA MED	$28.63	Data Warehouse
1040763	1-Jan-93	Employee Paid FICA Med	$28.63	Source
1040763	1-Jan-93	Employee Paid FICA OASDI	$71.98	Data Warehouse
1040763	1-Jan-93	Employee Paid FICA OASDI	$71.98	Source
1040763	1-Jan-93	Employee Paid Health Insurance	$66.85	Data Warehouse
1040763	1-Jan-93	Employee Paid Health Insurance	$66.85	Source
1040763	1-Jan-93	Employer Paid 401K Contribution	$50.14	Data Warehouse
1040763	1-Jan-93	Employer Paid 401K Contribution	$50.14	Source
1040763	1-Jan-93	Employer Paid Dental Insurance	$21.39	Data Warehouse
1040763	1-Jan-93	Employer Paid Dental Insurance	$21.39	Source
1040763	1-Jan-93	Employer Paid FICA MED	$28.63	Data Warehouse
1040763	1-Jan-93	Employer Paid FICA Med	$28.63	Source
1040763	1-Jan-93	Employer Paid FICA OASDI	$71.98	Data Warehouse
1040763	1-Jan-93	Employer Paid FICA OASDI	$71.98	Source
1040763	1-Jan-93	Employer Paid Health Insurance	$355.41	Data Warehouse
1040763	1-Jan-93	Employer Paid Health Insurance	$355.41	Source
1040763	1-Jan-93	Federal Withholding	$219.84	Data Warehouse
1040763	1-Jan-93	Federal Withholding	$219.84	Source
1040763	15-Jan-93	Employee Paid 401K Contribution	$50.14	Data Warehouse
1040763	15-Jan-93	Employee Paid 401K Contribution	$50.14	Source

EMPLOYEE_ NUMBER	DATE_PAID	TYPE	AMOUNT	'SOURCE'
1040763	15-Jan-93	Employee Paid Dental Insurance	$14.04	Data Warehouse
1040763	15-Jan-93	Employee Paid Dental Insurance	$14.04	Source
1040763	15-Jan-93	Employee Paid FICA MED	$28.63	Data Warehouse
1040763	15-Jan-93	Employee Paid FICA Med	$28.63	Source
1040763	15-Jan-93	Employee Paid FICA OASDI	$71.98	Data Warehouse
1040763	15-Jan-93	Employee Paid FICA OASDI	$71.98	Source
1040763	15-Jan-93	Employee Paid Health Insurance	$66.85	Data Warehouse
1040763	15-Jan-93	Employee Paid Health Insurance	$66.85	Source
1040763	15-Jan-93	Employer Paid 401K Contribution	$50.14	Data Warehouse
1040763	15-Jan-93	Employer Paid 401K Contribution	$50.14	Source
1040763	15-Jan-93	Employer Paid Dental Insurance	$21.39	Data Warehouse
1040763	15-Jan-93	Employer Paid Dental Insurance	$21.39	Source
1040763	15-Jan-93	Employer Paid FICA MED	$28.63	Data Warehouse
1040763	15-Jan-93	Employer Paid FICA Med	$28.63	Source
1040763	15-Jan-93	Employer Paid FICA OASDI	$71.98	Data Warehouse
1040763	15-Jan-93	Employer Paid FICA OASDI	$71.98	Source
1040763	15-Jan-93	Employer Paid Health Insurance	$355.41	Data Warehouse
1040763	15-Jan-93	Employer Paid Health Insurance	$355.41	Source
1040763	15-Jan-93	Federal Withholding	$219.84	Data Warehouse
1040763	15-Jan-93	Federal Withholding	$219.84	Source
1040763	29-Jan-93	Employee Paid 401K Contribution	$50.14	Data Warehouse
1040763	29-Jan-93	Employee Paid 401K Contribution	$50.14	Source
1040763	29-Jan-93	Employee Paid Dental Insurance	$14.04	Data Warehouse

EMPLOYEE_ NUMBER	DATE_PAID	TYPE	AMOUNT	'SOURCE'
1040763	29-Jan-93	Employee Paid Dental Insurance	$14.04	Source
1040763	29-Jan-93	Employee Paid FICA MED	$28.63	Data Warehouse
1040763	29-Jan-93	Employee Paid FICA Med	$28.63	Source
1040763	29-Jan-93	Employee Paid FICA OASDI	$71.98	Data Warehouse
1040763	29-Jan-93	Employee Paid FICA OASDI	$71.98	Source
1040763	29-Jan-93	Employee Paid Health Insurance	$66.85	Data Warehouse
1040763	29-Jan-93	Employee Paid Health Insurance	$66.85	Source
1040763	29-Jan-93	Employer Paid 401K Contribution	$50.14	Data Warehouse
1040763	29-Jan-93	Employer Paid 401K Contribution	$50.14	Source
1040763	29-Jan-93	Employer Paid Dental Insurance	$21.39	Data Warehouse
1040763	29-Jan-93	Employer Paid Dental Insurance	$21.39	Source
1040763	29-Jan-93	Employer Paid FICA MED	$28.63	Data Warehouse
1040763	29-Jan-93	Employer Paid FICA Med	$28.63	Source
1040763	29-Jan-93	Employer Paid FICA OASDI	$71.98	Data Warehouse
1040763	29-Jan-93	Employer Paid FICA OASDI	$71.98	Source
1040763	29-Jan-93	Employer Paid Health Insurance	$355.41	Data Warehouse
1040763	29-Jan-93	Employer Paid Health Insurance	$355.41	Source
1040763	29-Jan-93	Federal Withholding	$219.84	Data Warehouse
1040763	29-Jan-93	Federal Withholding	$219.84	Source

These groupings look good. We have already verified the gross wages grouping in the other select statements; however, we need to verify net pay.

```
SELECT     C.EMPLOYEE_NUMBER,
           A.DATE_PAID,
           'Source Gross Wages',
           SUM(B.AMOUNT) AMOUNT,
```

```
                'Source'
FROM            PAYCHECK_HEADER A,
                PAYCHECK_DETAIL B,
                EMPLOYEE C,
                APPOINTMENT D,
                PAY_TYPE E
WHERE           A.ID = B.PAYCHECK_HEADER_ID
                AND A.APPOINTMENT_ID = D.ID
                AND D.EMPLOYEE_ID = C.ID
                AND B.PAY_TYPE_ID = E.ID
                AND C.ID = 37136
                AND A.DATE_PAID = '01-JAN-1993'
                AND E.PAY_TYPE_NAME = 'Gross Wages'
GROUP BY        C.EMPLOYEE_NUMBER,
                A.DATE_PAID
UNION
SELECT          C.EMPLOYEE_NUMBER,
                A.DATE_PAID,
                'Source Withheld',
                SUM(B.AMOUNT) AMOUNT,
                'Source'
FROM            PAYCHECK_HEADER A,
                PAYCHECK_DETAIL B,
                EMPLOYEE C,
                APPOINTMENT D,
                PAY_TYPE E
WHERE           A.ID = B.PAYCHECK_HEADER_ID
                AND A.APPOINTMENT_ID = D.ID
                AND D.EMPLOYEE_ID = C.ID
                AND B.PAY_TYPE_ID = E.ID
                AND C.ID = 37136
                AND A.DATE_PAID = '01-JAN-1993'
                AND     (
                                E.PAY_TYPE_NAME = 'Federal Withholding'
                                OR
                                E.PAY_TYPE_NAME LIKE '%Employee%'
                        )
GROUP BY        C.EMPLOYEE_NUMBER, A.DATE_PAID
UNION
SELECT          B.EMPLOYEE_NUMBER,
                D.CALENDAR_DAY,
                C.PAY_CATEGORY_1,
                SUM(A.AMOUNT),
                'Data Warehouse'
FROM            FACT_SALARY_DAY A,
                DIM_EMPLOYEE B,
                DIM_PAY_TYPE C,
```

```
            DIM_DAY D,
            DIM_DAY E,
            DIM_DAY F
WHERE       A.KEY_EMPLOYEE = B.KEY_EMPLOYEE
            AND A.KEY_PAY_TYPE = C.KEY_PAY_TYPE
            AND A.KEY_DATE_PAID = D.KEY_DAY
            AND A.KEY_PAY_PERIOD_BEGIN_DATE = E.KEY_DAY
            AND A.KEY_PAY_PERIOD_END_DATE = F.KEY_DAY
            AND B.EMPLOYEE_ID = 37136
            AND D.CALENDAR_DAY = '01-JAN-1993'
            AND C.PAY_CATEGORY_1 = 'Net Pay'
GROUP BY    B.EMPLOYEE_NUMBER,
            D.CALENDAR_DAY,
            C.PAY_CATEGORY_1
ORDER BY    1,2,3,5
```

EMPLOYEE_NUMBER	DATE_PAID	'SOURCEGROSSWAGES'	AMOUNT	'SOURCE'
1040763	1-Jan-93	Net Pay	$1,614.25	Data Warehouse
1040763	1-Jan-93	Source Gross Wages	$2,065.73	Source
1040763	1-Jan-93	Source Withheld	$451.48	Source

As with the LOAD_SALARY_FACT table, the net pay will have to be verified manually. Subtracting $451.48 from $2,065.73 (amount withheld from gross pay) results in $1,614.25. This matches the net pay from the FACT_SALARY_DAY table. For ease of display, the select statement above only pulls data for one day. Feel free to verify the data for other time periods if desired.

The FACT_SALARY_DAY table includes the pay period begin and end dates, so those will need to be verified as well.

```
SELECT      C.EMPLOYEE_NUMBER,
            A.PAY_PERIOD_BEGIN_DATE,
            A.PAY_PERIOD_END_DATE,
            A.DATE_PAID,
            SUM(B.AMOUNT) AMOUNT,
            'Source'
FROM        PAYCHECK_HEADER A,
            PAYCHECK_DETAIL B,
            EMPLOYEE C,
            APPOINTMENT D,
            PAY_TYPE E,
            DEPARTMENT F,
            TITLE G
WHERE       A.ID = B.PAYCHECK_HEADER_ID
            AND A.APPOINTMENT_ID = D.ID
            AND D.EMPLOYEE_ID = C.ID
            AND B.PAY_TYPE_ID = E.ID
```

```
                AND D.DEPARTMENT_ID = F.ID
                AND D.TITLE_ID = G.ID
                AND C.ID = 37136
                AND E.PAY_TYPE_NAME = 'Gross Wages'
                AND EXTRACT(YEAR FROM A.DATE_PAID) = 1993
                AND EXTRACT(MONTH FROM A.DATE_PAID) = 1
GROUP BY        C.EMPLOYEE_NUMBER,
                A.PAY_PERIOD_BEGIN_DATE,
                A.PAY_PERIOD_END_DATE,
                A.DATE_PAID
UNION
SELECT          B.EMPLOYEE_NUMBER,
                E.CALENDAR_DAY,
                F.CALENDAR_DAY,
                D.CALENDAR_DAY,
                SUM(A.AMOUNT),
                'Data Warehouse'
FROM            FACT_SALARY_DAY A,
                DIM_EMPLOYEE B,
                DIM_PAY_TYPE C,
                DIM_DAY D,
                DIM_DAY E,
                DIM_DAY F
WHERE           A.KEY_EMPLOYEE = B.KEY_EMPLOYEE
                AND A.KEY_PAY_TYPE = C.KEY_PAY_TYPE
                AND A.KEY_DATE_PAID = D.KEY_DAY
                AND A.KEY_PAY_PERIOD_BEGIN_DATE = E.KEY_DAY
                AND A.KEY_PAY_PERIOD_END_DATE = F.KEY_DAY
                AND B.EMPLOYEE_ID = 37136
                AND C.COMPONENT_OF_GROSS_PAY = 'Yes'
                AND D.CALENDAR_YEAR = 1993
                AND D.CALENDAR_MONTH_NUMBER = 1
GROUP BY        B.EMPLOYEE_NUMBER,
                E.CALENDAR_DAY,
                F.CALENDAR_DAY,
                D.CALENDAR_DAY
ORDER BY        1,2,3,4,6
```

EMPLOYEE_ NUMBER	PAY_PERIOD_ BEGIN_DATE	PAY_PERIOD_ END_DATE	DATE_PAID	AMOUNT	'SOURCE'
1040763	14-Dec-92	27-Dec-92	1-Jan-93	$2,065.73	Data Warehouse
1040763	14-Dec-92	27-Dec-92	1-Jan-93	$2,065.73	Source
1040763	28-Dec-92	10-Jan-93	15-Jan-93	$2,065.73	Data Warehouse
1040763	28-Dec-92	10-Jan-93	15-Jan-93	$2,065.73	Source
1040763	11-Jan-93	24-Jan-93	29-Jan-93	$2,065.73	Data Warehouse

EMPLOYEE_ NUMBER	PAY_PERIOD_ BEGIN_DATE	PAY_PERIOD_ END_DATE	DATE_PAID	AMOUNT	'SOURCE'
1040763	11-Jan-93	24-Jan-93	29-Jan-93	$2,065.73	Source

The dollars appear to be correctly applied to the date dimensions. Finally, we need to consider the degenerate dimension, DD_CHECK_NUMBER.

```
SELECT      C.EMPLOYEE_NUMBER,
            A.CHECK_NUMBER,
            SUM(B.AMOUNT) AMOUNT,
            'Source'
FROM        PAYCHECK_HEADER A,
            PAYCHECK_DETAIL B,
            EMPLOYEE C,
            APPOINTMENT D,
            PAY_TYPE E,
            DEPARTMENT F,
            TITLE G
WHERE       A.ID = B.PAYCHECK_HEADER_ID
            AND A.APPOINTMENT_ID = D.ID
            AND D.EMPLOYEE_ID = C.ID
            AND B.PAY_TYPE_ID = E.ID
            AND D.DEPARTMENT_ID = F.ID
            AND D.TITLE_ID = G.ID
            AND C.ID = 37136
            AND E.PAY_TYPE_NAME = 'Gross Wages'
            AND EXTRACT(YEAR FROM A.DATE_PAID) = 1993
            AND EXTRACT(MONTH FROM A.DATE_PAID) = 1
GROUP BY    C.EMPLOYEE_NUMBER, A.CHECK_NUMBER, 'Source'
UNION
SELECT      B.EMPLOYEE_NUMBER,
            A.DD_CHECK_NUMBER,
            SUM(A.AMOUNT),
            'Data Warehouse'
FROM        FACT_SALARY_DAY A,
            DIM_EMPLOYEE B,
            DIM_PAY_TYPE C,
            DIM_DAY D,
            DIM_DAY E,
            DIM_DAY F
WHERE       A.KEY_EMPLOYEE = B.KEY_EMPLOYEE
            AND A.KEY_PAY_TYPE = C.KEY_PAY_TYPE
            AND A.KEY_DATE_PAID = D.KEY_DAY
            AND A.KEY_PAY_PERIOD_BEGIN_DATE = E.KEY_DAY
            AND A.KEY_PAY_PERIOD_END_DATE = F.KEY_DAY
            AND B.EMPLOYEE_ID = 37136
```

```
            AND C.COMPONENT_OF_GROSS_PAY = 'Yes'
            AND D.CALENDAR_YEAR = 1993
            AND D.CALENDAR_MONTH_NUMBER = 1
GROUP BY    B.EMPLOYEE_NUMBER,
            A.DD_CHECK_NUMBER
ORDER BY    1,2,4
```

EMPLOYEE_NUMBER	CHECK_NUMBER	AMOUNT	'SOURCE'
1040763	000001647	$2,065.73	Data Warehouse
1040763	000001647	$2,065.73	Source
1040763	000001648	$2,065.73	Data Warehouse
1040763	000001648	$2,065.73	Source
1040763	000001649	$2,065.73	Data Warehouse
1040763	000001649	$2,065.73	Source

The check number data also appears to be applied correctly. So, we have verified the data according to each of the dimensions and have found that it matches the star. As discussed in the previous chapter, this suggests that the ETL is working as designed, but not that the ETL is designed correctly. At this point in the process, a developer will hand the star to (or run some sample data for) a business user for his verification from a business perspective. Since that is outside of the scope of this book, we will consider this star complete. Once the data has been verified from a business perspective, it will be scheduled to run with a default value of 'Y' in the DEFAULT_TIMEPERIOD parameter. This way, it will always refresh the current month and the previous month. The LOAD_SALARY_FACT_TABLES procedure in its entirety is below.

Line	Code
1	CREATE OR REPLACE PROCEDURE LOAD_SALARY_FACT_TABLES
2	(
3	BEGIN_MONTH_OVERRIDE NUMBER,
4	BEGIN_YEAR_OVERRIDE NUMBER,
5	END_MONTH_OVERRIDE NUMBER,
6	END_YEAR_OVERRIDE NUMBER,
7	DEFAULT_TIMEPERIOD VARCHAR2
8	)
9	
10	AS
11	
12	SQLSTMT VARCHAR2(3000);
13	TBLCOUNT NUMBER := 0;

Line	Code
14	BEGIN_AS_OF_DATE DATE;
15	END_AS_OF_DATE DATE;
16	DATE_STRING VARCHAR(10);
17	ERR_MSG VARCHAR2(200);
18	PAY_TYPE_WAGES_KEY NUMBER := -1;
19	
20	BEGIN
21	--Log the beginning of the job
22	INSERT INTO ETL_JOB_STATUS
23	(
24	ID,
25	ETL_JOB_NAME,
26	STATUS_NAME,
27	STATUS_TIMESTAMP
28	)
29	VALUES
30	(
31	SEQ_ETL_JOB_STATUS.NEXTVAL,
32	'LOAD_SALARY_FACT_TABLES',
33	'IN PROGRESS',
34	SYSTIMESTAMP
35	);
36	
37	COMMIT;
38	
39	--If the table exists, drop it. If not, do nothing. The table will be created below.
40	SELECT COUNT(*) INTO TBLCOUNT
41	FROM ALL_TABLES
42	WHERE TABLE_NAME = 'STAGE_SALARY_DATA'
43	AND OWNER =
44	(
45	SELECT SYS_CONTEXT('USERENV', 'CURRENT_SCHEMA')
46	FROM DUAL

Line	Code
47	);
48	
49	IF TBLCOUNT > 0 THEN
50	EXECUTE IMMEDIATE 'DROP TABLE STAGE_SALARY_DATA';
51	END IF;
52	
53	--If the DEFAULT_PERIOD variable is set to 'Y', then the prior month and the current month are loaded or reloaded into the fact table.
54	--Otherwise, the overrides are used.
55	IF DEFAULT_TIMEPERIOD = 'Y' THEN
56	SELECT TRUNC(TRUNC(SYSDATE,'MM')-1,'MM') INTO BEGIN_AS_OF_DATE FROM DUAL;
57	SELECT LAST_DAY(TRUNC(SYSDATE)) INTO END_AS_OF_DATE FROM DUAL;
58	ELSE
59	--This IF statement is used to place a leading zero before the month number for those months less than 10
60	IF BEGIN_MONTH_OVERRIDE < 10 THEN
61	BEGIN_AS_OF_DATE := TO_DATE
62	(
63	'0'
64	|| TO_CHAR(BEGIN_MONTH_OVERRIDE)
65	|| '/01/'
66	|| TO_CHAR(BEGIN_YEAR_OVERRIDE),'MM/DD/YYYY'
67	);
68	ELSE
69	BEGIN_AS_OF_DATE := TO_DATE
70	(
71	TO_CHAR(BEGIN_MONTH_OVERRIDE)
72	|| '/01/'
73	|| TO_CHAR(BEGIN_YEAR_OVERRIDE),'MM/DD/YYYY'
74	);
75	END IF;
76	
77	IF END_MONTH_OVERRIDE < 10 THEN

Line	Code
78	END_AS_OF_DATE := LAST_DAY
79	(
80	TO_DATE
81	(
82	'0'
83	|| TO_CHAR(END_MONTH_OVERRIDE)
84	|| '/01/'
85	|| TO_CHAR(END_YEAR_OVERRIDE),'MM/DD/YYYY'
86	)
87	);
88	ELSE
89	END_AS_OF_DATE := LAST_DAY
90	(
91	TO_DATE
92	(
93	TO_CHAR(END_MONTH_OVERRIDE)
94	|| '/01/'
95	|| TO_CHAR(END_YEAR_OVERRIDE),'MM/DD/YYYY'
96	)
97	);
98	END IF;
99	
100	END IF;
101	
102	--Dump the data into the staging table and transform the PAY_TYPE_NAME into the values that are used in the DIM_PAY_TYPE table
103	SQLSTMT := 'CREATE TABLE STAGE_SALARY_DATA AS ('
104	|| 'SELECT E.EMPLOYEE_NUMBER, '
105	|| 'C.APPOINTMENT_BEGIN_DATE, '
106	|| 'F.TITLE_NAME, '
107	|| 'G.DEPARTMENT_NUMBER, '
108	|| 'D.PAY_TYPE_NAME, '
109	|| 'CASE WHEN PAY_TYPE_NAME = "Employer Paid - Dental Insurance" '
110	|| 'THEN "Employer Paid Dental Insurance" '

Line	Code
111	| | 'WHEN PAY_TYPE_NAME = "Employee Paid - Dental Insurance" '
112	| | 'THEN "Employee Paid Dental Insurance" '
113	| | 'WHEN PAY_TYPE_NAME = "Employer Paid - Health Insurance" '
114	| | 'THEN "Employer Paid Health Insurance" '
115	| | 'WHEN PAY_TYPE_NAME = "Employee Paid - Health Insurance" '
116	| | 'THEN "Employee Paid Health Insurance" '
117	| | 'WHEN PAY_TYPE_NAME = "Employer Paid - FICA OASDI" '
118	| | 'THEN "Employer Paid FICA OASDI" '
119	| | 'WHEN PAY_TYPE_NAME = "Employee Paid - FICA OASDI" '
120	| | 'THEN "Employee Paid FICA OASDI" '
121	| | 'WHEN PAY_TYPE_NAME = "Employer Paid - FICA Med" '
122	| | 'THEN "Employer Paid FICA MED" '
123	| | 'WHEN PAY_TYPE_NAME = "Employee Paid - FICA Med" '
124	| | 'THEN "Employee Paid FICA MED" '
125	| | 'WHEN PAY_TYPE_NAME = "401K Employee Contribution" '
126	| | 'THEN "Employee Paid 401K Contribution" '
127	| | 'WHEN PAY_TYPE_NAME = "401K Employer Contribution" '
128	| | 'THEN "Employer Paid 401K Contribution" '
129	| | 'WHEN PAY_TYPE_NAME = "Federal Withholding" '
130	| | 'THEN "Federal Withholding" '
131	| | 'ELSE NULL END AS PAY_TYPE_NAME_IN_STAR, '
132	| | 'A.DATE_PAID, '
133	| | 'A.PAY_PERIOD_BEGIN_DATE, '
134	| | 'A.PAY_PERIOD_END_DATE, '
135	| | 'A.CHECK_NUMBER, '
136	| | 'SUM(B.AMOUNT) AS AMOUNT '
137	| | 'FROM PAYCHECK_HEADER A, '
138	| | 'PAYCHECK_DETAIL B, '
139	| | 'APPOINTMENT C, '
140	| | 'PAY_TYPE D, '
141	| | 'EMPLOYEE E, '
142	| | 'TITLE F, '
143	| | 'DEPARTMENT G '

Line	Code
144	|| 'WHERE B.PAYCHECK_HEADER_ID = A.ID '
145	|| 'AND A.APPOINTMENT_ID = C.ID '
146	|| 'AND B.PAY_TYPE_ID = D.ID '
147	|| 'AND C.EMPLOYEE_ID = E.ID '
148	|| 'AND C.TITLE_ID = F.ID '
149	|| 'AND C.DEPARTMENT_ID = G.ID '
150	|| 'AND A.DATE_PAID BETWEEN '''
151	|| TO_CHAR(BEGIN_AS_OF_DATE,'DD-MON-YYYY')
152	|| ''' AND '''
153	|| to_char(END_AS_OF_DATE,'DD-MON-YYYY') || ''' '
154	|| 'GROUP BY E.EMPLOYEE_NUMBER, '
155	|| 'C.APPOINTMENT_BEGIN_DATE, '
156	|| 'F.TITLE_NAME, '
157	|| 'G.DEPARTMENT_NUMBER, '
158	|| 'D.PAY_TYPE_NAME, '
159	|| 'CASE WHEN PAY_TYPE_NAME = "Employer Paid - Dental Insurance" '
160	|| 'THEN "Employer Paid Dental Insurance" '
161	|| 'WHEN PAY_TYPE_NAME = "Employee Paid - Dental Insurance" '
162	|| 'THEN "Employee Paid Dental Insurance" '
163	|| 'WHEN PAY_TYPE_NAME = "Employer Paid - Health Insurance" '
164	|| 'THEN "Employer Paid Health Insurance" '
165	|| 'WHEN PAY_TYPE_NAME = "Employee Paid - Health Insurance" '
166	|| 'THEN "Employee Paid Health Insurance" '
167	|| 'WHEN PAY_TYPE_NAME = "Employer Paid - FICA OASDI" '
168	|| 'THEN "Employer Paid FICA OASDI" '
169	|| 'WHEN PAY_TYPE_NAME = "Employee Paid - FICA OASDI" '
170	|| 'THEN "Employee Paid FICA OASDI" '
171	|| 'WHEN PAY_TYPE_NAME = "Employer Paid - FICA Med" '
172	|| 'THEN "Employer Paid FICA MED" '
173	|| 'WHEN PAY_TYPE_NAME = "Employee Paid - FICA Med" '
174	|| 'THEN "Employee Paid FICA MED" '
175	|| 'WHEN PAY_TYPE_NAME = "401K Employee Contribution" '
176	|| 'THEN "Employee Paid 401K Contribution" '

Line	Code
177	|| 'WHEN PAY_TYPE_NAME = "401K Employer Contribution" '
178	|| 'THEN "Employer Paid 401K Contribution" '
179	|| 'WHEN PAY_TYPE_NAME = "Federal Withholding" '
180	|| 'THEN "Federal Withholding" '
181	|| 'ELSE NULL END, '
182	|| 'A.DATE_PAID, '
183	|| 'A.PAY_PERIOD_BEGIN_DATE, '
184	|| 'A.PAY_PERIOD_END_DATE, '
185	|| 'A.CHECK_NUMBER) ';
186	
187	EXECUTE IMMEDIATE SQLSTMT;
188	
189	--This index causes the SQL statement below, that creates the STAGE_SALARY_DATA_CALC_WAGES table, to run more efficiently
190	SQLSTMT := 'CREATE INDEX STAGE_SALARY_CHECK_NO ON STAGE_SALARY_DATA(CHECK_NUMBER)';
191	EXECUTE IMMEDIATE SQLSTMT;
192	
193	--If the table exists, drop it. If not, do nothing. The table will be created below.
194	SELECT COUNT(*) INTO TBLCOUNT
195	FROM ALL_TABLES
196	WHERE TABLE_NAME = 'STAGE_SALARY_DATA_CALC_WAGES'
197	AND OWNER =
198	(
199	SELECT SYS_CONTEXT('USERENV', 'CURRENT_SCHEMA')
200	FROM DUAL
201	);
202	
203	IF TBLCOUNT > 0 THEN
204	EXECUTE IMMEDIATE 'DROP TABLE STAGE_SALARY_DATA_CALC_WAGES';
205	END IF;
206	
207	--The source system stores the gross amount and the detail that is actually
208	--part of the gross total. The detail must be subtracted from the gross

Line	Code
209	--amount to get the net amount. Separating the gross pay from the amount
210	--withheld is done in the table below. The net amount will be calculated
211	--later.
212	SQLSTMT := 'CREATE TABLE STAGE_SALARY_DATA_CALC_WAGES AS ('
213	|| 'SELECT A.CHECK_NUMBER, '
214	|| 'SUM(A.AMOUNT) GROSS_PAY, '
215	|| ' (SELECT SUM(AMOUNT) '
216	|| 'FROM STAGE_SALARY_DATA AA '
217	|| 'WHERE AA.PAY_TYPE_NAME_IN_STAR IN '
218	|| '(
219	|| '"Federal Withholding", '
220	|| '"Employee Paid Health Insurance", '
221	|| '"Employee Paid Dental Insurance", '
222	|| '"Employee Paid 401K Contribution", '
223	|| '"Employee Paid FICA OASDI", '
224	|| '"Employee Paid FICA MED"'
225	|| ')'
226	|| 'AND AA.CHECK_NUMBER = A.CHECK_NUMBER) WITHHELD '
227	|| 'FROM STAGE_SALARY_DATA A '
228	|| 'WHERE A.PAY_TYPE_NAME = "Gross Wages" '
229	|| 'GROUP BY A.CHECK_NUMBER) ';
230	
231	EXECUTE IMMEDIATE SQLSTMT;
232	
233	--If the table exists, drop it. If not, do nothing. The table will be created below.
234	SELECT COUNT(*) INTO TBLCOUNT
235	FROM ALL_TABLES
236	WHERE TABLE_NAME = 'STAGE_SALARY_DATA_ADD_KEYS'
237	AND OWNER =
238	(
239	SELECT SYS_CONTEXT('USERENV', 'CURRENT_SCHEMA')
240	FROM DUAL
241	);

Line	Code
242	
243	IF TBLCOUNT > 0 THEN
244	EXECUTE IMMEDIATE 'DROP TABLE STAGE_SALARY_DATA_ADD_KEYS';
245	END IF;
246	
247	--The last staging table before the data is loaded into the fact table is
248	--created below. The keys are added via outer joins as opposed to separate
249	--subselects, since that is MUCH more efficient. A value of -1 is used as a
250	--foreign key if no value is found. This portion of the code only pulls in
251	--the withholdings for each check, not the net wages.
252	SQLSTMT := 'CREATE TABLE STAGE_SALARY_DATA_ADD_KEYS AS ('
253	|| 'SELECT NVL(B.KEY_EMPLOYEE,-1) KEY_EMPLOYEE,'
254	|| 'NVL(D.KEY_DAY,-1) KEY_PAY_PERIOD_BEGIN_DATE,'
255	|| 'NVL(E.KEY_DAY,-1) KEY_PAY_PERIOD_END_DATE,'
256	|| 'NVL(C.KEY_DAY,-1) KEY_DATE_PAID,'
257	|| 'NVL(F.KEY_PAY_TYPE,-1) KEY_PAY_TYPE,'
258	|| 'A.CHECK_NUMBER DD_CHECK_NUMBER,'
259	|| 'SUM(A.AMOUNT) AMOUNT'
260	|| 'FROM STAGE_SALARY_DATA A,'
261	|| 'DIM_EMPLOYEE B,'
262	|| 'DIM_DAY C,'
263	|| 'DIM_DAY D,'
264	|| 'DIM_DAY E,'
265	|| 'DIM_PAY_TYPE F'
266	|| 'WHERE A.PAY_TYPE_NAME <> "Gross Wages"'
267	|| 'AND A.EMPLOYEE_NUMBER = B.EMPLOYEE_NUMBER(+)'
268	|| 'AND A.APPOINTMENT_BEGIN_DATE = B.APPOINTMENT_BEGIN_DATE(+)'
269	|| 'AND A.TITLE_NAME = B.TITLE(+)'
270	|| 'AND A.DEPARTMENT_NUMBER = B.DEPARTMENT_NUMBER(+)'
271	|| 'AND A.DATE_PAID = C.CALENDAR_DAY(+)'
272	|| 'AND A.PAY_PERIOD_BEGIN_DATE = D.CALENDAR_DAY(+)'
273	|| 'AND A.PAY_PERIOD_END_DATE = E.CALENDAR_DAY(+)'
274	|| 'AND A.PAY_TYPE_NAME_IN_STAR = F.PAY_CATEGORY_2(+)'

Line	Code
275	|| 'GROUP BY NVL(B.KEY_EMPLOYEE,-1), NVL(C.KEY_DAY,-1), NVL(D.KEY_DAY,-1), '
276	|| 'NVL(E.KEY_DAY,-1), NVL(F.KEY_PAY_TYPE,-1), A.CHECK_NUMBER '
277	|| ') ';
278	
279	EXECUTE IMMEDIATE SQLSTMT;
280	
281	--The insert statement below is calculating the net wages and then adding the
282	--rows with the net wages into the STAGE_SALARY_DATA_ADD_KEYS table. The key
283	--that corresponds to the wages row in the DIM_PAY_TYPE table is inserted
284	--with EVERY record that is calculated. That is determined ahead of time by
285	--this SELECT INTO statement so that a subselect will not have to be used in
286	--the INSERT statement. The distinct keyword MUST be used in the sum in
287	--order to avoid double counting.
288	SELECT KEY_PAY_TYPE INTO PAY_TYPE_WAGES_KEY
289	FROM DIM_PAY_TYPE
290	WHERE PAY_CATEGORY_2 = 'Wages';
291	
292	SQLSTMT := 'INSERT INTO STAGE_SALARY_DATA_ADD_KEYS '
293	|| 'SELECT NVL(B.KEY_EMPLOYEE,-1), '
294	|| 'NVL(D.KEY_DAY,-1), '
295	|| 'NVL(E.KEY_DAY,-1), '
296	|| 'NVL(C.KEY_DAY,-1), '
297	|| PAY_TYPE_WAGES_KEY || ', '
298	|| 'A.CHECK_NUMBER, '
299	|| 'SUM(F.GROSS_PAY - F.WITHHELD) '
300	|| 'FROM '
301	|| '('
302	|| 'SELECT DISTINCT EMPLOYEE_NUMBER, '
303	|| 'APPOINTMENT_BEGIN_DATE, '
304	|| 'TITLE_NAME, '
305	|| 'DEPARTMENT_NUMBER, '
306	|| 'CHECK_NUMBER, '

Line	Code
307	|| 'DATE_PAID,'
308	|| 'PAY_PERIOD_BEGIN_DATE,'
309	|| 'PAY_PERIOD_END_DATE'
310	|| 'FROM STAGE_SALARY_DATA'
311	|| ') A,'
312	|| 'DIM_EMPLOYEE B,'
313	|| 'DIM_DAY C,'
314	|| 'DIM_DAY D,'
315	|| 'DIM_DAY E,'
316	|| 'STAGE_SALARY_DATA_CALC_WAGES F'
317	|| 'WHERE A.EMPLOYEE_NUMBER = B.EMPLOYEE_NUMBER(+)'
318	|| 'AND A.APPOINTMENT_BEGIN_DATE = B.APPOINTMENT_BEGIN_DATE(+)'
319	|| 'AND A.TITLE_NAME = B.TITLE(+)'
320	|| 'AND A.DEPARTMENT_NUMBER = B.DEPARTMENT_NUMBER(+)'
321	|| 'AND A.DATE_PAID = C.CALENDAR_DAY(+)'
322	|| 'AND A.PAY_PERIOD_BEGIN_DATE = D.CALENDAR_DAY(+)'
323	|| 'AND A.PAY_PERIOD_END_DATE = E.CALENDAR_DAY(+)'
324	|| 'AND A.CHECK_NUMBER = F.CHECK_NUMBER'
325	|| 'GROUP BY NVL(B.KEY_EMPLOYEE,-1), NVL(C.KEY_DAY,-1), NVL(D.KEY_DAY,-1),'
326	|| 'NVL(E.KEY_DAY,-1), A.CHECK_NUMBER';
327	
328	EXECUTE IMMEDIATE SQLSTMT;
329	COMMIT;
330	
331	--Updating the existing rows for months in which the amount has changed
332	--(i.e., an additional payroll was processed for that month since the last
333	--load) would be very inefficient. As a result, any existing data pertaining
334	--to the month(s) being pulled into the fact table is completely deleted from
335	--the fact table and reloaded.
336	SQLSTMT := 'DELETE'
337	|| 'FROM FACT_SALARY_DAY A'
338	|| 'WHERE A.KEY_DATE_PAID IN ('

Line	Code
339	|| 'SELECT KEY_DAY '
340	|| 'FROM DIM_DAY '
341	|| 'WHERE CALENDAR_DAY BETWEEN '''
342	|| TO_CHAR(BEGIN_AS_OF_DATE,'DD-MON-YYYY')
343	|| ''' AND '''
344	|| TO_CHAR(END_AS_OF_DATE,'DD-MON-YYYY')
345	|| ''') ';
346	
347	EXECUTE IMMEDIATE SQLSTMT;
348	COMMIT;
349	
350	--The fact table is loaded
351	SQLSTMT := 'INSERT INTO FACT_SALARY_DAY '
352	|| 'SELECT * FROM STAGE_SALARY_DATA_ADD_KEYS ';
353	
354	EXECUTE IMMEDIATE SQLSTMT;
355	COMMIT;
356	
357	SQLSTMT := 'DELETE '
358	|| 'FROM FACT_SALARY A '
359	|| 'WHERE A.KEY_MONTH IN ('
360	|| 'SELECT KEY_MONTH '
361	|| 'FROM DIM_MONTH '
362	|| 'WHERE FIRST_DAY BETWEEN '''
363	|| TO_CHAR(BEGIN_AS_OF_DATE,'DD-MON-YYYY')
364	|| ''' AND '''
365	|| TO_CHAR(END_AS_OF_DATE,'DD-MON-YYYY')
366	|| ''') ';
367	
368	EXECUTE IMMEDIATE SQLSTMT;
369	COMMIT;
370	
371	--The fact table is loaded

Line	Code
372	SQLSTMT := 'INSERT INTO FACT_SALARY '
373	|| 'SELECT A.KEY_EMPLOYEE, '
374	|| 'NVL(B.KEY_MONTH,-1), '
375	|| 'A.KEY_PAY_TYPE, '
376	|| 'SUM(A.AMOUNT) '
377	|| 'FROM STAGE_SALARY_DATA_ADD_KEYS A, '
378	|| 'DIM_MONTH B, '
379	|| 'DIM_DAY C '
380	|| 'WHERE A.KEY_DATE_PAID = C.KEY_DAY '
381	|| 'AND C.CALENDAR_DAY BETWEEN B.FIRST_DAY AND B.LAST_DAY '
382	|| 'GROUP BY A.KEY_EMPLOYEE, B.KEY_MONTH, A.KEY_PAY_TYPE ';
383	
384	EXECUTE IMMEDIATE SQLSTMT;
385	COMMIT;
386	
387	--Log the successful completion of the job.
388	INSERT INTO ETL_JOB_STATUS
389	(
390	ID,
391	ETL_JOB_NAME,
392	STATUS_NAME,
393	STATUS_TIMESTAMP
394	)
395	VALUES
396	(
397	SEQ_ETL_JOB_STATUS.NEXTVAL,
398	'LOAD_SALARY_FACT_TABLES',
399	'SUCCESSFULLY COMPLETED',
400	SYSTIMESTAMP
401	);
402	
403	COMMIT;
404	
405	--This is the equivalent of a catch block. Any errors are caught and logged.

Line	Code
406	EXCEPTION
407	WHEN OTHERS THEN
408	ERR_MSG := SUBSTR(SQLERRM, 1, 200);
409	INSERT INTO ETL_JOB_STATUS
410	(
411	ID,
412	ETL_JOB_NAME,
413	STATUS_NAME,
414	ERROR_MESSAGE,
415	STATUS_TIMESTAMP
416	)
417	VALUES
418	(
419	SEQ_ETL_JOB_STATUS.NEXTVAL,
420	'LOAD_SALARY_FACT_TABLES',
421	'ERROR',
422	ERR_MSG,
423	SYSTIMESTAMP
424	);
425	
426	COMMIT;
427	
428	END;

8
EVALUATION DATA

Description of the Evaluation Business Process

An employee may receive an evaluation once a year or several times a year. The evaluation can be administered for one of three reasons.

1.) Annual – This is the standard evaluation that each employee receives once per year
2.) Requested – An employee can request an evaluation
3.) Exit – An evaluation is administered when an employee leaves the company

Each evaluation consists of eight items about which the employee is rated from one to five. The EVALUATION_HEADER table contains the high-level data regarding the evaluation. Notice that the EVALUATOR column is used to store the name of the person administering the evaluation in varying formats. Because this system does not store the evaluator's employee number, providing a key to the DIM_EMPLOYEE dimension to conduct analysis based on the evaluator may not be possible. Also, notice that the EVAL_STATUS column stores the status for each evaluation in an inconsistent way. The EVALUATION_DETAIL table contains the detailed data regarding the evaluation, such as the score per item. The EVAL_REASON table contains a list of possible reasons to administer an evaluation. The EVALUATION_ITEM table contains a list of the eight items used in each evaluation.

Requirements

The users would like to perform analysis on the evaluation scores based on things like date, item, reason, status, and the people involved (evaluator and the one being evaluated). Based on these requirements, this is the table design of this star schema that our ETL will need to populate.

Figure 8-1

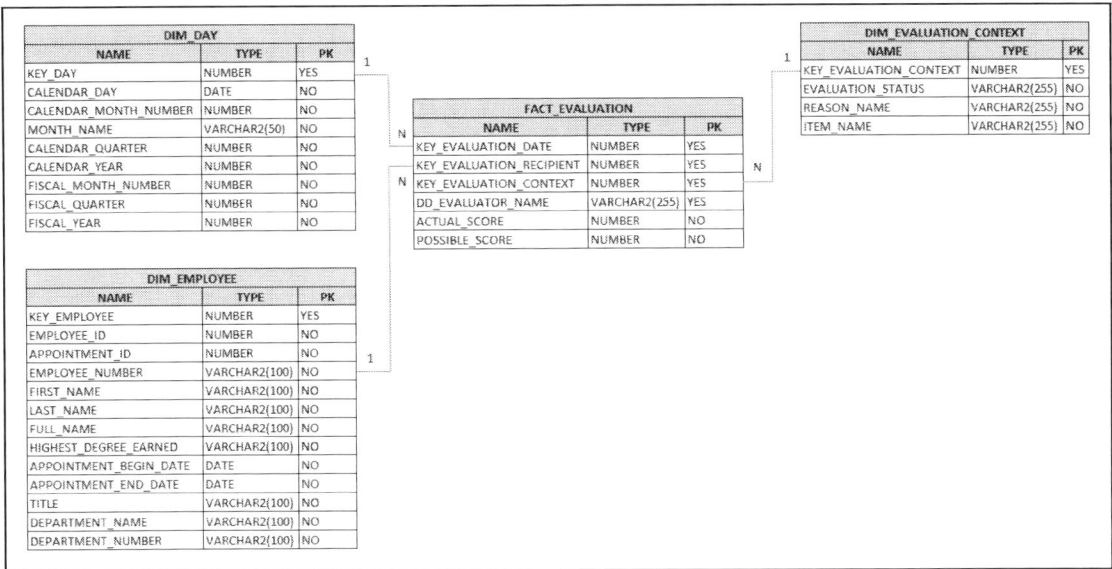

DIM_DAY: This is a standard type zero date dimension table, used to allow for analyzing data based on evaluation date. We can point to the DIM_DAY dimension table that was created for use with the salary star. Although creating a separate physical table with the same keys and data (or a subset of data) as the original DIM_DAY would not be wrong, for ease of use we will just reuse the original.

DIM_EMPLOYEE: This is the same type two slowly changing dimension as was used in the salary star. Although creating a separate physical table with the same keys and data (or a subset of data) as the original DIM_EMPLOYEE would not be wrong, for ease of use we will just reuse the original.

DIM_EVALUATION_CONTEXT: The source system contains three contextual elements that describe the evaluation score that do not fit into either of the above mentioned dimension tables. They are the reason, item, and status. While we could make each of these items degenerate dimensions, the data architects have opted to create a junk dimension table for these items. So, this table will contain every possible combination of the three values. The source of each column in the ERD above is in the table below.

Column Name	Source
EVALUATION_STATUS	EVALUATION_HEADER.EVAL_STATUS
REASON_NAME	EVAL_REASON.REASON_NAME
ITEM_NAME	EVALUATION_ITEM.ITEM_NAME

FACT_EVALUATION: This is a basic fact table that allows a user to analyze evaluation score data by evaluation recipient, evaluator, date, reason, item, and status. The ACTUAL_SCORE and POSSIBLE_SCORE columns will come from the EVALUATION_DETAIL.ACTUAL_SCORE and the EVALUATION_DETAIL.POSSIBLE_SCORE columns, respectively. The key values will point to their associated dimensions. The DD_EVALUATOR_NAME column is a degenerate dimension that is used to house the name of the evaluator. Remember from the source system analysis that the EVALUATION_HEADER.EVALUATOR column contains the name of the evaluator (not a numeric identifier), which is stored in an inconsistent format from record to record.

LOOKUP_EVAL_STATUS: One table that is not in the ERD since it is not officially a part of the star is called the LOOKUP_EVAL_STATUS table. Because the EVALUATION_HEADER.EVAL_STATUS column contains the status of each evaluation in an inconsistent manner, this table is used to map those inconsistencies to a standard format. When the ETL selects a status value from the source system, the matching value from this table is placed into the DIM_EVALUATION_CONTEXT.EVALUATION_STATUS column. The contents of the table will need to be maintained by the users in some way, perhaps directly or perhaps indirectly via a spreadsheet upload process. The initial contents are in the following table.

ID	ORIGINAL_EVAL_STATUS	WAREHOUSE_EVAL_STATUS
1	complete	Complete
2	Completed	Complete
3	Successful	Complete
4	In Progress	In Progress
5	IP	In Progress

So, when a record in the source system contains a value of 'Successful' a value of 'Complete' will be added to the DIM_EVALUATION_CONTEXT.EVALUATION_STATUS column. The following script can be used to create the sequence (if desired) and table structure. The data from the table above will need to be added manually.

```
CREATE SEQUENCE SEQ_DIM_LOOKUP_EVAL_STATUS
START WITH 0
MINVALUE 0
NOMAXVALUE
INCREMENT BY 1;

CREATE TABLE LOOKUP_EVAL_STATUS
(
    ID                      NUMBER,
    ORIGINAL_EVAL_STATUS    VARCHAR2(255),
    WAREHOUSE_EVAL_STATUS VARCHAR2(255)
);
```

Strategy for ETL

This star contains one fact table and three dimension tables. The DIM_DAY table is a standard type zero date dimension that is not populated by an ETL job. A job to populate the DIM_EMPLOYEE table (LOAD_EMPLOYEE_DIMENSION) has already been written. So, jobs will need to be written to populate the DIM_EVALUATION_CONTEXT and the

FACT_EVALUATION tables.

Populating the DIM_EVALUATION_CONTEXT Dimension

We will begin by populating the DIM_EVALUATION_CONTEXT table. Remember from chapter five that the goal of an ETL job that populates a dimension table is to accomplish the following.

1.) Select all of the necessary dimension attributes from the source
2.) Transform the data as needed
3.) Update any existing records
    a. Defined as records for which the natural key already exists in the dimension table, but having data that changed in the source system
4.) Add the surrogate key to any new rows
    a. Defined as records for which the natural key does not exist in the dimension table
5.) Add the new rows to the dimensions

In determining the approach to take when extracting the data, consider the amount of data involved. This select statement should give us an idea of the number of rows that will be included currently.

```
SELECT      DISTINCT C.ITEM_NAME,
            D.REASON_NAME,
            A.EVAL_STATUS
FROM        EVALUATION_HEADER A,
            EVALUATION_DETAIL B,
            EVALUATION_ITEM C,
            EVAL_REASON D
WHERE       A.ID = B.EVAL_HEADER_ID
            AND A.REASON_ID = D.ID
            AND B.EVAL_ITEM_ID = C.ID
```

This should return 96 rows. Because such a small number of rows return quickly, we can take the entire refresh approach discussed in chapter five. The processing needed to determine the as-of date for which this data should be extracted can be avoided. The ETL job will pull everything into the staging area and then compare that to the dimension table. Any rows not in the dimension table will be added.

Remember that we have been using the Oracle sequence feature to create new surrogate keys. This one should work well to create the KEY_EVALUATION_CONTEXT values in the DIM_EVALUATION_CONTEXT table.

```
CREATE SEQUENCE SEQ_DIM_EVALUATION_CONTEXT
START WITH 0
MINVALUE 0
NOMAXVALUE
INCREMENT BY 1;
```

The DIM_EVALUATION_CONTEXT table will need to be created as well. Run the following in Oracle to create it:

```
CREATE TABLE DIM_EVALUATION_CONTEXT
(
        KEY_EVALUATION_CONTEXT      NUMBER,
        EVALUATION_STATUS           VARCHAR2(255),
        REASON_NAME                 VARCHAR2(255),
        ITEM_NAME                   VARCHAR2(255)
);
```

Now that the infrastructure is available it is time to populate the dimension. We will name the job LOAD_EVALUATION_CONT_DIM.

Lines 1 – 29

Line	Code
1	CREATE OR REPLACE PROCEDURE LOAD_EVALUATION_CONT_DIM
2	
3	AS
4	
5	SQLSTMT VARCHAR2(2000);
6	TBLCOUNT NUMBER := 0;
7	ERR_MSG VARCHAR2(200);
8	MAX_KEY_EVALUATION_CONTEXT NUMBER;
9	NEXT_SEQ_VAL NUMBER;
10	
11	BEGIN
12	--Log the beginning of the job
13	INSERT INTO ETL_JOB_STATUS
14	(
15	ID,
16	ETL_JOB_NAME,
17	STATUS_NAME,
18	STATUS_TIMESTAMP
19	)
20	VALUES
21	(
22	SEQ_ETL_JOB_STATUS.NEXTVAL,
23	'LOAD_EVALUATION_CONT_DIMENSION',
24	'IN PROGRESS',

Line	Code
25	SYSTIMESTAMP
26	);
27	
28	COMMIT;
29	

These are the preliminary steps of the job. The variables are declared in lines 5-9 and the job is logged in the ETL_JOB_STATUS table as having begun in lines 13-26.

Lines 30 – 54

Line	Code
30	--Make sure that the sequence that populates the key_evaluation_context is
31	--set to begin at the next integer
32	SELECT NVL(MAX(KEY_EVALUATION_CONTEXT), 0) INTO MAX_KEY_EVALUATION_CONTEXT
33	FROM DIM_EVALUATION_CONTEXT;
34	
35	SELECT SEQ_DIM_EVALUATION_CONTEXT.NEXTVAL INTO NEXT_SEQ_VAL
36	FROM DUAL;
37	
38	IF NEXT_SEQ_VAL <> MAX_KEY_EVALUATION_CONTEXT THEN
39	SQLSTMT := 'ALTER SEQUENCE SEQ_DIM_EVALUATION_CONTEXT INCREMENT BY '
40	|| ((NEXT_SEQ_VAL - MAX_KEY_EVALUATION_CONTEXT) * -1)
41	|| ' MINVALUE 0';
42	
43	EXECUTE IMMEDIATE SQLSTMT;
44	
45	SELECT SEQ_DIM_EVALUATION_CONTEXT.NEXTVAL INTO NEXT_SEQ_VAL
46	FROM DUAL;
47	
48	SQLSTMT := 'ALTER SEQUENCE SEQ_DIM_EVALUATION_CONTEXT '
49	|| 'INCREMENT BY 1 MINVALUE 0';
50	
51	EXECUTE IMMEDIATE SQLSTMT;
52	

Line	Code
53	END IF;
54	

This piece of the job checks the sequence to make sure that it will begin at the number that equates to the highest KEY_EVALUATION_CONTEXT plus one. So, if the highest KEY_EVALUATION_CONTEXT value is 96, this code will set it to 97. This is not essential for a successful run of the code, but it will avoid large gaps between the surrogate keys.

Extract the Data
This piece of the job begins the process of extracting the data from the source system.

Lines 55 – 69

Line	Code
55	--If the table exists, drop it. If not, do nothing. The table will be
56	--created below.
57	SELECT COUNT(*) INTO TBLCOUNT
58	FROM ALL_TABLES
59	WHERE TABLE_NAME = 'STAGE_EVALUATION_CONT_DATA'
60	AND OWNER =
61	(
62	SELECT SYS_CONTEXT('USERENV', 'CURRENT_SCHEMA')
63	FROM DUAL
64	);
65	
66	IF TBLCOUNT > 0 THEN
67	EXECUTE IMMEDIATE 'DROP TABLE STAGE_EVALUATION_CONT_DATA';
68	END IF;
69	

The STAGE_EVALUATION_CONT_DATA table is dropped if it exists.

Lines 70 – 86

Line	Code
70	--Since this is a relatively small amount of data, the entire refresh
71	--approach can be taken. The data from the source system is "dumped"
72	--into the STAGE_EVALUATION_CONT_DATA table in the staging area.
73	SQLSTMT := 'CREATE TABLE STAGE_EVALUATION_CONT_DATA AS '

Line	Code
74	|| '(SELECT DISTINCT C.ITEM_NAME, '
75	|| 'D.REASON_NAME, '
76	|| 'A.EVAL_STATUS '
77	|| 'FROM EVALUATION_HEADER A, '
78	|| 'EVALUATION_DETAIL B, '
79	|| 'EVALUATION_ITEM C, '
80	|| 'EVAL_REASON D '
81	|| 'WHERE A.ID = B.EVAL_HEADER_ID '
82	|| 'AND A.REASON_ID = D.ID '
83	|| 'AND B.EVAL_ITEM_ID = C.ID) ';
84	
85	EXECUTE IMMEDIATE SQLSTMT;
86	

The STAGE_EVALUATION_CONT_DATA table is created and populated with all current combinations of the reason, status, and item.

Transform the Data

This piece of the job structures the data so that it will fit into DIM_EVALUATION_CONTEXT table.

Lines 87 – 103

Line	Code
87	--The status is compared to the LOOKUP_EVAL_STATUS table and the associated
88	--value is picked up. The data is then placed into the
89	--STAGE_EVAL_CONT_DATA_TRANSFORM table (table is dropped if it exists and
90	--then created below).
91	SELECT COUNT(*) INTO TBLCOUNT
92	FROM ALL_TABLES
93	WHERE TABLE_NAME = 'STAGE_EVAL_CONT_DATA_TRANSFORM'
94	AND OWNER =
95	(
96	SELECT SYS_CONTEXT('USERENV', 'CURRENT_SCHEMA')
97	FROM DUAL
98	);
99	
100	IF TBLCOUNT > 0 THEN

Line	Code
101	EXECUTE IMMEDIATE 'DROP TABLE STAGE_EVAL_CONT_DATA_TRANSFORM';
102	END IF;
103	

The STAGE_EVAL_CONT_DATA_TRANSFORM table is dropped if it exists.

Lines 104 – 115

Line	Code
104	SQLSTMT := 'CREATE TABLE STAGE_EVAL_CONT_DATA_TRANSFORM '
105	|| 'AS ('
106	|| 'SELECT DISTINCT '
107	|| 'B.WAREHOUSE_EVAL_STATUS EVALUATION_STATUS, '
108	|| 'A.REASON_NAME, '
109	|| 'A.ITEM_NAME '
110	|| 'FROM STAGE_EVALUATION_CONT_DATA A, '
111	|| 'LOOKUP_EVAL_STATUS B '
112	|| 'WHERE A.EVAL_STATUS = B.ORIGINAL_EVAL_STATUS)';
113	
114	EXECUTE IMMEDIATE SQLSTMT;
115	

The STAGE_EVALUATION_CONT_DATA.EVAL_STATUS column is compared to the LOOKUP_EVAL_STATUS.ORIGINAL_EVAL_STATUS column. The associated LOOKUP_EVAL_STATUS.WAREHOUSE_EVAL_STATUS column is then placed into the STAGE_EVAL_CONT_DATA_TRANSFORM column.

Lines 116 – 133

Line	Code
116	--Any new records that belong in this cont dimension table are given a key
117	--(using the sequence) and placed into the STAGE_EVAL_CONT_DATA_ADD_KEYS
118	--table. Since every column in this junk dimension table acts as the natural
119	--key, there is no way to update a row in this table as we would with another
120	--dimension table.
121	SELECT COUNT(*) INTO TBLCOUNT
122	FROM ALL_TABLES
123	WHERE TABLE_NAME = 'STAGE_EVAL_CONT_DATA_ADD_KEYS'

Line	Code
124	AND OWNER =
125	(
126	SELECT SYS_CONTEXT('USERENV', 'CURRENT_SCHEMA')
127	FROM DUAL
128	);
129	
130	IF TBLCOUNT > 0 THEN
131	EXECUTE IMMEDIATE 'DROP TABLE STAGE_EVAL_CONT_DATA_ADD_KEYS';
132	END IF;
133	

If the STAGE_EVAL_CONT_DATA_ADD_KEYS table exists, it is dropped.

Lines 134 – 148

Line	Code
134	SQLSTMT := 'CREATE TABLE STAGE_EVAL_CONT_DATA_ADD_KEYS '
135	|| 'AS ('
136	|| 'SELECT SEQ_DIM_EVALUATION_CONTEXT.NEXTVAL AS KEY_EVALUATION_CONTEXT, '
137	|| 'EVALUATION_STATUS, '
138	|| 'REASON_NAME, '
139	|| 'ITEM_NAME '
140	|| 'FROM STAGE_EVAL_CONT_DATA_TRANSFORM '
141	|| 'WHERE (EVALUATION_STATUS, REASON_NAME, ITEM_NAME)'
142	|| 'NOT IN '
143	|| '(SELECT EVALUATION_STATUS, REASON_NAME, ITEM_NAME '
144	|| 'FROM DIM_EVALUATION_CONTEXT)'
145	|| ') ';
146	
147	EXECUTE IMMEDIATE SQLSTMT;
148	

Normally when populating a dimension table, an ETL job will compare the natural keys between the source and the existing dimension records and update any of the other columns for those records that have been updated in the source system. Any records from the source that contain natural keys that are not in the dimension table are simply added. In this case, because each column acts as a natural key, the first step that performs the update cannot be done. So, this piece of code compares the contents of the STAGE_EVAL_CONT_DATA_TRANSFORM table to the

DIM_EVALUATION_CONTEXT table. If something exists in the STAGE_EVAL_CONT_DATA_TRANSFORM table that does not exist in the DIM_EVALUATION_CONTEXT table, a surrogate key is added via the Oracle sequence and that record is added to the STAGE_EVAL_CONT_DATA_ADD_KEYS table.

Insert the Data

This piece of the job inserts the data into the DIM_EVALUATION_CONTEXT table.

Lines 149 – 160

Line	Code
149	--Insert the new rows into the DIM_EVALUATION_CONTEXT dimension. Because
150	--this job cannot handle an update, if an eval_status is mapped to a new
151	--value this job will create a new row representing that. Another job will
152	--be created to handle the deletion of those old rows since the fact table
153	--rows that point to those old rows must first be repointed to the new ones.
154	SQLSTMT := 'INSERT INTO DIM_EVALUATION_CONTEXT '
155	|| 'SELECT * FROM STAGE_EVAL_CONT_DATA_ADD_KEYS ';
156	
157	EXECUTE IMMEDIATE SQLSTMT;
158	
159	COMMIT;
160	

This piece of code simply adds the records from the STAGE_EVAL_CONT_DATA_ADD_KEYS table to the DIM_EVALUATION_CONTEXT table.

Lines 161 – 178

Line	Code
161	--Log the successful completion of the job.
162	INSERT INTO ETL_JOB_STATUS
163	(
164	ID,
165	ETL_JOB_NAME,
166	STATUS_NAME,
167	STATUS_TIMESTAMP
168	)
169	VALUES
170	(

Line	Code
171	SEQ_ETL_JOB_STATUS.NEXTVAL,
172	'LOAD_EVALUATION_CONT_DIMENSION',
173	'SUCCESSFULLY COMPLETED',
174	SYSTIMESTAMP
175	);
176	
177	COMMIT;
178	

If the job reaches this point (line 161), it has finished successfully. The successful finish is logged in the ETL_JOB_STATUS table.

Lines 179 – 202

Line	Code
179	--This is the equivalent of a catch block. Any errors are caught and logged.
180	EXCEPTION
181	WHEN OTHERS THEN
182	ERR_MSG := SUBSTR(SQLERRM, 1, 200);
183	INSERT INTO ETL_JOB_STATUS
184	(
185	ID,
186	ETL_JOB_NAME,
187	STATUS_NAME,
188	ERROR_MESSAGE,
189	STATUS_TIMESTAMP
190	)
191	VALUES
192	(
193	SEQ_ETL_JOB_STATUS.NEXTVAL,
194	'LOAD_EVALUATION_CONT_DIMENSION',
195	'ERROR',
196	ERR_MSG,
197	SYSTIMESTAMP
198	);
199	
200	COMMIT;
201	

Line	Code
202	END;

These lines act as a catch block that will catch any errors encountered above and log them in the ETL_JOB_STATUS table.

Review the ETL Job

Running the job should result in 40 rows being placed into the DIM_EVALUATION_CONTEXT table.

1.) This job is designed to be run as many times as are necessary. In other words, running the job twice in a row will not result in erroneous rows being placed into the dimension.
2.) Because we have elected to go with the entire refresh approach, passing parameters to the job is not necessary. Notice that while we are taking the entire refresh approach with regards to pulling data from the source system, the job is not truncating the dimension table and repopulating. It is still comparing the dataset to the dimension table records and adding the new ones to the table.
3.) Remember that on page 153 we said that 96 records returned, which we can see in the STAGE_EVALUATION_CONT_DATA. However, only 40 ended up in the DIM_EVALUATION_CONTEXT table. This is due to the fact that while populating the STAGE_EVAL_CONT_DATA_TRANSFORM table the source system's status values are being replaced by the values in the LOOKUP_EVAL_STATUS. There are fewer distinct status values after this transformation, therefore resulting in a reduction in the number of rows.

Verify the ETL Job

Verifying a dimension table involves comparing all of its values to the source system. This will be slightly complex due to the role that the LOOKUP_EVAL_STATUS plays in transforming the data. The following SQL statement should be able to do this well.

```
SELECT      DISTINCT C.ITEM_NAME,
            D.REASON_NAME,
            E.WAREHOUSE_EVAL_STATUS,
            'Source'
FROM        EVALUATION_HEADER A,
            EVALUATION_DETAIL B,
            EVALUATION_ITEM C,
            EVAL_REASON D,
            LOOKUP_EVAL_STATUS E
WHERE       A.ID = B.EVAL_HEADER_ID
            AND A.REASON_ID = D.ID
            AND B.EVAL_ITEM_ID = C.ID
            AND E.ORIGINAL_EVAL_STATUS = A.EVAL_STATUS
UNION
SELECT      ITEM_NAME,
            REASON_NAME,
```

	EVALUATION_STATUS,
	'Data Warehouse'
FROM	DIM_EVALUATION_CONTEXT
ORDER BY	1,2,3,4

Partial Results – Due to space constraints only 8 of the 80 rows that this select statement returns are displayed below.

ITEM_NAME	REASON_NAME	WAREHOUSE_EVAL_STATUS	'SOURCE'
Additional Leadership Potential	Annual Evaluation	Complete	Data Warehouse
Additional Leadership Potential	Annual Evaluation	Complete	Source
Additional Leadership Potential	Annual Evaluation	In Progress	Data Warehouse
Additional Leadership Potential	Annual Evaluation	In Progress	Source
Additional Leadership Potential	Employee Requested Evaluation	Complete	Data Warehouse
Additional Leadership Potential	Employee Requested Evaluation	Complete	Source
Additional Leadership Potential	Employee Requested Evaluation	In Progress	Data Warehouse
Additional Leadership Potential	Employee Requested Evaluation	In Progress	Source

It appears that the dimension is being populated correctly.

Updates

Upon further review, there is an opportunity to improve the LOAD_EVALUATION_CONT_DIMENSION job, despite the fact that the job is working correctly. Remember that the select statement used to create and populate the STAGE_EVAL_CONT_DATA_TRANSFORM table joins to the LOOKUP_EVAL_STATUS table in order to pull the status value. Line 112 is a standard join.

Line	Code
112	SQLSTMT := SQLSTMT || 'WHERE A.EVAL_STATUS = B.ORIGINAL_EVAL_STATUS)';

This means that if a status value is in the source system (EVALUATION_HEADER.EVAL_STATUS) but not in the LOOKUP_EVAL_STATUS table, that record will not make it into the dimension. We can enhance the job in order to close this loophole through which records may potentially be dropped.

Enhancement to the **LOAD_EVALUATION_CONT_DIMENSION** Job

Line	Code
104	SQLSTMT := 'CREATE TABLE STAGE_EVAL_CONT_DATA_TRANSFORM '
105	|| 'AS ('
106	|| 'SELECT DISTINCT '
107 (updated)	|| 'NVL(B.WAREHOUSE_EVAL_STATUS, A.EVAL_STATUS) EVALUATION_STATUS, '
108	|| 'A.REASON_NAME, '
109	|| 'A.ITEM_NAME '
110	|| 'FROM STAGE_EVALUATION_CONT_DATA A, '
111	|| 'LOOKUP_EVAL_STATUS B '
112 (updated)	|| 'WHERE A.EVAL_STATUS = B.ORIGINAL_EVAL_STATUS(+))';
113	
114	EXECUTE IMMEDIATE SQLSTMT;
115	

Line 112 has been updated from a standard join to an outer join. This means that a record in the STAGE_EVALUATION_CONT_DATA table with an EVAL_STATUS value that is not in the LOOKUP_EVAL_STATUS table will not get dropped. If this were to happen, the users would prefer to see the source system's evaluation status value (EVALUATION_HEADER.EVAL_STATUS) instead of a null value. As a result, line 107 now includes the NVL() function. Until some additional data is added to the source system, this should have no impact on the current situation.

The LOAD_EVALUATION_CONT_DIMENSION in its entirety is available below.

Line	Code	
1	CREATE OR REPLACE PROCEDURE LOAD_EVALUATION_CONT_DIM	
2		
3	AS	
4		
5	SQLSTMT	VARCHAR2(2000);
6	TBLCOUNT	NUMBER := 0;
7	ERR_MSG	VARCHAR2(200);
8	MAX_KEY_EVALUATION_CONTEXT	NUMBER;
9	NEXT_SEQ_VAL	NUMBER;
10		
11	BEGIN	
12	--Log the beginning of the job	

Line	Code
13	INSERT INTO ETL_JOB_STATUS
14	(
15	ID,
16	ETL_JOB_NAME,
17	STATUS_NAME,
18	STATUS_TIMESTAMP
19	)
20	VALUES
21	(
22	SEQ_ETL_JOB_STATUS.NEXTVAL,
23	'LOAD_EVALUATION_CONT_DIMENSION',
24	'IN PROGRESS',
25	SYSTIMESTAMP
26	);
27	
28	COMMIT;
29	
30	--Make sure that the sequence that populates the key_evaluation_context is
31	--set to begin at the next integer
32	SELECT NVL(MAX(KEY_EVALUATION_CONTEXT), 0) INTO MAX_KEY_EVALUATION_CONTEXT
33	FROM DIM_EVALUATION_CONTEXT;
34	
35	SELECT SEQ_DIM_EVALUATION_CONTEXT.NEXTVAL INTO NEXT_SEQ_VAL
36	FROM DUAL;
37	
38	IF NEXT_SEQ_VAL <> MAX_KEY_EVALUATION_CONTEXT THEN
39	SQLSTMT := 'ALTER SEQUENCE SEQ_DIM_EVALUATION_CONTEXT INCREMENT BY '
40	|| ((NEXT_SEQ_VAL - MAX_KEY_EVALUATION_CONTEXT) * -1)
41	|| ' MINVALUE 0';
42	
43	EXECUTE IMMEDIATE SQLSTMT;
44	
45	SELECT SEQ_DIM_EVALUATION_CONTEXT.NEXTVAL INTO NEXT_SEQ_VAL
46	FROM DUAL;

Line	Code
47	
48	SQLSTMT := 'ALTER SEQUENCE SEQ_DIM_EVALUATION_CONTEXT '
49	|| 'INCREMENT BY 1 MINVALUE 0';
50	
51	EXECUTE IMMEDIATE SQLSTMT;
52	
53	END IF;
54	
55	--If the table exists, drop it. If not, do nothing. The table will be
56	--created below.
57	SELECT COUNT(*) INTO TBLCOUNT
58	FROM ALL_TABLES
59	WHERE TABLE_NAME = 'STAGE_EVALUATION_CONT_DATA'
60	AND OWNER =
61	(
62	SELECT SYS_CONTEXT('USERENV', 'CURRENT_SCHEMA')
63	FROM DUAL
64	);
65	
66	IF TBLCOUNT > 0 THEN
67	EXECUTE IMMEDIATE 'DROP TABLE STAGE_EVALUATION_CONT_DATA';
68	END IF;
69	
70	--Since this is a relatively small amount of data, the entire refresh
71	--approach can be taken. The data from the source system is "dumped"
72	--into the STAGE_EVALUATION_CONT_DATA table in the staging area.
73	SQLSTMT := 'CREATE TABLE STAGE_EVALUATION_CONT_DATA AS '
74	|| '(SELECT DISTINCT C.ITEM_NAME, '
75	|| 'D.REASON_NAME, '
76	|| 'A.EVAL_STATUS '
77	|| 'FROM EVALUATION_HEADER A, '
78	|| 'EVALUATION_DETAIL B, '
79	|| 'EVALUATION_ITEM C, '
80	|| 'EVAL_REASON D '
81	|| 'WHERE A.ID = B.EVAL_HEADER_ID '
82	|| 'AND A.REASON_ID = D.ID '

Line	Code
83	| | 'AND B.EVAL_ITEM_ID = C.ID) ';
84	
85	EXECUTE IMMEDIATE SQLSTMT;
86	
87	--The status is compared to the LOOKUP_EVAL_STATUS table and the associated
88	--value is picked up. The data is then placed into the
89	--STAGE_EVAL_CONT_DATA_TRANSFORM table (table is dropped if it exists and
90	--then created below).
91	SELECT COUNT(*) INTO TBLCOUNT
92	FROM ALL_TABLES
93	WHERE TABLE_NAME = 'STAGE_EVAL_CONT_DATA_TRANSFORM'
94	AND OWNER =
95	(
96	SELECT SYS_CONTEXT('USERENV', 'CURRENT_SCHEMA')
97	FROM DUAL
98	);
99	
100	IF TBLCOUNT > 0 THEN
101	EXECUTE IMMEDIATE 'DROP TABLE STAGE_EVAL_CONT_DATA_TRANSFORM';
102	END IF;
103	
104	SQLSTMT := 'CREATE TABLE STAGE_EVAL_CONT_DATA_TRANSFORM '
105	| | 'AS ('
106 (updated)	| | 'SELECT DISTINCT '
107	| | 'NVL(B.WAREHOUSE_EVAL_STATUS, A.EVAL_STATUS) EVALUATION_STATUS, '
108	| | 'A.REASON_NAME, '
109	| | 'A.ITEM_NAME '
110	| | 'FROM STAGE_EVALUATION_CONT_DATA A, '
111	| | 'LOOKUP_EVAL_STATUS B '
112 (updated)	| | 'WHERE A.EVAL_STATUS = B.ORIGINAL_EVAL_STATUS(+))';
113	
114	EXECUTE IMMEDIATE SQLSTMT;

Line	Code
115	
116	--Any new records that belong in this cont dimension table are given a key
117	--(using the sequence) and placed into the STAGE_EVAL_CONT_DATA_ADD_KEYS
118	--table. Since every column in this junk dimension table acts as the natural
119	--key, there is no way to update a row in this table as we would with another
120	--dimension table.
121	SELECT COUNT(*) INTO TBLCOUNT
122	FROM ALL_TABLES
123	WHERE TABLE_NAME = 'STAGE_EVAL_CONT_DATA_ADD_KEYS'
124	AND OWNER =
125	(
126	SELECT SYS_CONTEXT('USERENV', 'CURRENT_SCHEMA')
127	FROM DUAL
128	);
129	
130	IF TBLCOUNT > 0 THEN
131	EXECUTE IMMEDIATE 'DROP TABLE STAGE_EVAL_CONT_DATA_ADD_KEYS';
132	END IF;
133	
134	SQLSTMT := 'CREATE TABLE STAGE_EVAL_CONT_DATA_ADD_KEYS '
135	|| 'AS ('
136	|| 'SELECT SEQ_DIM_EVALUATION_CONTEXT.NEXTVAL AS KEY_EVALUATION_CONTEXT, '
137	|| 'EVALUATION_STATUS, '
138	|| 'REASON_NAME, '
139	|| 'ITEM_NAME '
140	|| 'FROM STAGE_EVAL_CONT_DATA_TRANSFORM '
141	|| 'WHERE (EVALUATION_STATUS, REASON_NAME, ITEM_NAME) '
142	|| 'NOT IN '
143	|| '(SELECT EVALUATION_STATUS, REASON_NAME, ITEM_NAME '
144	|| 'FROM DIM_EVALUATION_CONTEXT) '
145	|| ')';
146	
147	EXECUTE IMMEDIATE SQLSTMT;
148	
149	--Insert the new rows into the DIM_EVALUATION_CONTEXT dimension.

Line	Code
	Because
150	--this job cannot handle an update, if an eval_status is mapped to a new
151	--value this job will create a new row representing that. Another job will
152	--be created to handle the deletion of those old rows since the fact table
153	--rows that point to those old rows must first be repointed to the new ones.
154	SQLSTMT := 'INSERT INTO DIM_EVALUATION_CONTEXT '
155	|| 'SELECT * FROM STAGE_EVAL_CONT_DATA_ADD_KEYS ';
156	
157	EXECUTE IMMEDIATE SQLSTMT;
158	
159	COMMIT;
160	
161	--Log the successful completion of the job.
162	INSERT INTO ETL_JOB_STATUS
163	(
164	ID,
165	ETL_JOB_NAME,
166	STATUS_NAME,
167	STATUS_TIMESTAMP
168	)
169	VALUES
170	(
171	SEQ_ETL_JOB_STATUS.NEXTVAL,
172	'LOAD_EVALUATION_CONT_DIMENSION',
173	'SUCCESSFULLY COMPLETED',
174	SYSTIMESTAMP
175	);
176	
177	COMMIT;
178	
179	--This is the equivalent of a catch block. Any errors are caught and logged.
180	EXCEPTION
181	WHEN OTHERS THEN
182	ERR_MSG := SUBSTR(SQLERRM, 1, 200);
183	INSERT INTO ETL_JOB_STATUS
184	(

Line	Code
185	ID,
186	ETL_JOB_NAME,
187	STATUS_NAME,
188	ERROR_MESSAGE,
189	STATUS_TIMESTAMP
190	)
191	VALUES
192	(
193	SEQ_ETL_JOB_STATUS.NEXTVAL,
194	'LOAD_EVALUATION_CONT_DIMENSION',
195	'ERROR',
196	ERR_MSG,
197	SYSTIMESTAMP
198	);
199	
200	COMMIT;
201	
202	END;

Populating the FACT_EVALUATION Fact Table

Next we will populate the FACT_EVALUATION table. Remember from chapter five that the goal of an ETL job that populates a fact table is to accomplish the following.

1.) Select all necessary data from the source
  a. Measures
  b. Natural keys of the dimension objects
  c. Degenerate Dimension objects
2.) Transform the data as needed
  a. Aggregate measures and group by the appropriate objects
  b. Add foreign keys to dimension tables
3.) Delete any existing rows from the fact table that will be replaced by the new data
4.) Load the fact table

Because the Based on Timeframe approach worked well with the other fact tables, we can try that with this one as well. Use this script to create the FACT_EVALUATION table.

```
CREATE TABLE FACT_EVALUATION
  (
    KEY_EVALUATION_DATE          NUMBER,
    KEY_EVALUATION_RECIPIENT     NUMBER,
    KEY_EVALUATION_CONTEXT       NUMBER,
```

```
DD_EVALUATOR_NAME          VARCHAR2(255),
ACTUAL_SCORE               NUMBER,
POSSIBLE_SCORE             NUMBER
)
```

Now that the infrastructure has been created, we can move forward with actually populating the fact table. We will call the procedure LOAD_EVALUATION_FACT.

Lines 1-8

Line	Code
1	CREATE OR REPLACE PROCEDURE LOAD_EVALUATION_FACT
2	(
3	BEGIN_DAY_OVERRIDE DATE,
4	END_DAY_OVERRIDE DATE,
5	DEFAULT_TIMEPERIOD VARCHAR2,
6	ENTIRE_REFRESH VARCHAR2
7	)
8	

These are some of the preliminary activities needed at the beginning of a job. The job is written so that the following parameters can be passed.

1.) **BEGIN_DAY_OVERRIDE:** If this job is to be run for a specific date range, then this parameter is the beginning of that range.
2.) **END_DAY_OVERRIDE:** If this job is to be run for a specific date range, then this parameter is the end of that range.
3.) **DEFAULT_TIMEPERIOD:** If a value of 'Y' is passed here, then this job will be run for a default date range, which will be explained later. When the job is run as scheduled, a value of 'Y' will be passed here.
4.) **ENTIRE_REFRESH:** This has been added as a standard parameter for ETL jobs in order to make it easier to refresh a table in its entirety. Before this was added, the job runner would have to use the day override parameters to accomplish this. The problem is that the job runner would have to know the earliest and latest dates used in the source system. If a value of 'Y' is passed, the entire table is refreshed. We will see below that a value of 'Y' being passed here will trump a value of 'Y' being passed to the DEFAULT_TIMEPERIOD. In other words, this one takes precedence.

Lines 9 – 35

Line	Code
9	AS

Line	Code
10	
11	SQLSTMT VARCHAR2(3000);
12	TBLCOUNT NUMBER := 0;
13	BEGIN_AS_OF_DATE DATE;
14	END_AS_OF_DATE DATE;
15	ERR_MSG VARCHAR2(200);
16	
17	BEGIN
18	--Log the beginning of the job
19	INSERT INTO ETL_JOB_STATUS
20	(
21	ID,
22	ETL_JOB_NAME,
23	STATUS_NAME,
24	STATUS_TIMESTAMP
25	)
26	VALUES
27	(
28	SEQ_ETL_JOB_STATUS.NEXTVAL,
29	'LOAD_EVALUATION_FACT',
30	'IN PROGRESS',
31	SYSTIMESTAMP
32	);
33	
34	COMMIT;
35	

This piece of code declares the necessary variables and logs the beginning of the job in the ETL_JOB_STATUS table.

Extract the Data

This area of the code begins the process of extracting the data from the source system.

Lines 36 – 50

Line	Code
36	--If the table exists, drop it. If not, do nothing. The table will be
37	--created below.
38	SELECT COUNT(*) INTO TBLCOUNT
39	FROM ALL_TABLES
40	WHERE TABLE_NAME = 'STAGE_EVALUATION_DATA'
41	AND OWNER =
42	(
43	SELECT SYS_CONTEXT('USERENV', 'CURRENT_SCHEMA')
44	FROM DUAL
45	);
46	
47	IF TBLCOUNT > 0 THEN
48	EXECUTE IMMEDIATE 'DROP TABLE STAGE_EVALUATION_DATA';
49	END IF;
50	

If the STAGE_EVALUATION_DATA table exists drop it.

Lines 51 – 61

Line	Code
51	--If the DEFAULT_PERIOD variable is set to 'Y', then the prior month and the
52	--current month are loaded or reloaded into the fact table. Otherwise, the
53	--overrides are used.
54	IF DEFAULT_TIMEPERIOD = 'Y' THEN
55	SELECT TRUNC(TRUNC(SYSDATE,'MM')-1,'MM') INTO BEGIN_AS_OF_DATE FROM DUAL;
56	SELECT LAST_DAY(TRUNC(SYSDATE)) INTO END_AS_OF_DATE FROM DUAL;
57	ELSE
58	BEGIN_AS_OF_DATE := BEGIN_DAY_OVERRIDE;
59	END_AS_OF_DATE := END_DAY_OVERRIDE;
60	END IF;
61	

The date range for which the data will be extracted is defined here. If the DEFAULT_TIMEPERIOD = 'Y' then data pertaining to the current month and the previous month will be pulled. If not, the values passed as the BEGIN_DAY_OVERRIDE and the END_DAY_OVERRIDE are used to define that range. We will see below that if the ENTIRE_REFRESH = 'Y', that takes the most precedence.

Lines 62 – 94

Line	Code
62	--Dump the data into the staging table and transform the PAY_TYPE_NAME into
63	--the values that are used in the DIM_PAY_TYPE table
64	SQLSTMT := 'CREATE TABLE STAGE_EVALUATION_DATA AS ('
65	|| 'SELECT DISTINCT C.ITEM_NAME, '
66	|| 'D.REASON_NAME, '
67	|| 'A.EVAL_STATUS, '
68	|| 'A.EVALUATION_DATE, '
69	|| 'A.EVALUATOR, '
70	|| 'B.ACTUAL_SCORE, '
71	|| 'B.POSSIBLE_SCORE, '
72	|| 'E.EMPLOYEE_NUMBER, '
73	|| 'F.APPOINTMENT_BEGIN_DATE, '
74	|| 'H.TITLE_NAME, '
75	|| 'G.DEPARTMENT_NUMBER, '
76	|| 'I.WAREHOUSE_EVAL_STATUS '
77	|| 'FROM EVALUATION_HEADER A, '
78	|| 'EVALUATION_DETAIL B, '
79	|| 'EVALUATION_ITEM C, '
80	|| 'EVAL_REASON D, '
81	|| 'EMPLOYEE E, '
82	|| 'APPOINTMENT F, '
83	|| 'DEPARTMENT G, '
84	|| 'TITLE H, '
85	|| 'LOOKUP_EVAL_STATUS I '
86	|| 'WHERE A.ID = B.EVAL_HEADER_ID '
87	|| 'AND A.REASON_ID = D.ID '
88	|| 'AND B.EVAL_ITEM_ID = C.ID '

Line	Code
89	|| 'AND A.APPOINTMENT_ID = F.ID '
90	|| 'AND F.EMPLOYEE_ID = E.ID '
91	|| 'AND F.DEPARTMENT_ID = G.ID '
92	|| 'AND F.TITLE_ID = H.ID '
93	|| 'AND A.EVAL_STATUS = I.ORIGINAL_EVAL_STATUS(+) ';
94	

Remember that step one of populating a fact table involves pulling the measures, natural keys to the dimensions, and degenerate dimension values from the source system. This select statement accomplishes that.

Measures: EVALUATION_DETAIL.ACTUAL_SCORE (line 70) and EVALUATION.POSSIBLE_SCORE (line 71)

Natural Key To DIM_EMPLOYEE:
- EMPLOYEE.EMPLOYEE_NUMBER(line 72)
- APPOINTMENT.APPOINTMENT_BEGIN_DATE (line 73)
- TITLE.TITLE_NAME (line 74)
- DEPARTMENT.DEPARTMENT_NUMBER (line 75)

Natural Key To DIM_DAY: EVALUATION_HEADER.EVALUATION_DATE (line 68)

Natural Key To DIM_EVALUATION_CONTEXT:

- EVALUATION_ITEM.ITEM_NAME(line 65)
- EVAL_REASON.REASON_NAME(line 66)
- EVALUATION_HEADER.EVAL_STATUS(line 67) is joined to LOOKUP_EVAL_STATUS in order to pull the LOOKUP_EVAL_STATUS.WAREHOUSE_EVAL_STATUS(line 76)

Degenerate Dimension: EVALUATION_HEADER. EVALUATOR (line 69)

Also note that in keeping with our enhancement to the LOAD_EVALUATION_CONT_DIMENSION job line 93 uses an outer join to the LOOKUP_EVAL_STATUS table.

Lines 95 – 105

Line	Code
95	IF ENTIRE_REFRESH <> 'Y' THEN
96	SQLSTMT := SQLSTMT || 'AND A.EVALUATION_DATE BETWEEN '''

Line	Code
97	| | TO_CHAR(BEGIN_AS_OF_DATE,'DD-MON-YYYY')
98	| | "' AND "'
99	| | TO_CHAR(END_AS_OF_DATE,'DD-MON-YYYY') | | "' ';
100	END IF;
101	
102	SQLSTMT := SQLSTMT | | ')';
103	
104	EXECUTE IMMEDIATE SQLSTMT;
105	

If the ENTIRE_REFRESH parameter was passed a value of 'Y' then there is no date filtering done in the where clause. Otherwise, the data is pulled for the applicable date range.

Transform the Data

This piece of the job transforms the data so that it will fit into the FACT_EVALUATION table.

Lines 106 – 120

Line	Code
106	--If the table exists, drop it. If not, do nothing. The table will be
107	--created below.
108	SELECT COUNT(*) INTO TBLCOUNT
109	FROM ALL_TABLES
110	WHERE TABLE_NAME = 'STAGE_EVAL_DATA_ADD_KEYS'
111	AND OWNER =
112	(
113	SELECT SYS_CONTEXT('USERENV', 'CURRENT_SCHEMA')
114	FROM DUAL
115	);
116	
117	IF TBLCOUNT > 0 THEN
118	EXECUTE IMMEDIATE 'DROP TABLE STAGE_EVAL_DATA_ADD_KEYS';
119	END IF;
120	

If the STAGE_EVAL_DATA_ADD_KEYS table exists drop it.

Lines 121 – 142

Line	Code
121	SQLSTMT := 'CREATE TABLE STAGE_EVAL_DATA_ADD_KEYS AS ('
122	|| 'SELECT NVL(C.KEY_DAY,-1) KEY_EVALUATION_DATE, '
123	|| 'NVL(B.KEY_EMPLOYEE,-1) KEY_EVALUATION_RECIPIENT, '
124	|| 'NVL(D.KEY_EVALUATION_CONTEXT,-1) KEY_EVALUATION_CONTEXT, '
125	|| 'A.EVALUATOR AS DD_EVALUATOR_NAME, '
126	|| 'A.ACTUAL_SCORE, '
127	|| 'A.POSSIBLE_SCORE '
128	|| 'FROM STAGE_EVALUATION_DATA A, '
129	|| 'DIM_EMPLOYEE B, '
130	|| 'DIM_DAY C, '
131	|| 'DIM_EVALUATION_CONTEXT D '
132	|| 'WHERE A.EMPLOYEE_NUMBER = B.EMPLOYEE_NUMBER(+) '
133	|| 'AND A.DEPARTMENT_NUMBER = B.DEPARTMENT_NUMBER(+) '
134	|| 'AND A.TITLE_NAME = B.TITLE(+) '
135	|| 'AND A.APPOINTMENT_BEGIN_DATE = B.APPOINTMENT_BEGIN_DATE(+) '
136	|| 'AND A.EVALUATION_DATE = C.CALENDAR_DAY(+) '
137	|| 'AND A.ITEM_NAME = D.ITEM_NAME(+) '
138	|| 'AND A.REASON_NAME = D.REASON_NAME(+) '
139	|| 'AND NVL(A.WAREHOUSE_EVAL_STATUS,A.EVAL_STATUS) = D.EVALUATION_STATUS(+)) ';
140	
141	EXECUTE IMMEDIATE SQLSTMT;
142	

The extracted data is joined to the dimension tables so that the surrogate keys to those dimensions can be included. The results are placed into the STAGE_EVAL_DATA_ADD_KEYS table.

Load the Data

This piece of the job begins the process of loading the data into the fact table.

Lines 143 – 165

Line	Code
143	--Updating the existing rows for months in which the amount has changed
144	--(i.e., an additional payroll was processed for that month since the last
145	--load) would be very inefficient. As a result, any existing data pertaining
146	--to the month(s) being pulled into the fact table is completely deleted
147	--from the fact table and reloaded.
148	IF ENTIRE_REFRESH <> 'Y' THEN
149	SQLSTMT := 'DELETE '
150	|| 'FROM FACT_EVALUATION A '
151	|| 'WHERE A.KEY_EVALUATION_DATE IN ('
152	|| 'SELECT KEY_DAY '
153	|| 'FROM DIM_DAY '
154	|| 'WHERE CALENDAR_DAY BETWEEN '''
155	|| TO_CHAR(BEGIN_AS_OF_DATE,'DD-MON-YYYY')
156	|| ''' AND '''
157	|| TO_CHAR(END_AS_OF_DATE,'DD-MON-YYYY')
158	|| ''') ';
159	ELSE
160	SQLSTMT := 'TRUNCATE TABLE FACT_EVALUATION';
161	END IF;
162	
163	EXECUTE IMMEDIATE SQLSTMT;
164	COMMIT;
165	

The data is deleted from the fact table for the applicable timeframe. In the case of an entire refresh, the table is truncated.

Lines 166 – 172

Line	Code
166	--The fact table is loaded
167	SQLSTMT := 'INSERT INTO FACT_EVALUATION '
168	|| 'SELECT * FROM STAGE_EVAL_DATA_ADD_KEYS ';

Line	Code
169	
170	EXECUTE IMMEDIATE SQLSTMT;
171	COMMIT;
172	

The data is loaded into the FACT_EVALUATION table.

Lines 173 – 190

Line	Code
173	--Log the successful completion of the job.
174	INSERT INTO ETL_JOB_STATUS
175	(
176	ID,
177	ETL_JOB_NAME,
178	STATUS_NAME,
179	STATUS_TIMESTAMP
180	)
181	VALUES
182	(
183	SEQ_ETL_JOB_STATUS.NEXTVAL,
184	'LOAD_EVALUATION_FACT',
185	'SUCCESSFULLY COMPLETED',
186	SYSTIMESTAMP
187	);
188	
189	COMMIT;
190	

If the job reaches this point (line 174), it has finished successfully. The successful finish is logged in the ETL_JOB_STATUS table.

Lines 191 – 214

Line	Code
191	--This is the equivalent of a catch block. Any errors are caught and logged.

Line	Code
192	EXCEPTION
193	WHEN OTHERS THEN
194	ERR_MSG := SUBSTR(SQLERRM, 1, 200);
195	INSERT INTO ETL_JOB_STATUS
196	(
197	ID,
198	ETL_JOB_NAME,
199	STATUS_NAME,
200	ERROR_MESSAGE,
201	STATUS_TIMESTAMP
202	)
203	VALUES
204	(
205	SEQ_ETL_JOB_STATUS.NEXTVAL,
206	'LOAD_EVALUATION_FACT',
207	'ERROR',
208	ERR_MSG,
209	SYSTIMESTAMP
210	);
211	
212	COMMIT;
213	END;
214	

This area acts as a catch block that will catch any errors encountered above and log them in the ETL_JOB_STATUS table.

Review the ETL Job

Running the job should result in 3,563,048 rows being placed into the FACT_EVALUATION table.

1.) As with the other jobs that were created, this job is designed so that it can run multiple times without adding duplicate rows to the FACT_EVALUATION table.
2.) Although the FACT_EVALUATION table has a primary key, the primary key constraint has not been enabled so that inserts can occur quickly.

Verify the ETL Job

While verifying the salary fact tables we opted to write several select statements, one to verify against each dimension table. That approach can be taken here as well, although incorporating all of the dimensional elements into one select statement will also work. Since an example of several select statements was provided in chapter seven, we will verify the FACT_EVALUATION table with one.

```
SELECT      DISTINCT C.ITEM_NAME,
            D.REASON_NAME,
            I.WAREHOUSE_EVAL_STATUS,
            A.EVALUATION_DATE,
            E.EMPLOYEE_NUMBER,
            F.APPOINTMENT_BEGIN_DATE,
            H.TITLE_NAME,
            G.DEPARTMENT_NUMBER,
            B.ACTUAL_SCORE,
            B.POSSIBLE_SCORE,
            A.EVALUATOR,
            'Source'
FROM        EVALUATION_HEADER A,
            EVALUATION_DETAIL B,
            EVALUATION_ITEM C,
            EVAL_REASON D,
            EMPLOYEE E,
            APPOINTMENT F,
            DEPARTMENT G,
            TITLE H,
            LOOKUP_EVAL_STATUS I
WHERE       A.ID = B.EVAL_HEADER_ID
            AND A.REASON_ID = D.ID
            AND B.EVAL_ITEM_ID = C.ID
            AND A.APPOINTMENT_ID = F.ID
            AND F.EMPLOYEE_ID = E.ID
            AND F.DEPARTMENT_ID = G.ID
            AND F.TITLE_ID = H.ID
            AND A.EVAL_STATUS = I.ORIGINAL_EVAL_STATUS(+)
            AND E.EMPLOYEE_NUMBER = '1040763'
            AND A.EVALUATION_DATE = '14-OCT-2010'
UNION
SELECT      B.ITEM_NAME,
            B.REASON_NAME,
            B.EVALUATION_STATUS,
            D.CALENDAR_DAY,
            C.EMPLOYEE_NUMBER,
            C.APPOINTMENT_BEGIN_DATE,
            C.TITLE,
            C.DEPARTMENT_NUMBER,
            A.ACTUAL_SCORE,
            A.POSSIBLE_SCORE,
            A.DD_EVALUATOR_NAME,
```

```
                'Data Warehouse'
FROM            FACT_EVALUATION A,
                DIM_EVALUATION_CONTEXT B,
                DIM_EMPLOYEE C,
                DIM_DAY D
WHERE           A.KEY_EVALUATION_CONTEXT = B.KEY_EVALUATION_CONTEXT
                AND A.KEY_EVALUATION_RECIPIENT = C.KEY_EMPLOYEE
                AND A.KEY_EVALUATION_DATE = D.KEY_DAY
                AND C.EMPLOYEE_NUMBER = '1040763'
                AND D.CALENDAR_DAY = '14-OCT-2010'
```

Due to space limitations on the page, it is difficult to display an example of the results. However, this select statement should display 16 rows, 8 from the source and 8 from the data warehouse. So, it appears that everything is working as designed. Feel free to run this for different individuals, timeframes, etc. if desired. Also, break it up into several select statements if that will be more intuitive. At this point there are no updated requirements from the users or inefficiencies within the ETL job itself. As a result, it is time to hand this off to the business users for their verification. The LOAD_EVALUATION_FACT job in its entirety is below.

Line	Code
1	CREATE OR REPLACE PROCEDURE LOAD_EVALUATION_FACT
2	(
3	BEGIN_DAY_OVERRIDE DATE,
4	END_DAY_OVERRIDE DATE,
5	DEFAULT_TIMEPERIOD VARCHAR2,
6	ENTIRE_REFRESH VARCHAR2
7	)
8	
9	AS
10	
11	SQLSTMT VARCHAR2(3000);
12	TBLCOUNT NUMBER := 0;
13	BEGIN_AS_OF_DATE DATE;
14	END_AS_OF_DATE DATE;
15	ERR_MSG VARCHAR2(200);
16	
17	BEGIN
18	--Log the beginning of the job
19	INSERT INTO ETL_JOB_STATUS

Line	Code
20	(
21	ID,
22	ETL_JOB_NAME,
23	STATUS_NAME,
24	STATUS_TIMESTAMP
25	)
26	VALUES
27	(
28	SEQ_ETL_JOB_STATUS.NEXTVAL,
29	'LOAD_EVALUATION_FACT',
30	'IN PROGRESS',
31	SYSTIMESTAMP
32	);
33	
34	COMMIT;
35	
36	--If the table exists, drop it. If not, do nothing. The table will be
37	--created below.
38	SELECT COUNT(*) INTO TBLCOUNT
39	FROM ALL_TABLES
40	WHERE TABLE_NAME = 'STAGE_EVALUATION_DATA'
41	AND OWNER =
42	(
43	SELECT SYS_CONTEXT('USERENV', 'CURRENT_SCHEMA')
44	FROM DUAL
45	);
46	
47	IF TBLCOUNT > 0 THEN
48	EXECUTE IMMEDIATE 'DROP TABLE STAGE_EVALUATION_DATA';
49	END IF;
50	
51	--If the DEFAULT_PERIOD variable is set to 'Y', then the prior month and the
52	--current month are loaded or reloaded into the fact table. Otherwise, the

Line	Code
53	--overrides are used.
54	IF DEFAULT_TIMEPERIOD = 'Y' THEN
55	SELECT TRUNC(TRUNC(SYSDATE,'MM')-1,'MM') INTO BEGIN_AS_OF_DATE FROM DUAL;
56	SELECT LAST_DAY(TRUNC(SYSDATE)) INTO END_AS_OF_DATE FROM DUAL;
57	ELSE
58	BEGIN_AS_OF_DATE := BEGIN_DAY_OVERRIDE;
59	END_AS_OF_DATE := END_DAY_OVERRIDE;
60	END IF;
61	
62	--Dump the data into the staging table and transform the PAY_TYPE_NAME into
63	--the values that are used in the DIM_PAY_TYPE table
64	SQLSTMT := 'CREATE TABLE STAGE_EVALUATION_DATA AS ('
65	|| 'SELECT DISTINCT C.ITEM_NAME, '
66	|| 'D.REASON_NAME, '
67	|| 'A.EVAL_STATUS, '
68	|| 'A.EVALUATION_DATE, '
69	|| 'A.EVALUATOR, '
70	|| 'B.ACTUAL_SCORE, '
71	|| 'B.POSSIBLE_SCORE, '
72	|| 'E.EMPLOYEE_NUMBER, '
73	|| 'F.APPOINTMENT_BEGIN_DATE, '
74	|| 'H.TITLE_NAME, '
75	|| 'G.DEPARTMENT_NUMBER, '
76	|| 'I.WAREHOUSE_EVAL_STATUS '
77	|| 'FROM EVALUATION_HEADER A, '
78	|| 'EVALUATION_DETAIL B, '
79	|| 'EVALUATION_ITEM C, '
80	|| 'EVAL_REASON D, '
81	|| 'EMPLOYEE E, '
82	|| 'APPOINTMENT F, '
83	|| 'DEPARTMENT G, '
84	|| 'TITLE H, '

Line	Code
85	|| 'LOOKUP_EVAL_STATUS I '
86	|| 'WHERE A.ID = B.EVAL_HEADER_ID '
87	|| 'AND A.REASON_ID = D.ID '
88	|| 'AND B.EVAL_ITEM_ID = C.ID '
89	|| 'AND A.APPOINTMENT_ID = F.ID '
90	|| 'AND F.EMPLOYEE_ID = E.ID '
91	|| 'AND F.DEPARTMENT_ID = G.ID '
92	|| 'AND F.TITLE_ID = H.ID '
93	|| 'AND A.EVAL_STATUS = I.ORIGINAL_EVAL_STATUS(+) ';
94	
95	IF ENTIRE_REFRESH <> 'Y' THEN
96	SQLSTMT := SQLSTMT || 'AND A.EVALUATION_DATE BETWEEN '''
97	|| TO_CHAR(BEGIN_AS_OF_DATE,'DD-MON-YYYY')
98	|| ''' AND '''
99	|| TO_CHAR(END_AS_OF_DATE,'DD-MON-YYYY') || ''';
100	END IF;
101	
102	SQLSTMT := SQLSTMT || ')';
103	
104	EXECUTE IMMEDIATE SQLSTMT;
105	
106	--If the table exists, drop it. If not, do nothing. The table will be
107	--created below.
108	SELECT COUNT(*) INTO TBLCOUNT
109	FROM ALL_TABLES
110	WHERE TABLE_NAME = 'STAGE_EVAL_DATA_ADD_KEYS'
111	AND OWNER =
112	(
113	SELECT SYS_CONTEXT('USERENV', 'CURRENT_SCHEMA')
114	FROM DUAL
115	);
116	
117	IF TBLCOUNT > 0 THEN

Line	Code
118	EXECUTE IMMEDIATE 'DROP TABLE STAGE_EVAL_DATA_ADD_KEYS';
119	END IF;
120	
121	SQLSTMT := 'CREATE TABLE STAGE_EVAL_DATA_ADD_KEYS AS ('
122	|| 'SELECT NVL(C.KEY_DAY,-1) KEY_EVALUATION_DATE, '
123	|| 'NVL(B.KEY_EMPLOYEE,-1) KEY_EVALUATION_RECIPIENT, '
124	|| 'NVL(D.KEY_EVALUATION_CONTEXT,-1) KEY_EVALUATION_CONTEXT, '
125	|| 'A.EVALUATOR AS DD_EVALUATOR_NAME, '
126	|| 'A.ACTUAL_SCORE, '
127	|| 'A.POSSIBLE_SCORE '
128	|| 'FROM STAGE_EVALUATION_DATA A, '
129	|| 'DIM_EMPLOYEE B, '
130	|| 'DIM_DAY C, '
131	|| 'DIM_EVALUATION_CONTEXT D '
132	|| 'WHERE A.EMPLOYEE_NUMBER = B.EMPLOYEE_NUMBER(+) '
133	|| 'AND A.DEPARTMENT_NUMBER = B.DEPARTMENT_NUMBER(+) '
134	|| 'AND A.TITLE_NAME = B.TITLE(+) '
135	|| 'AND A.APPOINTMENT_BEGIN_DATE = B.APPOINTMENT_BEGIN_DATE(+) '
136	|| 'AND A.EVALUATION_DATE = C.CALENDAR_DAY(+) '
137	|| 'AND A.ITEM_NAME = D.ITEM_NAME(+) '
138	|| 'AND A.REASON_NAME = D.REASON_NAME(+) '
139	|| 'AND NVL(A.WAREHOUSE_EVAL_STATUS,A.EVAL_STATUS) = D.EVALUATION_STATUS(+)) ';
140	
141	EXECUTE IMMEDIATE SQLSTMT;
142	
143	--Updating the existing rows for months in which the amount has changed
144	--(i.e., an additional payroll was processed for that month since the last
145	--load) would be very inefficient. As a result, any existing data pertaining
146	--to the month(s) being pulled into the fact table is completely deleted
147	--from the fact table and reloaded.
148	IF ENTIRE_REFRESH <> 'Y' THEN
149	SQLSTMT := 'DELETE '

Line	Code
150	|| 'FROM FACT_EVALUATION A '
151	|| 'WHERE A.KEY_EVALUATION_DATE IN ('
152	|| 'SELECT KEY_DAY '
153	|| 'FROM DIM_DAY '
154	|| 'WHERE CALENDAR_DAY BETWEEN '''
155	|| TO_CHAR(BEGIN_AS_OF_DATE,'DD-MON-YYYY')
156	|| ''' AND '''
157	|| TO_CHAR(END_AS_OF_DATE,'DD-MON-YYYY')
158	|| ''') ';
159	ELSE
160	SQLSTMT := 'TRUNCATE TABLE FACT_EVALUATION';
161	END IF;
162	
163	EXECUTE IMMEDIATE SQLSTMT;
164	COMMIT;
165	
166	--The fact table is loaded
167	SQLSTMT := 'INSERT INTO FACT_EVALUATION '
168	|| 'SELECT * FROM STAGE_EVAL_DATA_ADD_KEYS ';
169	
170	EXECUTE IMMEDIATE SQLSTMT;
171	COMMIT;
172	
173	--Log the successful completion of the job.
174	INSERT INTO ETL_JOB_STATUS
175	(
176	ID,
177	ETL_JOB_NAME,
178	STATUS_NAME,
179	STATUS_TIMESTAMP
180	)
181	VALUES
182	(

Line	Code
183	SEQ_ETL_JOB_STATUS.NEXTVAL,
184	'LOAD_EVALUATION_FACT',
185	'SUCCESSFULLY COMPLETED',
186	SYSTIMESTAMP
187	);
188	
189	COMMIT;
190	
191	--This is the equivalent of a catch block. Any errors are caught and logged.
192	EXCEPTION
193	WHEN OTHERS THEN
194	ERR_MSG := SUBSTR(SQLERRM, 1, 200);
195	INSERT INTO ETL_JOB_STATUS
196	(
197	ID,
198	ETL_JOB_NAME,
199	STATUS_NAME,
200	ERROR_MESSAGE,
201	STATUS_TIMESTAMP
202	)
203	VALUES
204	(
205	SEQ_ETL_JOB_STATUS.NEXTVAL,
206	'LOAD_EVALUATION_FACT',
207	'ERROR',
208	ERR_MSG,
209	SYSTIMESTAMP
210	);
211	
212	COMMIT;
213	END;
214	

9
LEAVE DATA

Description of the Employee Leave Business Process

Every pay period, those employees that have worked less than five years receive four hours of personal time and three hours of sick time. Those that have worked for five years or longer receive six hours of personal time and five hours of sick time. An employee that leaves and then comes back has to begin accruing that seniority all over again. Also, the leave does not carry over when there is a gap in employment. If an employee moves to a new position with no gap in employment, then the leave accrual and seniority continues with no interruption. An employee may be paid for taking personal leave, sick leave, or comp time. Unpaid leave is also an option. The accrued leave becomes effective the last day of the pay period. The leave used is deducted from the leave bank (amount of accrued leave) the day that it is used. The ACTUAL_LEAVE table stores the amount of leave taken, who took it, and when it was taken. The leave bank is not stored in this source system. The LEAVE_TYPE table stores the types of leave.

Requirements

The users would like to see when leave is taken and accrued at the day level. Analyzing that data with respect to when it was taken, who took it, and the type of leave would be most valuable. Because the accrued leave is not stored in this source system it will have to be calculated by the ETL job. Based on these requirements, this is the design of the star schema that this ETL job will need to populate.

Figure 9-1

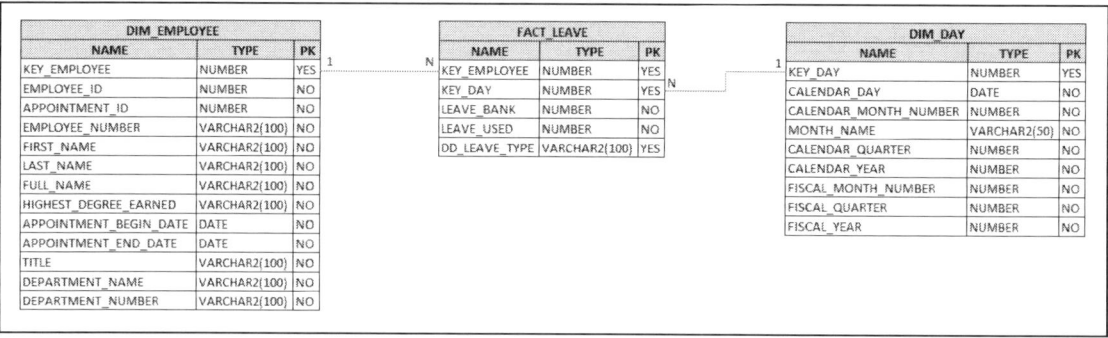

DIM_DAY: This is a standard date dimension table, used to allow for analyzing data based on the leave used or leave accrual date. We can point to the DIM_DAY dimension table that was created for use with the salary and evaluation stars. Although creating a separate physical table with the same keys and data (or a subset of data) as the original DIM_DAY table would not be wrong, for ease of use we will just reuse the original.

DIM_EMPLOYEE: This is the same type two slowly changing dimension as was used in the salary and evaluation stars. Although creating a separate physical table with the same keys and data (or a subset of data) as the original DIM_EMPLOYEE table would not be wrong, for ease of use we will just reuse the original.

FACT_LEAVE: This is a basic fact table that will allow a user to analyze leave hours accrued and taken by employee, date, and type. The source of the LEAVE_USED column is the source system's ACTUAL_LEAVE.HOURS_TAKEN column. The LEAVE_BANK column will be calculated by the ETL job. The key values will point to their associated dimensions. The source of the DD_LEAVE_TYPE column is the LEAVE_TYPE.TYPE column.

Strategy for ETL

This is a small star schema that consists of one fact table and two dimension tables. The DIM_DAY table is a standard date dimension that is not populated by an ETL job. A job to populate the DIM_EMPLOYEE table (LOAD_EMPLOYEE_DIMENSION) has already been written. So, a job will need to be written to populate the FACT_LEAVE table.

Populating the FACT_LEAVE Fact Table

Remember from chapter five that the goal of an ETL job that populates a fact table is to accomplish the following.

    1.) Select all necessary data from the source
        a. Measures
        b. Natural keys of the dimension objects
        c. Degenerate Dimension objects

2.) Transform the data as needed
    a. Aggregate measures and group by the appropriate objects
    b. Add foreign keys to dimension tables
3.) Delete any existing rows from the fact table that will be replaced by the new data
4.) Load the fact table

Because the Based on Timeframe approach worked well with the other fact tables, we can use that with this one as well. Use this script to create the FACT_LEAVE table.

```
CREATE TABLE FACT_LEAVE
(
    KEY_EMPLOYEE       NUMBER,
    KEY_DAY            NUMBER,
    LEAVE_BANK         NUMBER,
    LEAVE_USED         NUMBER,
    DD_LEAVE_TYPE      VARCHAR2(100)
)
```

Now that the infrastructure has been created, we can move forward with actually populating the fact table. We will call the procedure LOAD_LEAVE_FACT. Be aware that up until this point our ETL jobs have mainly consisted of copying data from source to target with some minor transformation performed in the middle. The transformation has usually involved reformatting text or adding some surrogate keys. In this case, however, we will have a much more involved piece of transformation. The ETL job will need to calculate the leave accrued. Because of the complexity, this ETL job will iterate through the four steps above in order to place the leave accrued into the fact table and then iterate through the four steps again to place the leave used into the fact table.

Lines 1 – 28

Line	Code
1	CREATE OR REPLACE PROCEDURE LOAD_LEAVE_FACT
2	(
3	BEGIN_DATE_OVERRIDE DATE,
4	END_DATE_OVERRIDE DATE,
5	DEFAULT_TIMEPERIOD VARCHAR2,
6	ENTIRE_REFRESH VARCHAR2
7	)
8	
9	AS
10	
11	SQLSTMT VARCHAR2(3000);
12	TBLCOUNT NUMBER := 0;

Line	Code	
13	BEGIN_AS_OF_DATE	DATE;
14	END_AS_OF_DATE	DATE;
15	DATE_STRING	VARCHAR(10);
16	ERR_MSG	VARCHAR2(200);
17	CURSOR_EMPL_ID	NUMBER;
18	CURSOR_APPT_ID	NUMBER;
19	PREVIOUS_APPT_END_DATE	DATE;
20	CURRENT_APPT_BEGIN_DATE	DATE;
21	CURRENT_LEAVE_DATE	DATE;
22	CONTINUOUS_EMPL_BEGIN_DATE	DATE;
23	MULTIPLE_FLAGS	EXCEPTION;
24	DATES_OUT_OF_ORDER	EXCEPTION;
25		
26	EE_ITERATION	NUMBER := 0;
27	APPT_ITERATION	NUMBER := 0;
28		

This piece of the code has the standard housekeeping activities performed at the beginning of an ETL job. The parameters are passed to indicate the timeframe to be used (same as the LOAD_EVALUATION_FACT) and the variables are declared.

Lines 29 – 44

Line	Code
29	--This cursor selects all employees who have more than one appointment.
30	CURSOR EMPLOYEES IS
31	SELECT EMPLOYEE_ID
32	FROM APPOINTMENT
33	GROUP BY EMPLOYEE_ID
34	HAVING COUNT(DISTINCT ID) > 1;
35	
36	--This cursor selects all appointments for each employee that is returned by
37	--the employees cursor. The employees cursor is an outer loop and this cursor
38	--is used in an inner loop later in the job.
39	CURSOR APPOINTMENTS IS

Line	Code
40	SELECT ID
41	FROM APPOINTMENT
42	WHERE EMPLOYEE_ID = CURSOR_EMPL_ID
43	ORDER BY APPOINTMENT_BEGIN_DATE;
44	

A later portion of the job will need to loop through those employees who have multiple appointments as well as their respective appointments. This portion of the code defines two Oracle cursors that allow that to happen. They will be referred to later.

Lines 45 – 63

Line	Code
45	BEGIN
46	--Log the beginning of the job
47	INSERT INTO ETL_JOB_STATUS
48	(
49	ID,
50	ETL_JOB_NAME,
51	STATUS_NAME,
52	STATUS_TIMESTAMP
53	)
54	VALUES
55	(
56	SEQ_ETL_JOB_STATUS.NEXTVAL,
57	'LOAD LEAVE FACT',
58	'IN PROGRESS',
59	SYSTIMESTAMP
60	);
61	
62	COMMIT;
63	

The beginning of the job is logged in the ETL_JOB_STATUS table.

Leave Accrued - Extract the Data

This portion of the job begins the process of extracting the data for the purposes of calculating the leave accrued.

Lines 64 – 78

Line	Code
64	--If the table exists, drop it. If not, do nothing. The table will be
65	--created below.
66	SELECT COUNT(*) INTO TBLCOUNT
67	FROM ALL_TABLES
68	WHERE TABLE_NAME = 'STAGE_LEAVE_BANK_EXTRACT'
69	AND OWNER =
70	(
71	SELECT SYS_CONTEXT('USERENV', 'CURRENT_SCHEMA')
72	FROM DUAL
73	);
74	
75	IF TBLCOUNT > 0 THEN
76	EXECUTE IMMEDIATE 'DROP TABLE STAGE_LEAVE_BANK_EXTRACT';
77	END IF;
78	

If the STAGE_LEAVE_BANK_EXTRACT table exists drop it.

Line 79 – 84

Line	Code
79	--The job cannot execute an entire refresh and the default time period at the
80	--same time, so if both flags are set to 'Y' then an exception is raised.
81	IF DEFAULT_TIMEPERIOD = 'Y' AND ENTIRE_REFRESH = 'Y' THEN
82	RAISE MULTIPLE_FLAGS;
83	END IF;
84	

It was decided that when the ENTIRE_REFRESH variable was introduced in the LOAD_EVALUATION_FACT job, it was not very intuitive that a value of 'Y' trumped a value of 'Y' for the DEFAULT_TIMEPERIOD. Therefore, this job will raise an exception if they are both

'Y', forcing the job runner to give only one of the variables a value of 'Y' if the default dates are not used.

Lines 85 – 101

Line	Code
85	--If the DEFAULT_PERIOD variable is set to 'Y', then the prior month and the
86	--current month are loaded or reloaded into the fact table. Otherwise, the
87	--overrides are used.
88	IF ENTIRE_REFRESH <> 'Y' THEN
89	IF DEFAULT_TIMEPERIOD = 'Y' THEN
90	SELECT TRUNC(TRUNC(SYSDATE,'MM')-1,'MM') INTO BEGIN_AS_OF_DATE FROM DUAL;
91	SELECT LAST_DAY(TRUNC(SYSDATE)) INTO END_AS_OF_DATE FROM DUAL;
92	--If the BEGIN_DATE_OVERRIDE variable is larger than the END_DATE_OVERRIDE
93	--then an exception is raised
94	ELSIF TRUNC(BEGIN_DATE_OVERRIDE) > TRUNC(END_DATE_OVERRIDE) THEN
95	RAISE DATES_OUT_OF_ORDER;
96	ELSE
97	BEGIN_AS_OF_DATE := BEGIN_DATE_OVERRIDE;
98	END_AS_OF_DATE := END_DATE_OVERRIDE;
99	END IF;
100	END IF;
101	

If an entire refresh is not being run, the time periods are set. If the DEFAULT_TIMEPERIOD is set to 'Y' then the default time period is set to the previous month and the current month. Otherwise, the dates assigned to the BEGIN_DATE_OVERRIDE and the END_DATE_OVERRIDE parameters are used.

Lines 102 – 163

Line	Code
102	--The data needed to calculate the leave bank amounts is extracted. Those
103	--employees who have been employed for less than 5 years receive 4 hours of
104	--personal leave and 3 hours of sick leave every 2 weeks (each pay period).
105	--Those employees who have been employed for 5 years or longer receive 6

Line	Code
106	--hours of personal leave and 5 hours of sick leave every two weeks (each
107	--pay period). The code below compares the appointment being date to the
108	--pay period end date to make that calculation. That is complicated when
109	--somebody has been employed for more than 5 years and then moved to a
110	--different appointment. That situation is handled later in the job. This
111	--code simply pulls those who have one appointment.
112	SQLSTMT := 'CREATE TABLE STAGE_LEAVE_BANK_EXTRACT AS ('
113	|| 'SELECT B.EMPLOYEE_NUMBER, '
114	|| 'E.TITLE_NAME, '
115	|| 'D.DEPARTMENT_NUMBER, '
116	|| 'A.APPOINTMENT_BEGIN_DATE, '
117	|| 'C.PAY_PERIOD_END_DATE, '
118	|| 'CASE WHEN ROUND'
119	||'('
120	||'MONTHS_BETWEEN'
121	||'('
122	||'C.PAY_PERIOD_END_DATE,'
123	||'A.APPOINTMENT_BEGIN_DATE'
124	||')'
125	||'/12,2'
126	||') < 5 THEN 4 ELSE 6 END AS PERSONAL_BANK, '
127	|| 'CASE WHEN ROUND'
128	||'('
129	||'MONTHS_BETWEEN'
130	||'('
131	||'C.PAY_PERIOD_END_DATE,'
132	||'A.APPOINTMENT_BEGIN_DATE'
133	||')'
134	||'/12,2'
135	||') < 5 THEN 3 ELSE 5 END AS SICK_BANK '
136	|| 'FROM APPOINTMENT A, '
137	|| 'EMPLOYEE B, '
138	|| 'PAYCHECK_HEADER C, '

Line	Code
139	|| 'DEPARTMENT D, '
140	|| 'TITLE E '
141	|| 'WHERE A.EMPLOYEE_ID = B.ID '
142	|| 'AND C.APPOINTMENT_ID = A.ID '
143	|| 'AND A.DEPARTMENT_ID = D.ID '
144	|| 'AND A.TITLE_ID = E.ID ';
145	
146	--The date logic is not needed if an entire refresh is being done
147	IF ENTIRE_REFRESH <> 'Y' THEN
148	SQLSTMT := SQLSTMT || 'AND C.PAY_PERIOD_END_DATE BETWEEN ''
149	|| TO_CHAR(BEGIN_AS_OF_DATE,'DD-MON-YYYY')
150	|| '' AND ''
151	|| TO_CHAR(END_AS_OF_DATE,'DD-MON-YYYY')
152	|| '' ';
153	END IF;
154	
155	SQLSTMT := SQLSTMT || 'AND A.EMPLOYEE_ID '
156	|| 'IN '
157	|| '(SELECT A.EMPLOYEE_ID '
158	|| 'FROM APPOINTMENT A '
159	|| 'GROUP BY A.EMPLOYEE_ID '
160	|| 'HAVING COUNT(DISTINCT A.ID) <= 1)) ';
161	
162	EXECUTE IMMEDIATE SQLSTMT;
163	

This portion of the job pulls the measure and natural keys to the dimensions for those employees who have or have had only one appointment. Those with multiple appointments will be handled later due to their complexity. This job looks at the number of paychecks received, since leave is accrued at the end of a pay period.

Measures:
- Either four or six hours of personal leave are applied based on whether or not the employee has been employed five years (line 118).
- Either three or five hours of sick leave are applied based on whether or not the employee has been employed five years (line 127).

Natural Key to DIM_EMPLOYEE:
- EMPLOYEE.EMPLOYEE_NUMBER(line 113)
- APPOINTMENT.APPOINTMENT_BEGIN_DATE (line 116)
- TITLE.TITLE_NAME (line 114)
- DEPARTMENT.DEPARTMENT_NUMBER (line 115)

Natural Key to DIM_DAY: PAYCHECK_HEADER. PAY_PERIOD_END_DATE (line 117)

Degenerate Dimension: There is a different column for each type on lines 118 and 127. Later, this will be merged into one dimension, with a textual description describing the type of leave (sick vs. personal).

Lines 155 – 160 ensure that we are only pulling records for those individuals who have one appointment.

Lines 164 – 176

Line	Code
164	--This cursor iterates through all employees who have multiple appointments.
165	--A second cursor, named APPOINTMENTS, iterates inside this one to iterate
166	--through all appointments for each employee that has multiple appointments.
167	--This approach is taken since the business rule states that if an employee
168	--is employed for at least 5 years and reaches the point at which he begins
169	--to accumulate more days off and then moves to a new appointment in the
170	--company, that level of seniority still applies. However, if that employee
171	--were to leave the company and then come back, he will start all over.
172	OPEN EMPLOYEES;
173	LOOP
174	FETCH EMPLOYEES INTO CURSOR_EMPL_ID;
175	EXIT WHEN EMPLOYEES%NOTFOUND;
176	

Because the business rules specify that a gap in employment causes the accrual to start all over, the ETL job must loop through those appointments belonging to individuals with multiple appointments in order to see if the appointments are consecutive. The EMPLOYEES and APPOINTMENTS cursors that were created on lines 29 – 43 are used to do that. A cursor basically contains a set of data, allowing the procedure to iterate through those records.

Lines 177 – 201

Line	Code
177	--This variable holds the appointment end date of the previous iteration of
178	--the loop below. Since we haven't entered the loop yet (meaning that
179	--there was no previous appointment) it is set to null.
180	PREVIOUS_APPT_END_DATE := null;
181	
182	/*This variable holds the earliest appointment begin date that falls after
183	any gaps in employment or the earliest employment begin date if there are
184	no gaps in employment. This variable is important since the business rule
185	states that seniority with regards to the number of personal/sick hours
186	that are accrued each pay period only applies to continuous employment.
187	So, if an employee has these appointments...
188	
189	Appointment 1: 1/1/1985 through 5/1/1995
190	Appointment 2: 2/3/2001 through 7/6/2002
191	Appointment 3: 7/7/2002 through current
192	
193	...then for records that occur within Appointment 1, the pay period end
194	date is compared to 1/1/1985 in order to find the number of hours that
195	should be placed into the leave bank. For records that occur within
196	Appointment 2, the pay period end date is compared to 2/3/2001 since there
197	was a gap in employment between Appointments 1 and 2. For records that
198	occur within Appointment 3, the pay period end date is compared to 2/3/2001
199	since there was no gap in employment between Appointments 2 and 3.*/
200	CONTINUOUS_EMPL_BEGIN_DATE := null;
201	

The beginning of that loop contains two variables. They are the PREVIOUS_APPT_END_DATE and the CONTINUOUS_EMPL_BEGIN_DATE. The PREVIOUS_APPT_END_DATE contains the previous appointment's end date for a given employee. This allows the next begin date to be compared to this date. If there is more than one day between the two, then the accrual of leave will start over. The CONTINUOUS_EMPL_BEGIN_DATE contains the begin date for the earliest appointment after any gaps in employment. This is needed so that the correct duration of employment can be derived. For example, if an employee has the following appointments:

Appointment 1: 1/1/1985 through 5/1/1995
Appointment 2: 2/3/2001 through 7/6/2002
Appointment 3: 7/7/2002 through current

…then, a PAYCHECK_DETAIL record that falls in March of 2002 will be compared to the 2/3/2001 date. Since that duration is less than 5 years, then 4 hours of personal time and 3 hours of sick time are applied. However, a PAYCHECK_DETAIL record that falls in March of 2008 will be compared to the 2/3/2001 date as well. Although a new appointment began on 7/7/2002, there has been continuous employment since 2/3/2001. In this example, the CONTINUOUS_EMPL_BEGIN_DATE will have a value of 1/1/1985 until the loop notices a gap between appointments 1 and 2. When appointment 2 begins, the CONTINUOUS_EMPL_BEGIN_DATE will be reset to 2/3/2001 and will remain that way through the duration of this employee's records.

Lines 202 – 208

Line	Code
202	--This cursor iterates through all appointments for a given employee who
203	--has multiple appointments.
204	OPEN APPOINTMENTS;
205	LOOP
206	FETCH APPOINTMENTS INTO CURSOR_APPT_ID;
207	EXIT WHEN APPOINTMENTS%NOTFOUND;
208	

The APPOINTMENTS cursor opens inside of the EMPLOYEES cursor as an inner loop and iterates through each appointment for those employees who have multiple appointments.

Lines 209 – 262

Line	Code
209	--This SQL statement pulls data related to the first appointment in the
210	--loop. The appointment begin date is compared to the pay period end
211	--date to determine how many
212	--hours to place into the bank.
213	IF PREVIOUS_APPT_END_DATE IS NULL THEN
214	SQLSTMT := 'INSERT INTO STAGE_LEAVE_BANK_EXTRACT '
215	|| 'SELECT B.EMPLOYEE_NUMBER, '
216	|| 'E.TITLE_NAME, '
217	|| 'D.DEPARTMENT_NUMBER, '

Line	Code
218	|| 'A.APPOINTMENT_BEGIN_DATE, '
219	|| 'C.PAY_PERIOD_END_DATE, '
220	|| 'CASE WHEN ROUND'
221	||'('
222	||'MONTHS_BETWEEN'
223	||'('
224	||'C.PAY_PERIOD_END_DATE,'
225	||'A.APPOINTMENT_BEGIN_DATE'
226	||')'
227	||'/12,2'
228	||') < 5 THEN 4 ELSE 6 END AS PERSONAL_BANK, '
229	|| 'CASE WHEN ROUND'
230	||'('
231	||'MONTHS_BETWEEN'
232	||'('
233	||'C.PAY_PERIOD_END_DATE,'
234	||'A.APPOINTMENT_BEGIN_DATE'
235	||')'
236	||'/12,2'
237	||') < 5 THEN 3 ELSE 5 END AS SICK_BANK '
238	|| 'FROM APPOINTMENT A, '
239	|| 'EMPLOYEE B, '
240	|| 'PAYCHECK_HEADER C, '
241	|| 'DEPARTMENT D, '
242	|| 'TITLE E '
243	|| 'WHERE A.EMPLOYEE_ID = B.ID '
244	|| 'AND C.APPOINTMENT_ID = A.ID '
245	|| 'AND A.DEPARTMENT_ID = D.ID '
246	|| 'AND A.TITLE_ID = E.ID ';
247	
248	IF ENTIRE_REFRESH <> 'Y' THEN
249	SQLSTMT := SQLSTMT
250	|| 'AND C.PAY_PERIOD_END_DATE BETWEEN ''

Line	Code
251	|| TO_CHAR(BEGIN_AS_OF_DATE,'DD-MON-YYYY')
252	|| "' AND '"
253	|| TO_CHAR(END_AS_OF_DATE,'DD-MON-YYYY')
254	|| "' ';
255	END IF;
256	
257	SQLSTMT := SQLSTMT || 'AND A.ID = ' || CURSOR_APPT_ID;
258	
259	EXECUTE IMMEDIATE SQLSTMT;
260	
261	COMMIT;
262	

This select statement calculates the leave hours for the first appointment in the loop, which should always equate to the four hours of personal time and three hours of sick time. Notice that this select statement pulls the same measure and dimension objects as was discussed in lines 102 – 163. It serves the same purpose as that select statement, other than the fact that it is pulling data for individuals with multiple appointments only.

Lines 263 – 275

Line	Code
263	--The current APPOINTMENT_END_DATE is placed into the
264	--PREVIOUS_APPT_END_DATE variable for use in the next iteration.
265	SELECT APPOINTMENT_END_DATE INTO PREVIOUS_APPT_END_DATE
266	FROM APPOINTMENT
267	WHERE ID = CURSOR_APPT_ID;
268	
269	--The current APPOINTMENT_BEGIN_DATE is placed into the
270	--CONTINUOUS_EMPL_BEGIN_DATE variable for use in the next iteration.
271	--It will only be reset when a gap in employment is detected.
272	SELECT APPOINTMENT_BEGIN_DATE INTO CONTINUOUS_EMPL_BEGIN_DATE
273	FROM APPOINTMENT
274	WHERE ID = CURSOR_APPT_ID;
275	

The APPOINTMENT_END_DATE and the APPOINTMENT_BEGIN_DATE are assigned to the PREVIOUS_APPT_END_DATE and the CONTINUOUS_EMPL_BEGIN_DATE variables, respectively, for the next iteration of the loop.

Lines 276 – 290

Line	Code
276	ELSE
277	--This part of the IF statement pertains to subsequent appointments for
278	--those individuals who have multiple appointments. The current
279	--appointment begin date is added to the CURRENT_APPT_BEGIN_DATE
280	--variable. This is then compared to the PREVIOUS_APPT_END_DATE
281	--variable to see if this appointment began right after the previous
282	--appointment ended (meaning that employment was continuous) or if
283	--there was a gap in employment. If there is a gap in employment, the
284	--current appointment begin date is compared to the pay period end
285	--date to calculate the number of hours that should be added to the
286	--bank.
287	SELECT APPOINTMENT_BEGIN_DATE INTO CURRENT_APPT_BEGIN_DATE
288	FROM APPOINTMENT
289	WHERE ID = CURSOR_APPT_ID;
290	

This portion of the loop (lines 276 – 402) pertains to those appointments that are not the first appointment in the batch. The APPOINTMENT_BEGIN_DATE is assigned to the CURRENT_APPT_BEGIN_DATE variable.

Lines 291 – 340

Line	Code
291	IF TRUNC(CURRENT_APPT_BEGIN_DATE) - TRUNC(PREVIOUS_APPT_END_DATE) > 1 THEN
292	SQLSTMT := 'INSERT INTO STAGE_LEAVE_BANK_EXTRACT '
293	| | 'SELECT B.EMPLOYEE_NUMBER, '
294	| | 'E.TITLE_NAME, '
295	| | 'D.DEPARTMENT_NUMBER, '
296	| | 'A.APPOINTMENT_BEGIN_DATE, '
297	| | 'C.PAY_PERIOD_END_DATE, '

Line	Code
298	|| 'CASE WHEN ROUND'
299	||'(
300	||'MONTHS_BETWEEN'
301	||'(
302	||'C.PAY_PERIOD_END_DATE,'
303	||'A.APPOINTMENT_BEGIN_DATE'
304	||')'
305	||'/12,2'
306	||') < 5 THEN 4 ELSE 6 END AS PERSONAL_BANK, '
307	|| 'CASE WHEN ROUND'
308	||'(
309	||'MONTHS_BETWEEN'
310	||'(
311	||'C.PAY_PERIOD_END_DATE,'
312	||'A.APPOINTMENT_BEGIN_DATE'
313	||')'
314	||'/12,2'
315	||') < 5 THEN 3 ELSE 5 END AS SICK_BANK '
316	|| 'FROM APPOINTMENT A, '
317	|| 'EMPLOYEE B, '
318	|| 'PAYCHECK_HEADER C, '
319	|| 'DEPARTMENT D, '
320	|| 'TITLE E '
321	|| 'WHERE A.EMPLOYEE_ID = B.ID '
322	|| 'AND C.APPOINTMENT_ID = A.ID '
323	|| 'AND A.DEPARTMENT_ID = D.ID '
324	|| 'AND A.TITLE_ID = E.ID ';
325	
326	IF ENTIRE_REFRESH <> 'Y' THEN
327	SQLSTMT := SQLSTMT
328	|| 'AND C.PAY_PERIOD_END_DATE BETWEEN '''
329	|| TO_CHAR(BEGIN_AS_OF_DATE,'DD-MON-YYYY')
330	|| ''' AND '''

Line	Code
331	|| TO_CHAR(END_AS_OF_DATE,'DD-MON-YYYY')
332	|| '"';
333	END IF;
334	
335	SQLSTMT := SQLSTMT || 'AND A.ID = ' || CURSOR_APPT_ID;
336	
337	EXECUTE IMMEDIATE SQLSTMT;
338	
339	COMMIT;
340	

This portion of the loop pertains to those appointments that are the first appointment after a break in employment. If the difference between the previous appointment's end and the current appointment's begin is greater than one day (line 291) then this piece of the code executes. When the leave is calculated on lines 298 and 307, notice that the PAY_PERIOD_END_DATE is not compared to the CONTINUOUS_EMPL_BEGIN_DATE. Because there was a gap in employment, the PAY_PERIOD_END_DATE is compared to the current appointment's begin date (CURRENT_APPT_BEGIN_DATE).

Lines 341 – 347

Line	Code
341	--Since this piece of the IF statement pertains to those appointments
342	--falling after a gap in employment, the CONTINUOUS_EMPL_BEGIN_DATE
343	--is overwritten with the current APPOINTMENT_BEGIN_DATE.
344	SELECT APPOINTMENT_BEGIN_DATE INTO CONTINUOUS_EMPL_BEGIN_DATE
345	FROM APPOINTMENT
346	WHERE ID = CURSOR_APPT_ID;
347	

The   APPOINTMENT_BEGIN_DATE   is   assigned   to   the CONTINUOUS_EMPL_BEGIN_DATE variable for use by the next iteration of the loop.

Lines 348 – 394

Line	Code
348	ELSE

Line	Code
349	--If there is no gap in employment, the minimum appointment begin
350	--date that falls after any gaps in employment (or the minimum
351	--appointment begin date if there are not gaps) is compared to the
352	--pay period end date to calculate the number of hours that should be
353	--added to the bank.
354	SQLSTMT := 'INSERT INTO STAGE_LEAVE_BANK_EXTRACT '
355	|| 'SELECT B.EMPLOYEE_NUMBER, '
356	|| 'E.TITLE_NAME, '
357	|| 'D.DEPARTMENT_NUMBER, '
358	|| 'A.APPOINTMENT_BEGIN_DATE, '
359	|| 'C.PAY_PERIOD_END_DATE, '
360	|| 'CASE WHEN ROUND(MONTHS_BETWEEN(C.PAY_PERIOD_END_DATE, '''
361	|| TO_CHAR(CONTINUOUS_EMPL_BEGIN_DATE,'DD-MON-YYYY')
362	|| ''') '
363	|| '/12,2) < 5 THEN 4 ELSE 6 END AS PERSONAL, '
364	|| 'CASE WHEN ROUND(MONTHS_BETWEEN(C.PAY_PERIOD_END_DATE, '''
365	|| TO_CHAR(CONTINUOUS_EMPL_BEGIN_DATE,'DD-MON-YYYY')
366	|| ''') '
367	|| '/12,2) < 5 THEN 3 ELSE 5 END AS SICK '
368	|| 'FROM APPOINTMENT A, '
369	|| 'EMPLOYEE B, '
370	|| 'PAYCHECK_HEADER C, '
371	|| 'DEPARTMENT D, '
372	|| 'TITLE E '
373	|| 'WHERE A.EMPLOYEE_ID = B.ID '
374	|| 'AND C.APPOINTMENT_ID = A.ID '
375	|| 'AND A.DEPARTMENT_ID = D.ID '
376	|| 'AND A.TITLE_ID = E.ID ';
377	
378	IF ENTIRE_REFRESH <> 'Y' THEN
379	SQLSTMT := SQLSTMT
380	|| 'AND C.PAY_PERIOD_END_DATE BETWEEN '''

Line	Code
381	|| TO_CHAR(BEGIN_AS_OF_DATE,'DD-MON-YYYY')
382	|| ''' AND '''
383	|| TO_CHAR(END_AS_OF_DATE,'DD-MON-YYYY')
384	|| ''';
385	END IF;
386	
387	SQLSTMT := SQLSTMT || 'AND A.ID = ' || CURSOR_APPT_ID;
388	
389	EXECUTE IMMEDIATE SQLSTMT;
390	
391	COMMIT;
392	
393	END IF;
394	

This portion of the loop pertains to appointments that are not the first appointment for an individual but that do not represent a gap in employment. Therefore the current PAY_PERIOD_END_DATE is compared to the CONTINUOUS_EMPL_BEGIN_DATE when making the calculation on lines 360 – 367.

Lines 395 – 400

Line	Code
395	--Before moving to a new appointment, the PREVIOUS_APPT_END_DATE is
396	--overwritten with the current APPOINTMENT_END_DATE
397	SELECT APPOINTMENT_END_DATE INTO PREVIOUS_APPT_END_DATE
398	FROM APPOINTMENT
399	WHERE ID = CURSOR_APPT_ID;
400	

The APPOINTMENT_END_DATE is assigned to the PREVIOUS_APPT_END_DATE for use by the next iteration. Since this iteration represents a subsequent appointment with no gap in employment, the CONTINUOUS_EMPL_BEGIN_DATE is not overwritten. If the next appointment for this employee falls directly after this one (with no gap in between) then this portion of the loop will be used for that appointment as well, meaning that the same CONTINUOUS_EMPL_BEGIN_DATE will be needed for the comparison.

Lines 401 – 407

Line	Code
401	END IF;
402	END LOOP;
403	CLOSE APPOINTMENTS;
404	
405	END LOOP;
406	CLOSE EMPLOYEES;
407	

The loops are ended and the cursors are closed. The leave calculations are complete.

Leave Accrued – Transform the Data

This portion of the job begins the process of transforming the data for the leave accrual process.

Lines 408 – 422

Line	Code
408	--If the table exists, drop it. If not, do nothing. The table will be
409	--created below.
410	SELECT COUNT(*) INTO TBLCOUNT
411	FROM ALL_TABLES
412	WHERE TABLE_NAME = 'STAGE_LEAVE_ADD_KEYS_BANK'
413	AND OWNER =
414	(
415	SELECT SYS_CONTEXT('USERENV', 'CURRENT_SCHEMA')
416	from dual
417	);
418	
419	IF TBLCOUNT > 0 THEN
420	EXECUTE IMMEDIATE 'DROP TABLE STAGE_LEAVE_ADD_KEYS_BANK';
421	END IF;
422	

This portion of the job drops the STAGE_LEAVE_ADD_KEYS_BANK table if it exists.

Lines 423 – 452

Line	Code
423	--Add the surrogate keys to the leave bank data
424	SQLSTMT := 'CREATE TABLE STAGE_LEAVE_ADD_KEYS_BANK AS ('
425	|| 'SELECT NVL(B.EMPLOYEE_ID,-1) KEY_EMPLOYEE,'
426	|| 'NVL(C.KEY_DAY,-1) KEY_DAY,'
427	|| 'A.PERSONAL_BANK LEAVE_BANK,'
428	|| '''Personal Leave'' DD_LEAVE_TYPE '
429	|| 'FROM STAGE_LEAVE_BANK_EXTRACT A,'
430	|| 'DIM_EMPLOYEE B,'
431	|| 'DIM_DAY C '
432	|| 'WHERE A.EMPLOYEE_NUMBER = B.EMPLOYEE_NUMBER(+)'
433	|| 'AND A.APPOINTMENT_BEGIN_DATE = B.APPOINTMENT_BEGIN_DATE(+)'
434	|| 'AND A.TITLE_NAME = B.TITLE(+)'
435	|| 'AND A.DEPARTMENT_NUMBER = B.DEPARTMENT_NUMBER(+)'
436	|| 'AND A.PAY_PERIOD_END_DATE = C.CALENDAR_DAY(+)'
437	|| 'UNION '
438	|| 'SELECT NVL(B.EMPLOYEE_ID,-1),'
439	|| 'NVL(C.KEY_DAY,-1),'
440	|| 'A.SICK_BANK,'
441	|| '''Sick Leave'' '
442	|| 'FROM STAGE_LEAVE_BANK_EXTRACT A,'
443	|| 'DIM_EMPLOYEE B,'
444	|| 'DIM_DAY C '
445	|| 'WHERE A.EMPLOYEE_NUMBER = B.EMPLOYEE_NUMBER(+) '
446	|| 'AND A.APPOINTMENT_BEGIN_DATE = B.APPOINTMENT_BEGIN_DATE(+) '
447	|| 'AND A.TITLE_NAME = B.TITLE(+) '
448	|| 'AND A.DEPARTMENT_NUMBER = B.DEPARTMENT_NUMBER(+) '
449	|| 'AND A.PAY_PERIOD_END_DATE = C.CALENDAR_DAY(+))';
450	
451	EXECUTE IMMEDIATE SQLSTMT;
452	

This portion of the job adds the dimension keys to the leave accrued (or leave bank) data. Notice that the select statement that is used to create and populate the STAGE_LEAVE_ADD_KEYS_BANK table is actually two select statements "unioned" together. Remember that the STAGE_LEAVE_ADD_KEYS_BANK table stores the personal leave and sick leave amounts in two separate columns per person and pay period on the same record. Because the fact table is designed so that all of the accrued leave data will be placed into a single LEAVE_BANK column with the DD_LEAVE_TYPE dimension value specifying which type of leave that record refers to, this data needs to be restructured. The first select statement of the union selects the keys as well as the personal leave while the second select statement of the union selects the keys as well as the sick leave. Lines 432 – 435 and lines 445 – 448 join the data to the DIM_EMPLOYEE table via the natural key (EMPLOYEE_NUMBER, APPOINTMENT_BEGIN_DATE, TITLE_NAME, and DEPARTMENT_NUMBER) so that the KEY_EMPLOYEE can be included. As was done in other areas of the job, an outer join is used so that facts related to employees that are not in the DIM_EMPLOYEE table will not be excluded. Lines 436 and 449 accomplish the same thing for the DIM_DAY dimension table.

Lines 453 – 467

Line	Code
453	--If the table exists, drop it. If not, do nothing. The table will be
454	--created below.
455	SELECT COUNT(*) INTO TBLCOUNT
456	FROM ALL_TABLES
457	WHERE TABLE_NAME = 'STAGE_LEAVE_HOURS_USED'
458	AND OWNER =
459	(
460	SELECT SYS_CONTEXT('USERENV', 'CURRENT_SCHEMA')
461	FROM DUAL
462	);
463	
464	IF TBLCOUNT > 0 THEN
465	EXECUTE IMMEDIATE 'DROP TABLE STAGE_LEAVE_HOURS_USED';
466	END IF;
467	

If the STAGE_LEAVE_HOURS_USED table exists, it is dropped.

Lines 468 – 483

Line	Code
468	--Rather than use the typical "create table as" statement, a "create table"
469	--statement is used instead. This table is populated via a loop with some
470	--iterations populating something and other iterations not populating
471	--anything. Because it is not a one-time creation, this approach is needed
472	--here.
473	SQLSTMT := 'CREATE TABLE STAGE_LEAVE_HOURS_USED '
474	|| '(EMPLOYEE_NUMBER VARCHAR2(50), '
475	|| 'TITLE_NAME VARCHAR2(255), '
476	|| 'DEPARTMENT_NUMBER VARCHAR2(100), '
477	|| 'APPOINTMENT_BEGIN_DATE DATE, '
478	|| 'LEAVE_DATE DATE, '
479	|| 'LEAVE_TYPE VARCHAR2(255), '
480	|| 'HOURS_PER_DAY NUMBER)';
481	
482	EXECUTE IMMEDIATE SQLSTMT;
483	

Usually, a staging table is created using the "create table as" syntax, so that it is created and populated at the same time. In this case, the select statement needed to populate that table will need to be placed inside of a loop as variables are updated with each iteration. In other words, executing this select statement only once will not be enough to populate this table. It must be executed over and over again (the reason will be explained later). As a result, it will work best to just create the table manually and then use the loop to populate it.

Lines 484 – 508

Line	Code
484	/*The loop below uses the begin and end dates passed to the job (or derived
485	by the job in the case of the default time period) to iterate through all
486	days between those dates and insert the appropriate data into the staging
487	table. The ACTUAL_LEAVE table stores the begin and end dates of an
488	employee's leave and the total number of hours taken. This ETL job breaks
489	that down and stores the average per day for the begin date, the end date,
490	and each day in between. So, if a record in the ACTUAL_LEAVE table looks

Line	Code
491	like this...
492	
493	BEGIN DATE END DATE HOURS TAKEN
494	2/4/2006 2/8/2006 40
495	
496	...it will result in the data looking this way in the staging table...
497	
498	DATE HOURS TAKEN
499	2/4/2006 8
500	2/5/2006 8
501	2/6/2006 8
502	2/7/2006 8
503	2/8/2006 8
504	
505	The IF statement immediately below will place the minimum date for which
506	leave was taken and the maximum date for which leave was taken into the
507	variables in the case of an entire refresh. The loop is below that.
508	*/

These lines contain comments explaining the code that follows.

Lines 509 – 513

Line	Code
509	IF ENTIRE_REFRESH = 'Y' THEN
510	SELECT MIN(LEAVE_BEGIN_DATE) INTO BEGIN_AS_OF_DATE FROM ACTUAL_LEAVE;
511	SELECT MAX(LEAVE_END_DATE) INTO END_AS_OF_DATE FROM ACTUAL_LEAVE;
512	END IF;
513	

If the ENTIRE_REFRESH variable is set to 'Y', the BEGIN_AS_OF_DATE and the END_AS_OF_DATE variables are set to the earliest LEAVE_BEGIN_DATE and latest LEAVE_END_DATE available, respectively.

Lines 514 – 548

Line	Code
514	CURRENT_LEAVE_DATE := BEGIN_AS_OF_DATE;
515	WHILE CURRENT_LEAVE_DATE <= END_AS_OF_DATE
516	LOOP
517	SQLSTMT := 'INSERT INTO STAGE_LEAVE_HOURS_USED '
518	|| 'SELECT B.EMPLOYEE_NUMBER, '
519	|| 'E.TITLE_NAME, '
520	|| 'D.DEPARTMENT_NUMBER, '
521	|| 'A.APPOINTMENT_BEGIN_DATE, '
522	|| 'TO_DATE(''' || CURRENT_LEAVE_DATE || ''',''DD-MON-RR''), '
523	|| 'F.TYPE, '
524	|| 'C.HOURS_TAKEN / (C.LEAVE_END_DATE - C.LEAVE_BEGIN_DATE + 1) '
525	|| 'HOURS_PER_DAY '
526	|| 'FROM APPOINTMENT A, '
527	|| 'EMPLOYEE B, '
528	|| 'ACTUAL_LEAVE C, '
529	|| 'DEPARTMENT D, '
530	|| 'TITLE E, '
531	|| 'LEAVE_TYPE F '
532	|| 'WHERE A.EMPLOYEE_ID = B.ID '
533	|| 'AND A.DEPARTMENT_ID = D.ID '
534	|| 'AND A.TITLE_ID = E.ID '
535	|| 'AND A.ID = C.APPOINTMENT_ID '
536	|| 'AND C.LEAVE_TYPE_ID = F.ID '
537	|| 'AND TO_DATE('''
538	|| CURRENT_LEAVE_DATE
539	|| ''',''DD-MON-RR'') BETWEEN C.LEAVE_BEGIN_DATE AND C.LEAVE_END_DATE';
540	
541	EXECUTE IMMEDIATE SQLSTMT;
542	
543	COMMIT;
544	

Line	Code
545	CURRENT_LEAVE_DATE := CURRENT_LEAVE_DATE + 1;
546	
547	END LOOP;
548	

The code loops through this select statement for each date that falls between the BEGIN_AS_OF_DATE and END_AS_OF_DATE. As is documented in the comments, the source system will store the begin date and end date of a span of leave along with the total leave taken during that span.

Begin Date	End Date	Hours
3/2/2005	3/3/2005	10

It is unclear from this how the hours were distributed between the two days (i.e., five hours on one day and five the other, three hours on one day and seven the other, etc.). The data warehouse needs this at a daily grain, so the ETL must calculate an average per day. Line 524 performs this calculation so that the data in the warehouse will look this way:

Day	Hours
3/2/2005	5
3/3/2005	5

Add Foreign Keys To The Fact Table

Lines 549 – 563

Line	Code
549	--If the table exists, drop it. If not, do nothing. The table will be
550	--created below.
551	SELECT COUNT(*) INTO TBLCOUNT
552	FROM ALL_TABLES
553	WHERE TABLE_NAME = 'STAGE_LEAVE_ADD_KEYS_HRS_USED'
554	AND OWNER =
555	(
556	SELECT SYS_CONTEXT('USERENV', 'CURRENT_SCHEMA')
557	FROM DUAL
558	);
559	
560	IF TBLCOUNT > 0 THEN

Line	Code
561	EXECUTE IMMEDIATE 'DROP TABLE STAGE_LEAVE_ADD_KEYS_HRS_USED';
562	END IF;
563	

If the STAGE_LEAVE_ADD_KEYS_HRS_USED table exists then drop it.

Lines 564 – 580

Line	Code
564	--This table adds surrogate keys to the hours used data
565	SQLSTMT := 'CREATE TABLE STAGE_LEAVE_ADD_KEYS_HRS_USED AS '
566	|| '(SELECT NVL(B.KEY_EMPLOYEE,-1) KEY_EMPLOYEE,'
567	|| 'NVL(C.KEY_DAY,-1) KEY_DAY,'
568	|| 'A.LEAVE_TYPE DD_LEAVE_TYPE,'
569	|| 'A.HOURS_PER_DAY LEAVE_USED '
570	|| 'FROM STAGE_LEAVE_HOURS_USED A,'
571	|| 'DIM_EMPLOYEE B,'
572	|| 'DIM_DAY C '
573	|| 'WHERE A.EMPLOYEE_NUMBER = B.EMPLOYEE_NUMBER(+) '
574	|| 'AND A.TITLE_NAME = B.TITLE(+) '
575	|| 'AND A.DEPARTMENT_NUMBER = B.DEPARTMENT_NUMBER(+) '
576	|| 'AND A.APPOINTMENT_BEGIN_DATE = B.APPOINTMENT_BEGIN_DATE(+) '
577	|| 'AND A.LEAVE_DATE = C.CALENDAR_DAY(+))';
578	
579	EXECUTE IMMEDIATE SQLSTMT;
580	

The STAGE_LEAVE_HOURS_USED table is joined to the various dimension tables by the natural keys in order to pick up the foreign keys (surrogate keys) that are needed by the fact table. Notice that outer joins are used so that a fact record will not be excluded from the result set if its corresponding dimension is, for some reason, not present in the dimension table.

Load The Fact Table

Lines 581 – 603

Line	Code
581	--If the ENTIRE_REFRESH variable is set to Y, then the fact table is
582	--truncated. Otherwise, only the rows that pertain to the time period being
583	--added or refreshed are deleted from the fact table.
584	IF ENTIRE_REFRESH = 'Y' THEN
585	SQLSTMT := 'TRUNCATE TABLE FACT_LEAVE';
586	EXECUTE IMMEDIATE SQLSTMT;
587	ELSE
588	SQLSTMT := 'DELETE FROM FACT_LEAVE '
589	|| 'WHERE KEY_DAY IN ('
590	|| 'SELECT KEY_DAY '
591	|| 'FROM DIM_DAY '
592	|| 'WHERE CALENDAR_DAY BETWEEN '''
593	|| TO_CHAR(BEGIN_AS_OF_DATE, 'DD-MON-YYYY')
594	|| ''' AND '''
595	|| TO_CHAR(END_AS_OF_DATE, 'DD-MON-YYYY')
596	|| ''')';
597	
598	EXECUTE IMMEDIATE SQLSTMT;
599	
600	COMMIT;
601	
602	END IF;
603	

These lines of code make room in the fact table for the new fact records. If the ENTIRE_REFRESH variable is set to Y, meaning that the entire fact table needs to be refreshed, then the table is truncated. Otherwise, only those existing records that fall between the BEGIN_AS_OF_DATE and the END_AS_OF_DATE are deleted.

216

Lines 604 – 631

Line	Code
604	--The records are inserted into the fact table
605	SQLSTMT := 'INSERT INTO FACT_LEAVE '
606	|| 'SELECT KEY_EMPLOYEE, '
607	|| 'KEY_DAY, '
608	|| 'SUM(LEAVE_BANK), '
609	|| 'SUM(LEAVE_USED), '
610	|| 'DD_LEAVE_TYPE '
611	|| 'FROM '
612	|| '('
613	|| 'SELECT A.KEY_EMPLOYEE, '
614	|| 'A.KEY_DAY, '
615	|| 'A.DD_LEAVE_TYPE, '
616	|| '0 LEAVE_USED, '
617	|| 'A.LEAVE_BANK '
618	|| 'FROM STAGE_LEAVE_ADD_KEYS_BANK A '
619	|| 'UNION '
620	|| 'SELECT A.KEY_EMPLOYEE, '
621	|| 'A.KEY_DAY, '
622	|| 'A.DD_LEAVE_TYPE, '
623	|| 'A.LEAVE_USED, '
624	|| '0 '
625	|| 'FROM STAGE_LEAVE_ADD_KEYS_HRS_USED A '
626	|| ') '
627	|| 'GROUP BY KEY_EMPLOYEE, KEY_DAY, DD_LEAVE_TYPE';
628	
629	EXECUTE IMMEDIATE SQLSTMT;
630	COMMIT;
631	

The records from the STAGE_LEAVE_ADD_KEYS_HRS_USED table are added to the FACT_LEAVE table.

Lines 632 – 649

Line	Code
632	--Log the successful completion of the job.
633	INSERT INTO ETL_JOB_STATUS
634	(
635	ID,
636	ETL_JOB_NAME,
637	STATUS_NAME,
638	STATUS_TIMESTAMP
639	)
640	VALUES
641	(
642	SEQ_ETL_JOB_STATUS.NEXTVAL,
643	'LOAD_LEAVE_FACT',
644	'SUCCESSFULLY COMPLETED',
645	SYSTIMESTAMP
646	);
647	
648	COMMIT;
649	

The end of the job is logged.

Lines 650 – 719

Line	Code
650	--This is the equivalent of a catch block. Any errors are caught and logged.
651	EXCEPTION
652	--The MULTIPLE_FLAGS exception is raised here
653	WHEN MULTIPLE_FLAGS THEN
654	ERR_MSG := 'The ENTIRE_REFRESH and DEFAULT_TIMEPERIOD flags are both set '
655	||'to "Y". Please set only one to "Y" or set both to "N" with two '
656	||'override dates.';
657	INSERT INTO ETL_JOB_STATUS

Line	Code
658	(
659	ID,
660	ETL_JOB_NAME,
661	STATUS_NAME,
662	ERROR_MESSAGE,
663	STATUS_TIMESTAMP
664	)
665	VALUES
666	(
667	SEQ_ETL_JOB_STATUS.NEXTVAL,
668	'LOAD_LEAVE_FACT',
669	'ERROR',
670	ERR_MSG,
671	SYSTIMESTAMP
672	);
673	
674	COMMIT;
675	--The DATES_OUT_OF_ORDER exception is raised here
676	WHEN DATES_OUT_OF_ORDER THEN
677	ERR_MSG := 'The date provided for the BEGIN_DATE_OVERRIDE falls after the '
678	|| 'END_DATE_OVERRIDE.';
679	INSERT INTO ETL_JOB_STATUS
680	(
681	ID,
682	ETL_JOB_NAME,
683	STATUS_NAME,
684	ERROR_MESSAGE,
685	STATUS_TIMESTAMP
686	)
687	VALUES
688	(
689	SEQ_ETL_JOB_STATUS.NEXTVAL,
690	'LOAD_LEAVE_FACT',

Line	Code
691	'ERROR',
692	ERR_MSG,
693	SYSTIMESTAMP
694	);
695	
696	COMMIT;
697	
698	WHEN OTHERS THEN
699	ERR_MSG := SUBSTR(SQLERRM, 1, 200);
700	INSERT INTO ETL_JOB_STATUS
701	(
702	ID,
703	ETL_JOB_NAME,
704	STATUS_NAME,
705	ERROR_MESSAGE,
706	STATUS_TIMESTAMP
707	)
708	VALUES
709	(
710	SEQ_ETL_JOB_STATUS.NEXTVAL,
711	'LOAD_LEAVE_FACT',
712	'ERROR',
713	ERR_MSG,
714	SYSTIMESTAMP
715	);
716	
717	COMMIT;
718	
719	END;

These lines are written to catch any exceptions thrown by the job and log those exceptions in the ETL_JOB_STATUS table.

Review The ETL Job

Running this job should result in 2,182,724 rows being placed into the FACT_LEAVE table.

1.) This ETL job is designed to be run as many times as necessary. Running this job multiple times will not cause rows to be duplicated.
2.) By default, the prior month and the current month are refreshed. However, variables may be passed that will cause the fact table to be refreshed for data between certain dates or the entire fact table to be refreshed.
3.) Because the source system only stores the total number of hours of leave taken within a date span, the job will calculate the average number of hours taken per day.

Verify The ETL Job

Because of the complexity of this ETL job, a couple of SQL statements are needed to verify the results. The statement below should help to verify the leave bank data.

```
SELECT      B.EMPLOYEE_NUMBER,
            SUM(A.LEAVE_BANK),
            'DATA WAREHOUSE'
FROM        FACT_LEAVE A,
            DIM_EMPLOYEE B
WHERE       A.KEY_EMPLOYEE = B.KEY_EMPLOYEE
GROUP BY    B.EMPLOYEE_NUMBER
UNION
SELECT      EMPLOYEE_NUMBER,
            SUM(PERSONAL_BANK + SICK_BANK),
            'SOURCE'
FROM        STAGE_LEAVE_BANK_EXTRACT
GROUP BY    EMPLOYEE_NUMBER
ORDER BY    1, 3
```

While there are several matches, notice that the results are not matching in some cases, alerting us to the fact that there is an error in our code. The error probably has to do with a mismatch of some sort regarding the association of leave bank hours to employees. After combing through the code, notice lines 425 and 438:

Line	Code
425	|| 'SELECT NVL(B.EMPLOYEE_ID,-1) KEY_EMPLOYEE '
438	|| 'SELECT NVL(B.EMPLOYEE_ID,-1) '

These lines are part of the SQL statement used to populate the STAGE_LEAVE_ADD_KEYS_BANK table. The intent is that the surrogate keys are added to the extract. The error above is that the surrogate key, KEY_EMPLOYEE, should be selected (and inserted into the staging table) instead of the natural key, EMPLOYEE_ID. So, these two lines should become:

221

Line	Code
425 (updated)	|| 'SELECT NVL(B.KEY_EMPLOYEE,-1) KEY_EMPLOYEE,'
438 (updated)	|| 'SELECT NVL(B.KEY_EMPLOYEE,-1),'

Running the updated procedure and verifying the data again will result in 2,182,936 rows being placed into the FACT_LEAVE table. As you can see, the data now seems to make sense.

An additional item that needs verification is the hours used piece. This SQL statement should allow us to verify that data.

```
SELECT      B.FULL_NAME,
            SUM(A.LEAVE_USED),
            'DATA WAREHOUSE'
FROM        FACT_LEAVE A,
            DIM_EMPLOYEE B
WHERE       A.KEY_EMPLOYEE = B.KEY_EMPLOYEE
GROUP BY    B.FULL_NAME
UNION
SELECT      C.FIRST_NAME || ' ' || C.LAST_NAME,
            SUM(HOURS_TAKEN),
            'SOURCE'
FROM        ACTUAL_LEAVE A,
            APPOINTMENT B,
            EMPLOYEE C
WHERE       A.APPOINTMENT_ID = B.ID
            AND B.EMPLOYEE_ID = C.ID
GROUP BY    C.FIRST_NAME || ' ' || C.LAST_NAME
ORDER BY    1
```

Running the SQL will show that the warehoused data appears to match the source system in most cases. However, run the above SQL and limit it to an EMPLOYEE_NUMBER value of 1003720 (Travis Abernethy). The results are below:

FULL_NAME	SUM(A.LEAVE_USED)	'DATAWAREHOUSE'
Travis Abernethy	6112	DATA WAREHOUSE
Travis Abernethy	6296	SOURCE

As a result of this discrepancy, we will need to trace backward through our staging tables to find the cause.

The STAGE_LEAVE_ADD_KEYS_HRS_USED table is the table used to populate the fact. The following is a modified version of the SQL used to create that table (lines 565 – 577) so that only Travis Abernethy's data displays.

```
SELECT      NVL(B.KEY_EMPLOYEE,-1) KEY_EMPLOYEE,
            SUM(A.HOURS_PER_DAY) LEAVE_USED,
            B.FULL_NAME
```

```
FROM        STAGE_LEAVE_HOURS_USED A,
            DIM_EMPLOYEE B,
            DIM_DAY C
WHERE       A.EMPLOYEE_NUMBER = B.EMPLOYEE_NUMBER(+)
            AND A.TITLE_NAME = B.TITLE(+)
            AND A.DEPARTMENT_NUMBER = B.DEPARTMENT_NUMBER(+)
            AND A.APPOINTMENT_BEGIN_DATE =
            B.APPOINTMENT_BEGIN_DATE(+)
            AND A.LEAVE_DATE = C.CALENDAR_DAY(+)
            AND B.FULL_NAME = UPPER('TRAVIS ABERNETHY')
GROUP BY    NVL(B.KEY_EMPLOYEE,-1), B.FULL_NAME
```

The results are below (your KEY_EMPLOYEE value may differ).

KEY_EMPLOYEE	LEAVE_USED	FULL_NAME
263	6296	Travis Abernethy

Because these results match the source, the error must fall after this step of the ETL job. The only step remaining is the actual insertion into the fact table (lines 605 – 627). This code, limited to Travis Abernethy (you may need to manually look up his KEY_EMPLOYEE value) and grouped only by employee, is below.

```
SELECT      KEY_EMPLOYEE,
            SUM(LEAVE_BANK),
            SUM(LEAVE_USED)
FROM
(
            SELECT      A.KEY_EMPLOYEE,
                        A.KEY_DAY,
                        A.DD_LEAVE_TYPE,
                        0 LEAVE_USED,
                        A.LEAVE_BANK
            FROM        STAGE_LEAVE_ADD_KEYS_BANK A
            UNION
            SELECT      A.KEY_EMPLOYEE,
                        A.KEY_DAY,
                        A.DD_LEAVE_TYPE,
                        A.LEAVE_USED,
                        0
            FROM        STAGE_LEAVE_ADD_KEYS_HRS_USED A
)
WHERE       KEY_EMPLOYEE = 263
GROUP BY    KEY_EMPLOYEE
```

The results are below.

KEY_EMPLOYEE	SUM(LEAVE_BANK)	SUM(LEAVE_USED)
263	14	6112

This SQL statement is interpreting the sum of the LEAVE_USED column to be a value of 6,112 as opposed to the 6,296, which is present in the source system. To dig a bit deeper, remove the top part of the union.

```
SELECT      KEY_EMPLOYEE,
            SUM(LEAVE_BANK),
            SUM(LEAVE_USED)
FROM
(
            SELECT      A.KEY_EMPLOYEE,
                        A.KEY_DAY,
                        A.DD_LEAVE_TYPE,
                        A.LEAVE_USED,
                        0 LEAVE_BANK
            FROM        STAGE_LEAVE_ADD_KEYS_HRS_USED A
)
WHERE       KEY_EMPLOYEE = 263
GROUP BY    KEY_EMPLOYEE
```

The results are below.

KEY_EMPLOYEE	SUM(LEAVE_BANK)	SUM(LEAVE_USED)
263	14	6296

These results suggest that the SQL statement used to select the LEAVE_USED in and of itself is correct. However, when "unioned" with the SQL statement used to select the LEAVE_BALANCE, an incorrect result is returned. Remember that if multiple SQL statements in a UNION return the same record, that record will appear in the result set only once. In order for ALL occurrences to be returned, a UNION ALL will need to be used. Now, edit the above SQL statement to use a UNION ALL as opposed to a UNION.

```
SELECT      KEY_EMPLOYEE,
            SUM(LEAVE_BANK),
            SUM(LEAVE_USED)
FROM
(
            SELECT      A.KEY_EMPLOYEE,
                        A.KEY_DAY,
                        A.DD_LEAVE_TYPE,
                        0 LEAVE_USED,
                        A.LEAVE_BANK
            FROM        STAGE_LEAVE_ADD_KEYS_BANK A
```

```
                UNION ALL
                SELECT      A.KEY_EMPLOYEE,
                            A.KEY_DAY,
                            A.DD_LEAVE_TYPE,
                            A.LEAVE_USED,
                            0
                FROM        STAGE_LEAVE_ADD_KEYS_HRS_USED A
)
WHERE       KEY_EMPLOYEE = 263
GROUP BY    KEY_EMPLOYEE
```

The results, shown below, match the source system.

KEY_EMPLOYEE	SUM(LEAVE_BANK)	SUM(LEAVE_USED)
263	14	6296

This suggests that some rows in the result set are duplicates of each other. This also suggests that we need those duplicates in order to match the source system. Digging through the source system's data will show some puzzling results. The SQL below will display one example of those puzzling results.

```
SELECT      *
FROM        ACTUAL_LEAVE A
WHERE       A.ID IN (4799, 4729)
```

The results are below.

ID	LEAVE_BEGIN_DATE	LEAVE_END_DATE	APPOINTMENT_ID	LEAVE_TYPE_ID	HOURS_TAKEN	INSERT_DATE
4729	18-Nov-01	23-Nov-01	100	1	48	13-Nov-01
4799	21-Nov-01	28 Nov-01	100	1	64	9-Nov-01

It appears that 24 hours of leave taken between 11/21/2001 and 11/23/2001 are recorded twice (essentially double-counted) in the source system. At this point, the users will need to be consulted since they own the source system data. There may or may not be a scenario in which this apparent duplication is legitimate. For now, we will update line 619 so that it uses a UNION ALL instead of a UNION. This will ensure that the fact table matches the source system, pending any updates in data and/or business rules by the users.

Re-running the updated procedure will still result in 2,182,936 rows being placed into the FACT_LEAVE table. The row count did not change since the UNION ALL affects the sum of the LEAVE_USED column but does not affect the number of rows returned. Rerun the SQL statement used to verify the results for Travis Abernethy (shown below).

```
SELECT      B.FULL_NAME,
            SUM(A.LEAVE_USED),
```

	'DATA WAREHOUSE'
FROM	FACT_LEAVE A,
	DIM_EMPLOYEE B
WHERE	A.KEY_EMPLOYEE = B.KEY_EMPLOYEE
	AND UPPER(B.FULL_NAME) = 'TRAVIS ABERNETHY'
GROUP BY	B.FULL_NAME
UNION	
SELECT	C.FIRST_NAME || ' ' || C.LAST_NAME,
	SUM(HOURS_TAKEN),
	'SOURCE'
FROM	ACTUAL_LEAVE A,
	APPOINTMENT B,
	EMPLOYEE C
WHERE	A.APPOINTMENT_ID = B.ID
	AND B.EMPLOYEE_ID = C.ID
	AND UPPER(C.FIRST_NAME || ' ' || C.LAST_NAME) = 'TRAVIS ABERNETHY'
GROUP BY	C.FIRST_NAME || ' ' || C.LAST_NAME

FULL_NAME	SUM(A.LEAVE_USED)	'DATAWAREHOUSE'
Travis Abernethy	6296	DATA WAREHOUSE
Travis Abernethy	6296	SOURCE

As you can see, the star now matches the source system. To test more thoroughly, remove the limitation on name and do not group by name in the SQL statement above.

SELECT	SUM(A.LEAVE_USED),
	'DATA WAREHOUSE'
FROM	FACT_LEAVE A,
	DIM_EMPLOYEE B
WHERE	A.KEY_EMPLOYEE = B.KEY_EMPLOYEE
UNION	
SELECT	SUM(HOURS_TAKEN),
	'SOURCE'
FROM	ACTUAL_LEAVE A,
	APPOINTMENT B,
	EMPLOYEE C
WHERE	A.APPOINTMENT_ID = B.ID
	AND B.EMPLOYEE_ID = C.ID
	AND EXTRACT(YEAR FROM A.LEAVE_BEGIN_DATE) >= 1985

The results are shown below. Everything looks good.

SUM(A.LEAVE_USED)	'DATAWAREHOUSE'
15660152	DATA WAREHOUSE
15660152	SOURCE

The LOAD_LEAVE_FACT procedure in its entirety is shown below.

Line	Code
1	CREATE OR REPLACE PROCEDURE LOAD_LEAVE_FACT
2	(
3	BEGIN_DATE_OVERRIDE DATE,
4	END_DATE_OVERRIDE DATE,
5	DEFAULT_TIMEPERIOD VARCHAR2,
6	ENTIRE_REFRESH VARCHAR2
7	)
8	
9	AS
10	
11	SQLSTMT VARCHAR2(3000);
12	TBLCOUNT NUMBER := 0;
13	BEGIN_AS_OF_DATE DATE;
14	END_AS_OF_DATE DATE;
15	DATE_STRING VARCHAR(10);
16	ERR_MSG VARCHAR2(200);
17	CURSOR_EMPL_ID NUMBER;
18	CURSOR_APPT_ID NUMBER;
19	PREVIOUS_APPT_END_DATE DATE;
20	CURRENT_APPT_BEGIN_DATE DATE;
21	CURRENT_LEAVE_DATE DATE;
22	CONTINUOUS_EMPL_BEGIN_DATE DATE;
23	MULTIPLE_FLAGS EXCEPTION;
24	DATES_OUT_OF_ORDER EXCEPTION;
25	
26	EE_ITERATION NUMBER := 0;
27	APPT_ITERATION NUMBER := 0;
28	
29	--This cursor selects all employees who have more than one appointment.
30	CURSOR EMPLOYEES IS
31	SELECT EMPLOYEE_ID
32	FROM APPOINTMENT

Line	Code
33	GROUP BY EMPLOYEE_ID
34	HAVING COUNT(DISTINCT ID) > 1;
35	
36	--This cursor selects all appointments for each employee that is returned by
37	--the employees cursor. The employees cursor is an outer loop and this cursor
38	--is used in an inner loop later in the job.
39	CURSOR APPOINTMENTS IS
40	SELECT ID
41	FROM APPOINTMENT
42	WHERE EMPLOYEE_ID = CURSOR_EMPL_ID
43	ORDER BY APPOINTMENT_BEGIN_DATE;
44	
45	BEGIN
46	--Log the beginning of the job
47	INSERT INTO ETL_JOB_STATUS
48	(
49	ID,
50	ETL_JOB_NAME,
51	STATUS_NAME,
52	STATUS_TIMESTAMP
53	)
54	VALUES
55	(
56	SEQ_ETL_JOB_STATUS.NEXTVAL,
57	'LOAD_LEAVE_FACT',
58	'IN PROGRESS',
59	SYSTIMESTAMP
60	);
61	
62	COMMIT;
63	
64	--If the table exists, drop it. If not, do nothing. The table will be
65	--created below.

Line	Code
66	SELECT COUNT(*) INTO TBLCOUNT
67	FROM ALL_TABLES
68	WHERE TABLE_NAME = 'STAGE_LEAVE_BANK_EXTRACT'
69	AND OWNER =
70	(
71	SELECT SYS_CONTEXT('USERENV', 'CURRENT_SCHEMA')
72	FROM DUAL
73	);
74	
75	IF TBLCOUNT > 0 THEN
76	EXECUTE IMMEDIATE 'DROP TABLE STAGE_LEAVE_BANK_EXTRACT';
77	END IF;
78	
79	--The job cannot execute an entire refresh and the default time period at the
80	--same time, so if both flags are set to 'Y' then an exception is raised.
81	IF DEFAULT_TIMEPERIOD = 'Y' AND ENTIRE_REFRESH = 'Y' THEN
82	RAISE MULTIPLE_FLAGS;
83	END IF;
84	
85	--If the DEFAULT_PERIOD variable is set to 'Y', then the prior month and the
86	--current month are loaded or reloaded into the fact table. Otherwise, the
87	--overrides are used.
88	IF ENTIRE_REFRESH <> 'Y' THEN
89	IF DEFAULT_TIMEPERIOD = 'Y' THEN
90	SELECT TRUNC(TRUNC(SYSDATE,'MM')-1,'MM') INTO BEGIN_AS_OF_DATE FROM DUAL;
91	SELECT LAST_DAY(TRUNC(SYSDATE)) INTO END_AS_OF_DATE FROM DUAL;
92	--If the BEGIN_DATE_OVERRIDE variable is larger than the END_DATE_OVERRIDE
93	--then an exception is raised
94	ELSIF TRUNC(BEGIN_DATE_OVERRIDE) > TRUNC(END_DATE_OVERRIDE) THEN
95	RAISE DATES_OUT_OF_ORDER;
96	ELSE

Line	Code
97	BEGIN_AS_OF_DATE := BEGIN_DATE_OVERRIDE;
98	END_AS_OF_DATE := END_DATE_OVERRIDE;
99	END IF;
100	END IF;
101	
102	--The data needed to calculate the leave bank amounts is extracted. Those
103	--employees who have been employed for less than 5 years receive 4 hours of
104	--personal leave and 3 hours of sick leave every 2 weeks (each pay period).
105	--Those employees who have been employed for 5 years or longer receive 6
106	--hours of personal leave and 5 hours of sick leave every two weeks (each
107	--pay period). The code below compares the appointment being date to the
108	--pay period end date to make that calculation. That is complicated when
109	--somebody has been employed for more than 5 years and then moved to a
110	--different appointment. That situation is handled later in the job. This
111	--code simply pulls those who have one appointment.
112	SQLSTMT := 'CREATE TABLE STAGE_LEAVE_BANK_EXTRACT AS ('
113	|| 'SELECT B.EMPLOYEE_NUMBER, '
114	|| 'E.TITLE_NAME, '
115	|| 'D.DEPARTMENT_NUMBER, '
116	|| 'A.APPOINTMENT_BEGIN_DATE, '
117	|| 'C.PAY_PERIOD_END_DATE, '
118	|| 'CASE WHEN ROUND'
119	||'('
120	||'MONTHS_BETWEEN'
121	||'('
122	||'C.PAY_PERIOD_END_DATE,'
123	||'A.APPOINTMENT_BEGIN_DATE'
124	||')'
125	||'/12,2'
126	||') < 5 THEN 4 ELSE 6 END AS PERSONAL_BANK, '
127	|| 'CASE WHEN ROUND'
128	||'('
129	||'MONTHS_BETWEEN'

Line	Code
130	||'('
131	||'C.PAY_PERIOD_END_DATE,'
132	||'A.APPOINTMENT_BEGIN_DATE'
133	||')'
134	||'/12,2'
135	||') < 5 THEN 3 ELSE 5 END AS SICK_BANK '
136	|| 'FROM APPOINTMENT A, '
137	|| 'EMPLOYEE B, '
138	|| 'PAYCHECK_HEADER C, '
139	|| 'DEPARTMENT D, '
140	|| 'TITLE E '
141	|| 'WHERE A.EMPLOYEE_ID = B.ID '
142	|| 'AND C.APPOINTMENT_ID = A.ID '
143	|| 'AND A.DEPARTMENT_ID = D.ID '
144	|| 'AND A.TITLE_ID = E.ID ';
145	
146	--The date logic is not needed if an entire refresh is being done
147	IF ENTIRE_REFRESH <> 'Y' THEN
148	SQLSTMT := SQLSTMT || 'AND C.PAY_PERIOD_END_DATE BETWEEN '''
149	|| TO_CHAR(BEGIN_AS_OF_DATE,'DD-MON-YYYY')
150	|| ''' AND '''
151	|| TO_CHAR(END_AS_OF_DATE,'DD-MON-YYYY')
152	|| ''' ';
153	END IF;
154	
155	SQLSTMT := SQLSTMT || 'AND A.EMPLOYEE_ID '
156	|| 'IN '
157	|| '(SELECT A.EMPLOYEE_ID '
158	|| 'FROM APPOINTMENT A '
159	|| 'GROUP BY A.EMPLOYEE_ID '
160	|| 'HAVING COUNT(DISTINCT A.ID) <= 1)) ';
161	
162	EXECUTE IMMEDIATE SQLSTMT;

Line	Code
163	
164	--This cursor iterates through all employees who have multiple appointments.
165	--A second cursor, named APPOINTMENTS, iterates inside this one to iterate
166	--through all appointments for each employee that has multiple appointments.
167	--This approach is taken since the business rule states that if an employee
168	--is employed for at least 5 years and reaches the point at which he begins
169	--to accumulate more days off and then moves to a new appointment in the
170	--company, that level of seniority still applies. However, if that employee
171	--were to leave the company and then come back, he will start all over.
172	OPEN EMPLOYEES;
173	LOOP
174	FETCH EMPLOYEES INTO CURSOR_EMPL_ID;
175	EXIT WHEN EMPLOYEES%NOTFOUND;
176	
177	--This variable holds the appointment end date of the previous iteration of
178	--the loop below. Since we haven't entered the loop yet (meaning that
179	--there was no previous appointment) it is set to null.
180	PREVIOUS_APPT_END_DATE := null;
181	
182	/*This variable holds the earliest appointment begin date that falls after
183	any gaps in employment or the earliest employment begin date if there are
184	no gaps in employment. This variable is important since the business rule
185	states that seniority with regards to the number of personal/sick hours
186	that are accrued each pay period only applies to continuous employment.
187	So, if an employee has these appointments...
188	
189	Appointment 1: 1/1/1985 through 5/1/1995
190	Appointment 2: 2/3/2001 through 7/6/2002
191	Appointment 3: 7/7/2002 through current
192	
193	...then for records that occur within Appointment 1, the pay period end
194	date is compared to 1/1/1985 in order to find the number of hours that
195	should be placed into the leave bank. For records that occur within

Line	Code
196	Appointment 2, the pay period end date is compared to 2/3/2001 since there
197	was a gap in employment between Appointments 1 and 2. For records that
198	occur within Appointment 3, the pay period end date is compared to 2/3/2001
199	since there was no gap in employment between Appointments 2 and 3.*/
200	CONTINUOUS_EMPL_BEGIN_DATE := null;
201	
202	--This cursor iterates through all appointments for a given employee who
203	--has multiple appointments.
204	OPEN APPOINTMENTS;
205	LOOP
206	FETCH APPOINTMENTS INTO CURSOR_APPT_ID;
207	EXIT WHEN APPOINTMENTS%NOTFOUND;
208	
209	--This SQL statement pulls data related to the first appointment in the
210	--loop. The appointment begin date is compared to the pay period end
211	--date to determine how many
212	--hours to place into the bank.
213	IF PREVIOUS_APPT_END_DATE IS NULL THEN
214	SQLSTMT := 'INSERT INTO STAGE_LEAVE_BANK_EXTRACT '
215	|| 'SELECT B.EMPLOYEE_NUMBER, '
216	|| 'E.TITLE_NAME, '
217	|| 'D.DEPARTMENT_NUMBER, '
218	|| 'A.APPOINTMENT_BEGIN_DATE, '
219	|| 'C.PAY_PERIOD_END_DATE, '
220	|| 'CASE WHEN ROUND'
221	||'('
222	||'MONTHS_BETWEEN'
223	||'('
224	||'C.PAY_PERIOD_END_DATE,'
225	||'A.APPOINTMENT_BEGIN_DATE'
226	||')'
227	||'/12,2'
228	||') < 5 THEN 4 ELSE 6 END AS PERSONAL_BANK, '

Line	Code
229	|| 'CASE WHEN ROUND'
230	||'('
231	||'MONTHS_BETWEEN'
232	||'('
233	||'C.PAY_PERIOD_END_DATE,'
234	||'A.APPOINTMENT_BEGIN_DATE'
235	||')'
236	||'/12,2'
237	||') < 5 THEN 3 ELSE 5 END AS SICK_BANK '
238	|| 'FROM APPOINTMENT A, '
239	|| 'EMPLOYEE B, '
240	|| 'PAYCHECK_HEADER C, '
241	|| 'DEPARTMENT D, '
242	|| 'TITLE E '
243	|| 'WHERE A.EMPLOYEE_ID = B.ID '
244	|| 'AND C.APPOINTMENT_ID = A.ID '
245	|| 'AND A.DEPARTMENT_ID = D.ID '
246	|| 'AND A.TITLE_ID = E.ID ';
247	
248	IF ENTIRE_REFRESH <> 'Y' THEN
249	SQLSTMT := SQLSTMT
250	|| 'AND C.PAY_PERIOD_END_DATE BETWEEN ''
251	|| TO_CHAR(BEGIN_AS_OF_DATE,'DD-MON-YYYY')
252	|| ''' AND '''
253	|| TO_CHAR(END_AS_OF_DATE,'DD-MON-YYYY')
254	|| ''' ';
255	END IF;
256	
257	SQLSTMT := SQLSTMT || 'AND A.ID = ' || CURSOR_APPT_ID;
258	
259	EXECUTE IMMEDIATE SQLSTMT;
260	
261	COMMIT;

Line	Code
262	
263	--The current APPOINTMENT_END_DATE is placed into the
264	--PREVIOUS_APPT_END_DATE variable for use in the next iteration.
265	SELECT APPOINTMENT_END_DATE INTO PREVIOUS_APPT_END_DATE
266	FROM APPOINTMENT
267	WHERE ID = CURSOR_APPT_ID;
268	
269	--The current APPOINTMENT_BEGIN_DATE is placed into the
270	--CONTINUOUS_EMPL_BEGIN_DATE variable for use in the next iteration.
271	--It will only be reset when a gap in employment is detected.
272	SELECT APPOINTMENT_BEGIN_DATE INTO CONTINUOUS_EMPL_BEGIN_DATE
273	FROM APPOINTMENT
274	WHERE ID = CURSOR_APPT_ID;
275	
276	ELSE
277	--This part of the IF statement pertains to subsequent appointments for
278	--those individuals who have multiple appointments. The current
279	--appointment begin date is added to the CURRENT_APPT_BEGIN_DATE
280	--variable. This is then compared to the PREVIOUS_APPT_END_DATE
281	--variable to see if this appointment began right after the previous
282	--appointment ended (meaning that employment was continuous) or if
283	--there was a gap in employment. If there is a gap in employment, the
284	--current appointment begin date is compared to the pay period end
285	--date to calculate the number of hours that should be added to the
286	--bank.
287	SELECT APPOINTMENT_BEGIN_DATE INTO CURRENT_APPT_BEGIN_DATE
288	FROM APPOINTMENT
289	WHERE ID = CURSOR_APPT_ID;
290	
291	IF TRUNC(CURRENT_APPT_BEGIN_DATE) - TRUNC(PREVIOUS_APPT_END_DATE) > 1 THEN
292	SQLSTMT := 'INSERT INTO STAGE_LEAVE_BANK_EXTRACT '

Line	Code
293	|| 'SELECT B.EMPLOYEE_NUMBER, '
294	|| 'E.TITLE_NAME, '
295	|| 'D.DEPARTMENT_NUMBER, '
296	|| 'A.APPOINTMENT_BEGIN_DATE, '
297	|| 'C.PAY_PERIOD_END_DATE, '
298	|| 'CASE WHEN ROUND'
299	||'('
300	||'MONTHS_BETWEEN'
301	||'('
302	||'C.PAY_PERIOD_END_DATE,'
303	||'A.APPOINTMENT_BEGIN_DATE'
304	||')'
305	||'/12,2'
306	||') < 5 THEN 4 ELSE 6 END AS PERSONAL_BANK, '
307	|| 'CASE WHEN ROUND'
308	||'('
309	||'MONTHS_BETWEEN'
310	||'('
311	||'C.PAY_PERIOD_END_DATE,'
312	||'A.APPOINTMENT_BEGIN_DATE'
313	||')'
314	||'/12,2'
315	||') < 5 THEN 3 ELSE 5 END AS SICK_BANK '
316	|| 'FROM APPOINTMENT A, '
317	|| 'EMPLOYEE B, '
318	|| 'PAYCHECK_HEADER C, '
319	|| 'DEPARTMENT D, '
320	|| 'TITLE E '
321	|| 'WHERE A.EMPLOYEE_ID = B.ID '
322	|| 'AND C.APPOINTMENT_ID = A.ID '
323	|| 'AND A.DEPARTMENT_ID = D.ID '
324	|| 'AND A.TITLE_ID = E.ID ';
325	

Line	Code
326	IF ENTIRE_REFRESH <> 'Y' THEN
327	SQLSTMT := SQLSTMT
328	|| 'AND C.PAY_PERIOD_END_DATE BETWEEN '''
329	|| TO_CHAR(BEGIN_AS_OF_DATE,'DD-MON-YYYY')
330	|| ''' AND '''
331	|| TO_CHAR(END_AS_OF_DATE,'DD-MON-YYYY')
332	|| ''' ';
333	END IF;
334	
335	SQLSTMT := SQLSTMT || 'AND A.ID = ' || CURSOR_APPT_ID;
336	
337	EXECUTE IMMEDIATE SQLSTMT;
338	
339	COMMIT;
340	
341	--Since this piece of the IF statement pertains to those appointments
342	--falling after a gap in employment, the CONTINUOUS_EMPL_BEGIN_DATE
343	--is overwritten with the current APPOINTMENT_BEGIN_DATE.
344	SELECT APPOINTMENT_BEGIN_DATE INTO CONTINUOUS_EMPL_BEGIN_DATE
345	FROM APPOINTMENT
346	WHERE ID = CURSOR_APPT_ID;
347	
348	ELSE
349	--If there is no gap in employment, the minimum appointment begin
350	--date that falls after any gaps in employment (or the minimum
351	--appointment begin date if there are not gaps) is compared to the
352	--pay period end date to calculate the number of hours that should be
353	--added to the bank.
354	SQLSTMT := 'INSERT INTO STAGE_LEAVE_BANK_EXTRACT '
355	|| 'SELECT B.EMPLOYEE_NUMBER, '
356	|| 'E.TITLE_NAME, '
357	|| 'D.DEPARTMENT_NUMBER, '

Line	Code
358	|| 'A.APPOINTMENT_BEGIN_DATE, '
359	|| 'C.PAY_PERIOD_END_DATE, '
360	|| 'CASE WHEN ROUND(MONTHS_BETWEEN(C.PAY_PERIOD_END_DATE, '''
361	|| TO_CHAR(CONTINUOUS_EMPL_BEGIN_DATE,'DD-MON-YYYY')
362	|| ''') '
363	|| '/12,2) < 5 THEN 4 ELSE 6 END AS PERSONAL, '
364	|| 'CASE WHEN ROUND(MONTHS_BETWEEN(C.PAY_PERIOD_END_DATE, '''
365	|| TO_CHAR(CONTINUOUS_EMPL_BEGIN_DATE,'DD-MON-YYYY')
366	|| ''') '
367	|| '/12,2) < 5 THEN 3 ELSE 5 END AS SICK '
368	|| 'FROM APPOINTMENT A, '
369	|| 'EMPLOYEE B, '
370	|| 'PAYCHECK_HEADER C, '
371	|| 'DEPARTMENT D, '
372	|| 'TITLE E '
373	|| 'WHERE A.EMPLOYEE_ID = B.ID '
374	|| 'AND C.APPOINTMENT_ID = A.ID '
375	|| 'AND A.DEPARTMENT_ID = D.ID '
376	|| 'AND A.TITLE_ID = E.ID ';
377	
378	IF ENTIRE_REFRESH <> 'Y' THEN
379	SQLSTMT := SQLSTMT
380	|| 'AND C.PAY_PERIOD_END_DATE BETWEEN '''
381	|| TO_CHAR(BEGIN_AS_OF_DATE,'DD-MON-YYYY')
382	|| ''' AND '''
383	|| TO_CHAR(END_AS_OF_DATE,'DD-MON-YYYY')
384	|| ''' ';
385	END IF;
386	
387	SQLSTMT := SQLSTMT || 'AND A.ID = ' || CURSOR_APPT_ID;
388	

Line	Code
389	EXECUTE IMMEDIATE SQLSTMT;
390	
391	COMMIT;
392	
393	END IF;
394	
395	--Before moving to a new appointment, the PREVIOUS_APPT_END_DATE is
396	--overwritten with the current APPOINTMENT_END_DATE
397	SELECT APPOINTMENT_END_DATE INTO PREVIOUS_APPT_END_DATE
398	FROM APPOINTMENT
399	WHERE ID = CURSOR_APPT_ID;
400	
401	END IF;
402	END LOOP;
403	CLOSE APPOINTMENTS;
404	
405	END LOOP;
406	CLOSE EMPLOYEES;
407	
408	--If the table exists, drop it. If not, do nothing. The table will be
409	--created below.
410	SELECT COUNT(*) INTO TBLCOUNT
411	FROM ALL_TABLES
412	WHERE TABLE_NAME = 'STAGE_LEAVE_ADD_KEYS_BANK'
413	AND OWNER =
414	(
415	SELECT SYS_CONTEXT('USERENV', 'CURRENT_SCHEMA')
416	from dual
417	);
418	
419	IF TBLCOUNT > 0 THEN
420	EXECUTE IMMEDIATE 'DROP TABLE STAGE_LEAVE_ADD_KEYS_BANK';

Line	Code
421	END IF;
422	
423	--Add the surrogate keys to the leave bank data
424	SQLSTMT := 'CREATE TABLE STAGE_LEAVE_ADD_KEYS_BANK AS ('
425 (updated)	|| 'SELECT NVL(B.KEY_EMPLOYEE,-1) KEY_EMPLOYEE, '
426	|| 'NVL(C.KEY_DAY,-1) KEY_DAY, '
427	|| 'A.PERSONAL_BANK LEAVE_BANK, '
428	|| '"Personal Leave" DD_LEAVE_TYPE '
429	|| 'FROM STAGE_LEAVE_BANK_EXTRACT A, '
430	|| 'DIM_EMPLOYEE B, '
431	|| 'DIM_DAY C '
432	|| 'WHERE A.EMPLOYEE_NUMBER = B.EMPLOYEE_NUMBER(+)'
433	|| 'AND A.APPOINTMENT_BEGIN_DATE = B.APPOINTMENT_BEGIN_DATE(+)'
434	|| 'AND A.TITLE_NAME = B.TITLE(+)'
435	|| 'AND A.DEPARTMENT_NUMBER = B.DEPARTMENT_NUMBER(+)'
436	|| 'AND A.PAY_PERIOD_END_DATE = C.CALENDAR_DAY(+)'
437	|| 'UNION '
438 (updated)	|| 'SELECT NVL(B.KEY_EMPLOYEE,-1), '
439	|| 'NVL(C.KEY_DAY,-1), '
440	|| 'A.SICK_BANK, '
441	|| '"Sick Leave" '
442	|| 'FROM STAGE_LEAVE_BANK_EXTRACT A, '
443	|| 'DIM_EMPLOYEE B, '
444	|| 'DIM_DAY C '
445	|| 'WHERE A.EMPLOYEE_NUMBER = B.EMPLOYEE_NUMBER(+) '
446	|| 'AND A.APPOINTMENT_BEGIN_DATE = B.APPOINTMENT_BEGIN_DATE(+) '
447	|| 'AND A.TITLE_NAME = B.TITLE(+) '
448	|| 'AND A.DEPARTMENT_NUMBER = B.DEPARTMENT_NUMBER(+) '
449	|| 'AND A.PAY_PERIOD_END_DATE = C.CALENDAR_DAY(+))';
450	
451	EXECUTE IMMEDIATE SQLSTMT;

Line	Code
452	
453	--If the table exists, drop it. If not, do nothing. The table will be
454	--created below.
455	SELECT COUNT(*) INTO TBLCOUNT
456	FROM ALL_TABLES
457	WHERE TABLE_NAME = 'STAGE_LEAVE_HOURS_USED'
458	AND OWNER =
459	(
460	SELECT SYS_CONTEXT('USERENV', 'CURRENT_SCHEMA')
461	FROM DUAL
462	);
463	
464	IF TBLCOUNT > 0 THEN
465	EXECUTE IMMEDIATE 'DROP TABLE STAGE_LEAVE_HOURS_USED';
466	END IF;
467	
468	--Rather than use the typical "create table as" statement, a "create table"
469	--statement is used instead. This table is populated via a loop with some
470	--iterations populating something and other iterations not populating
471	--anything. Because it is not a one-time creation, this approach is needed
472	--here.
473	SQLSTMT := 'CREATE TABLE STAGE_LEAVE_HOURS_USED '
474	|| '(EMPLOYEE_NUMBER VARCHAR2(50), '
475	|| 'TITLE_NAME VARCHAR2(255), '
476	|| 'DEPARTMENT_NUMBER VARCHAR2(100), '
477	|| 'APPOINTMENT_BEGIN_DATE DATE, '
478	|| 'LEAVE_DATE DATE, '
479	|| 'LEAVE_TYPE VARCHAR2(255), '
480	|| 'HOURS_PER_DAY NUMBER)';
481	
482	EXECUTE IMMEDIATE SQLSTMT;
483	
484	/*The loop below uses the begin and end dates passed to the job (or derived

Line	Code
485	by the job in the case of the default time period) to iterate through all
486	days between those dates and insert the appropriate data into the staging
487	table. The ACTUAL_LEAVE table stores the begin and end dates of an
488	employee's leave and the total number of hours taken. This ETL job breaks
489	that down and stores the average per day for the begin date, the end date,
490	and each day in between. So, if a record in the ACTUAL_LEAVE table looks
491	like this...
492	
493	BEGIN DATE END DATE HOURS TAKEN
494	2/4/2006 2/8/2006 40
495	
496	...it will result in the data looking this way in the staging table...
497	
498	DATE HOURS TAKEN
499	2/4/2006 8
500	2/5/2006 8
501	2/6/2006 8
502	2/7/2006 8
503	2/8/2006 8
504	
505	The IF statement immediately below will place the minimum date for which
506	leave was taken and the maximum date for which leave was taken into the
507	variables in the case of an entire refresh. The loop is below that.
508	*/
509	IF ENTIRE_REFRESH = 'Y' THEN
510	SELECT MIN(LEAVE_BEGIN_DATE) INTO BEGIN_AS_OF_DATE FROM ACTUAL_LEAVE;
511	SELECT MAX(LEAVE_END_DATE) INTO END_AS_OF_DATE FROM ACTUAL_LEAVE;
512	END IF;
513	
514	CURRENT_LEAVE_DATE := BEGIN_AS_OF_DATE;
515	WHILE CURRENT_LEAVE_DATE <= END_AS_OF_DATE
516	LOOP

Line	Code
517	SQLSTMT := 'INSERT INTO STAGE_LEAVE_HOURS_USED '
518	|| 'SELECT B.EMPLOYEE_NUMBER, '
519	|| 'E.TITLE_NAME, '
520	|| 'D.DEPARTMENT_NUMBER, '
521	|| 'A.APPOINTMENT_BEGIN_DATE, '
522	|| 'TO_DATE('" || CURRENT_LEAVE_DATE || '","DD-MON-RR"), '
523	|| 'F.TYPE, '
524	|| 'C.HOURS_TAKEN / (C.LEAVE_END_DATE - C.LEAVE_BEGIN_DATE + 1) '
525	|| 'HOURS_PER_DAY '
526	|| 'FROM APPOINTMENT A, '
527	|| 'EMPLOYEE B, '
528	|| 'ACTUAL_LEAVE C, '
529	|| 'DEPARTMENT D, '
530	|| 'TITLE E, '
531	|| 'LEAVE_TYPE F '
532	|| 'WHERE A.EMPLOYEE_ID = B.ID '
533	|| 'AND A.DEPARTMENT_ID = D.ID '
534	|| 'AND A.TITLE_ID = E.ID '
535	|| 'AND A.ID = C.APPOINTMENT_ID '
536	|| 'AND C.LEAVE_TYPE_ID = F.ID '
537	|| 'AND TO_DATE('"
538	|| CURRENT_LEAVE_DATE
539	|| '","DD-MON-RR") BETWEEN C.LEAVE_BEGIN_DATE AND C.LEAVE_END_DATE';
540	
541	EXECUTE IMMEDIATE SQLSTMT;
542	
543	COMMIT;
544	
545	CURRENT_LEAVE_DATE := CURRENT_LEAVE_DATE + 1;
546	
547	END LOOP;
548	

Line	Code
549	--If the table exists, drop it. If not, do nothing. The table will be
550	--created below.
551	SELECT COUNT(*) INTO TBLCOUNT
552	FROM ALL_TABLES
553	WHERE TABLE_NAME = 'STAGE_LEAVE_ADD_KEYS_HRS_USED'
554	AND OWNER =
555	(
556	SELECT SYS_CONTEXT('USERENV', 'CURRENT_SCHEMA')
557	FROM DUAL
558	);
559	
560	IF TBLCOUNT > 0 THEN
561	EXECUTE IMMEDIATE 'DROP TABLE STAGE_LEAVE_ADD_KEYS_HRS_USED';
562	END IF;
563	
564	--This table adds surrogate keys to the hours used data
565	SQLSTMT := 'CREATE TABLE STAGE_LEAVE_ADD_KEYS_HRS_USED AS '
566	|| '(SELECT NVL(B.KEY_EMPLOYEE,-1) KEY_EMPLOYEE, '
567	|| 'NVL(C.KEY_DAY,-1) KEY_DAY, '
568	|| 'A.LEAVE_TYPE DD_LEAVE_TYPE, '
569	|| 'A.HOURS_PER_DAY LEAVE_USED '
570	|| 'FROM STAGE_LEAVE_HOURS_USED A, '
571	|| 'DIM_EMPLOYEE B, '
572	|| 'DIM_DAY C '
573	|| 'WHERE A.EMPLOYEE_NUMBER = B.EMPLOYEE_NUMBER(+) '
574	|| 'AND A.TITLE_NAME = B.TITLE(+) '
575	|| 'AND A.DEPARTMENT_NUMBER = B.DEPARTMENT_NUMBER(+) '
576	|| 'AND A.APPOINTMENT_BEGIN_DATE = B.APPOINTMENT_BEGIN_DATE(+) '
577	|| 'AND A.LEAVE_DATE = C.CALENDAR_DAY(+))';
578	
579	EXECUTE IMMEDIATE SQLSTMT;
580	

Line	Code
581	--If the ENTIRE_REFRESH variable is set to Y, then the fact table is
582	--truncated. Otherwise, only the rows that pertain to the time period being
583	--added or refreshed are deleted from the fact table.
584	IF ENTIRE_REFRESH = 'Y' THEN
585	SQLSTMT := 'TRUNCATE TABLE FACT_LEAVE';
586	EXECUTE IMMEDIATE SQLSTMT;
587	ELSE
588	SQLSTMT := 'DELETE FROM FACT_LEAVE '
589	|| 'WHERE KEY_DAY IN ('
590	|| 'SELECT KEY_DAY '
591	|| 'FROM DIM_DAY '
592	|| 'WHERE CALENDAR_DAY BETWEEN '''
593	|| TO_CHAR(BEGIN_AS_OF_DATE, 'DD-MON-YYYY')
594	|| ''' AND '''
595	|| TO_CHAR(END_AS_OF_DATE, 'DD-MON-YYYY')
596	|| ''')';
597	
598	EXECUTE IMMEDIATE SQLSTMT;
599	
600	COMMIT;
601	
602	END IF;
603	
604	--The records are inserted into the fact table
605	SQLSTMT := 'INSERT INTO FACT_LEAVE '
606	|| 'SELECT KEY_EMPLOYEE, '
607	|| 'KEY_DAY, '
608	|| 'SUM(LEAVE_BANK), '
609	|| 'SUM(LEAVE_USED), '
610	|| 'DD_LEAVE_TYPE '
611	|| 'FROM '
612	|| '('
613	|| 'SELECT A.KEY_EMPLOYEE, '

Line	Code
614	|| 'A.KEY_DAY, '
615	|| 'A.DD_LEAVE_TYPE, '
616	|| '0 LEAVE_USED, '
617	|| 'A.LEAVE_BANK '
618	|| 'FROM STAGE_LEAVE_ADD_KEYS_BANK A '
619 (updated)	|| 'UNION ALL'
620	|| 'SELECT A.KEY_EMPLOYEE, '
621	|| 'A.KEY_DAY, '
622	|| 'A.DD_LEAVE_TYPE, '
623	|| 'A.LEAVE_USED, '
624	|| '0 '
625	|| 'FROM STAGE_LEAVE_ADD_KEYS_HRS_USED A '
626	|| ') '
627	|| 'GROUP BY KEY_EMPLOYEE, KEY_DAY, DD_LEAVE_TYPE';
628	
629	EXECUTE IMMEDIATE SQLSTMT;
630	COMMIT;
631	
632	--Log the successful completion of the job.
633	INSERT INTO ETL_JOB_STATUS
634	(
635	ID,
636	ETL_JOB_NAME,
637	STATUS_NAME,
638	STATUS_TIMESTAMP
639	)
640	VALUES
641	(
642	SEQ_ETL_JOB_STATUS.NEXTVAL,
643	'LOAD_LEAVE_FACT',
644	'SUCCESSFULLY COMPLETED',
645	SYSTIMESTAMP
646	);

Line	Code
647	
648	COMMIT;
649	
650	--This is the equivalent of a catch block. Any errors are caught and logged.
651	EXCEPTION
652	--The MULTIPLE_FLAGS exception is raised here
653	WHEN MULTIPLE_FLAGS THEN
654	ERR_MSG := 'The ENTIRE_REFRESH and DEFAULT_TIMEPERIOD flags are both set '
655	||'to "Y". Please set only one to "Y" or set both to "N" with two '
656	||'override dates.';
657	INSERT INTO ETL_JOB_STATUS
658	(
659	ID,
660	ETL_JOB_NAME,
661	STATUS_NAME,
662	ERROR_MESSAGE,
663	STATUS_TIMESTAMP
664	)
665	VALUES
666	(
667	SEQ_ETL_JOB_STATUS.NEXTVAL,
668	'LOAD_LEAVE_FACT',
669	'ERROR',
670	ERR_MSG,
671	SYSTIMESTAMP
672	);
673	
674	COMMIT;
675	--The DATES_OUT_OF_ORDER exception is raised here
676	WHEN DATES_OUT_OF_ORDER THEN
677	ERR_MSG := 'The date provided for the BEGIN_DATE_OVERRIDE falls after the '
678	|| 'END_DATE_OVERRIDE.';

Line	Code
679	INSERT INTO ETL_JOB_STATUS
680	(
681	ID,
682	ETL_JOB_NAME,
683	STATUS_NAME,
684	ERROR_MESSAGE,
685	STATUS_TIMESTAMP
686	)
687	VALUES
688	(
689	SEQ_ETL_JOB_STATUS.NEXTVAL,
690	'LOAD_LEAVE_FACT',
691	'ERROR',
692	ERR_MSG,
693	SYSTIMESTAMP
694	);
695	
696	COMMIT;
697	
698	WHEN OTHERS THEN
699	ERR_MSG := SUBSTR(SQLERRM, 1, 200);
700	INSERT INTO ETL_JOB_STATUS
701	(
702	ID,
703	ETL_JOB_NAME,
704	STATUS_NAME,
705	ERROR_MESSAGE,
706	STATUS_TIMESTAMP
707	)
708	VALUES
709	(
710	SEQ_ETL_JOB_STATUS.NEXTVAL,
711	'LOAD_LEAVE_FACT',
712	'ERROR',

Line	Code
713	ERR_MSG,
714	SYSTIMESTAMP
715	);
716	
717	COMMIT;
718	
719	END;

10
EVALUATION VS. PAY DATA

Description of the Employee Pay vs. Evaluation Business Process

This business process is really a comparison that involves two other business processes. Chapters six and eight discuss the pay and evaluation business processes, respectively. The users would like to be able to easily compare an individual's difference in pay from year-to-year to their difference in evaluation score from year-to-year. While some SQL can be written off of the existing stars, the logic will be very complex and the code will probably be inefficient. A fact table can be created specifically for this comparison.

Requirements

As discussed, the users would like to compare an individual's delta in pay to his/her delta in evaluation score. These two measures will be defined as the employee's total evaluation score (independent of the number of evaluations he was given) along with the total gross pay in a given year. The employee's total evaluation score will need to be stored as a percentage of the possible evaluation score. The star will need to provide the user with the ability to see the prior year's evaluation score and salary along with the percentage difference between the current year and the prior year. Based on these requirements this is the design of the star schema that this ETL job will need to populate.

Figure 10-1

DIM_EMPLOYEE		
NAME	TYPE	PK
KEY_EMPLOYEE	NUMBER	YES
EMPLOYEE_ID	NUMBER	NO
APPOINTMENT_ID	NUMBER	NO
EMPLOYEE_NUMBER	VARCHAR2(100)	NO
FIRST_NAME	VARCHAR2(100)	NO
LAST_NAME	VARCHAR2(100)	NO
FULL_NAME	VARCHAR2(100)	NO
HIGHEST_DEGREE_EARNED	VARCHAR2(100)	NO
APPOINTMENT_BEGIN_DATE	DATE	NO
APPOINTMENT_END_DATE	DATE	NO
TITLE	VARCHAR2(100)	NO
DEPARTMENT_NAME	VARCHAR2(100)	NO
DEPARTMENT_NUMBER	VARCHAR2(100)	NO

FACT_EVAL_PAY_COMPARISON		
NAME	TYPE	PK
KEY_EMPLOYEE	NUMBER	YES
KEY_CURRENT_CALENDAR_YEAR	NUMBER	YES
KEY_PRIOR_CALENDAR_YEAR	NUMBER	YES
PRIOR_YEAR_EVAL_SCORE	NUMBER	NO
PRIOR_YEAR_SALARY	NUMBER	NO
CURRENT_YEAR_EVAL_SCORE	NUMBER	NO
CURRENT_YEAR_SALARY	NUMBER	NO
EVAL_PERCENTAGE_CHANGE	NUMBER	NO
SALARY_PERCENTAGE_CHANGE	NUMBER	NO

DIM_CALENDAR_YEAR		
NAME	TYPE	PK
KEY_CALENDAR_YEAR	NUMBER	YES
CALENDAR_YEAR	NUMBER	NO
FIRST_DAY	DATE	NO
LAST_DAY	DATE	NO

DIM_CALENDAR_YEAR		
NAME	TYPE	PK
KEY_CALENDAR_YEAR	NUMBER	YES
CALENDAR_YEAR	NUMBER	NO
FIRST_DAY	DATE	NO
LAST_DAY	DATE	NO

DIM_EMPLOYEE: This is the same type two slowly changing dimension as was used in the salary, evaluation, and leave stars. Although creating a separate physical table with the same keys and data (or a subset of data) as the original DIM_EMPLOYEE would not be wrong, for ease of use we will just reuse the original.

DIM_CALENDAR_YEAR: This is a dimension table that contains one row per calendar year. This dimension has no source system and will be populated by the ETL developer.

FACT_EVAL_PAY_COMPARISON: This is a basic fact table that will allow a user to analyze the prior year's salary and evaluation score, the current year's salary and evaluation score, and the delta in salary and evaluation score between the prior year and current year. The source of the PRIOR_YEAR_EVAL_SCORE and the CURRENT_YEAR_EVAL_SCORE columns is the FACT_EVALUATION.ACTUAL_SCORE divided by the FACT_EVALUATION.POSSIBLE_SCORE, for the appropriate years. The source of the PRIOR_YEAR_SALARY and the CURRENT_YEAR_SALARY columns is the FACT_SALARY.AMOUNT column, for the appropriate years. The key values will point to their associated dimensions. The EVAL_PERCENTAGE_CHANGE and the SALARY_PERCENTAGE_CHANGE columns will store the delta between the prior year and the current year. The EVAL_PERCENTAGE_CHANGE is calculated by subtracting the prior year's evaluation score from the current year's evaluation score and then dividing that by the prior year's evaluation score. The SALARY_PERCENTAGE_CHANGE is calculated by subtracting the prior year's salary from the current year's salary and then dividing that by the prior year's salary.

Strategy for ETL

This is a small star schema that consists of one fact table and two dimension tables (one will need to be aliased and used twice). The DIM_CALENDAR_YEAR table is a standard date dimension that is not populated by an ETL job. A job to populate the DIM_EMPLOYEE table (LOAD_EMPLOYEE_DIMENSION) has already been written. So, a job will need to be written to populate the FACT_EVAL_PAY_COMPARISON table.

Populating the FACT_EVAL_PAY_COMPARISON Fact Table

Remember from chapter five that the goal of an ETL job that populates a fact table is to accomplish the following.

1.) Select all necessary data from the source
    a. Measures
    b. Natural keys of the dimension objects
    c. Degenerate Dimension objects
2.) Transform the data as needed
    a. Aggregate measures and group by the appropriate objects
    b. Add foreign keys to dimension tables
3.) Delete any existing rows from the fact table that will be replaced by the new data
4.) Load the fact table

Because the Based on Timeframe approach worked well with the other fact tables, we can use that with this one as well. Use this script to create the FACT_EVAL_PAY_COMPARISON table.

```
CREATE TABLE FACT_EVAL_PAY_COMPARISON
(
    KEY_EMPLOYEE                    NUMBER,
    KEY_CURRENT_CALENDAR_YEAR       NUMBER,
    KEY_PRIOR_CALENDAR_YEAR         NUMBER,
    PRIOR_YEAR_EVAL_SCORE           NUMBER,
    PRIOR_YEAR_SALARY               NUMBER,
    CURRENT_YEAR_EVAL_SCORE         NUMBER,
    CURRENT_YEAR_SALARY             NUMBER,
    EVAL_PERCENTAGE_CHANGE          NUMBER,
    SALARY_PERCENTAGE_CHANGE        NUMBER
)
```

Now that the infrastructure has been created, we can move forward with populating the fact table. We will call the procedure LOAD_EVAL_PAY_COMPARISON_FACT. Unlike the ETL that has been written up until this point, which has consisted of copying data from a source system's tables to the data warehouse, this job will not pull from a source system. The salary and evaluation stars that already exist in the data warehouse will serve as the source.

Lines 1 – 19

Line	Code
1	CREATE OR REPLACE PROCEDURE LOAD_EVAL_PAY_COMP_FACT
2	(
3	BEGIN_YEAR_OVERRIDE NUMBER,
4	END_YEAR_OVERRIDE NUMBER,
5	DEFAULT_TIMEPERIOD VARCHAR2,
6	ENTIRE_REFRESH VARCHAR2
7	)
8	
9	AS
10	
11	SQLSTMT VARCHAR2(3000);
12	TBLCOUNT NUMBER := 0;
13	BEGIN_YEAR NUMBER;
14	END_YEAR NUMBER;
15	ERR_MSG VARCHAR2(200);
16	YEARS_OUT_OF_ORDER EXCEPTION;
17	MULTIPLE_FLAGS EXCEPTION;
18	CURR_YEAR NUMBER;

Line	Code
19	

This piece of the code has the standard housekeeping activities performed at the beginning of an ETL job. The parameters are passed to indicate the timeframe to be used (same as the LOAD_LEAVE_FACT procedure) and the variables are declared.

Lines 20 – 38

Line	Code
20	BEGIN
21	--Log the beginning of the job
22	INSERT INTO ETL_JOB_STATUS
23	(
24	ID,
25	ETL_JOB_NAME,
26	STATUS_NAME,
27	STATUS_TIMESTAMP
28	)
29	VALUES
30	(
31	SEQ_ETL_JOB_STATUS.NEXTVAL,
32	'LOAD_EVAL_PAY_COMPARISON_FACT',
33	'IN PROGRESS',
34	SYSTIMESTAMP
35	);
36	
37	COMMIT;
38	

The beginning of the job is logged in the ETL_JOB_STATUS table.

Lines 39 – 44

Line	Code
39	--The job cannot execute an entire refresh and the default time period at the
40	--same time, so if both flags are set to 'Y' then an exception is raised.

Line	Code
41	IF DEFAULT_TIMEPERIOD = 'Y' AND ENTIRE_REFRESH = 'Y' THEN
42	RAISE MULTIPLE_FLAGS;
43	END IF;
44	

It was decided that when the ENTIRE_REFRESH was introduced in the LOAD_EVALUATION_FACT job, it was not very intuitive that a value of 'Y' trumped a value of 'Y' for the DEFAULT_TIMEPERIOD. Therefore, this job will raise an exception if they are both 'Y', forcing the job runner to give only one of the variables a value of 'Y' if the default dates are not used.

Lines 45 – 65

Line	Code
45	--If the DEFAULT_PERIOD variable is set to 'Y', then the prior year and the
46	--current year are loaded or reloaded into the fact table. If the
47	--ENTIRE_REFRESH variable is set to 'Y', then the entire fact table is
48	--truncated and reloaded. Otherwise, the overrides are used.
49	IF DEFAULT_TIMEPERIOD = 'Y' THEN
50	SELECT EXTRACT(YEAR FROM SYSDATE) - 1 INTO BEGIN_YEAR FROM DUAL;
51	SELECT EXTRACT(YEAR FROM SYSDATE) INTO END_YEAR FROM DUAL;
52	ELSIF ENTIRE_REFRESH = 'Y' THEN
53	SELECT MIN(CALENDAR_YEAR) INTO BEGIN_YEAR FROM DIM_CALENDAR_YEAR;
54	SELECT EXTRACT(YEAR FROM TRUNC(SYSDATE)) INTO END_YEAR FROM DUAL;
55	ELSE
56	--If the BEGIN_YEAR_OVERRIDE variable is larger than the END_YEAR_OVERRIDE
57	--then an exception is raised
58	IF BEGIN_YEAR_OVERRIDE > END_YEAR_OVERRIDE THEN
59	RAISE YEARS_OUT_OF_ORDER;
60	END IF;
61	
62	BEGIN_YEAR := BEGIN_YEAR_OVERRIDE;
63	END_YEAR := END_YEAR_OVERRIDE;
64	END IF;

Line	Code
65	

If an entire refresh is not being run, the time periods are set. If the DEFAULT_TIMEPERIOD is set to 'Y' then the default time period is set to the previous year and the current year (where the KEY_CURRENT_CALENDAR_YEAR equals the previous and current year, that is). Otherwise, the dates assigned to the BEGIN_YEAR_OVERRIDE and the END_YEAR_OVERRIDE variables are used. If the BEGIN_YEAR_OVERRIDE is greater than the END_YEAR_OVERRIDE, an exception is thrown.

Extract The Data

This portion of the job begins the process of extracting the data from the source system.

Lines 66 – 72

Line	Code
66	--The fact table is loaded one year at a time using a while loop. The
67	--CURR_YEAR is set to the first year in the range before entering the loop.
68	CURR_YEAR := BEGIN_YEAR;
69	
70	--The WHILE LOOP begins
71	WHILE CURR_YEAR <= END_YEAR
72	LOOP

If an individual had a salary of $100,000 in 2006, then that will be the value of the CURRENT_YEAR_SALARY column where the KEY_CURRENT_CALENDAR_YEAR column contains a surrogate key that refers to the year 2006. That same $100,000 will be the value of the PRIOR_YEAR_SALARY where the KEY_PRIOR_CALENDAR_YEAR column contains a surrogate key that refers to the year 2007. The same is true of the evaluation score logic that is being stored in this table as well. Because of the nature of this type of data storage, a loop must be used to populate this data one year at a time.

Line 68 sets the CURR_YEAR variable (a variable that essentially contains the current position of the loop) to the first year for which the job is being run. It will be incremented by one for each iteration of the loop (see lines 341 – 345). Lines 71 and 72 begin the WHILE loop, which will continue until the CURR_YEAR variable exceeds the END_YEAR variable. As this code is discussed throughout this chapter, when we refer to the current year we will be referring to the value of the CURR_YEAR variable. When we refer to the prior year in this chapter, we will be referring to the year prior to the current year (the value of CURR_YEAR minus one).

Lines 73 – 102

Line	Code
73	--If the table exists, drop it. If not, do nothing. The table will be
74	--created below.
75	SELECT COUNT(*) INTO TBLCOUNT
76	FROM ALL_TABLES
77	WHERE TABLE_NAME = 'STAGE_EVAL_COMPARISON_PY'
78	AND OWNER =
79	(
80	SELECT SYS_CONTEXT('USERENV', 'CURRENT_SCHEMA')
81	FROM DUAL
82	);
83	
84	IF TBLCOUNT > 0 THEN
85	EXECUTE IMMEDIATE 'DROP TABLE STAGE_EVAL_COMPARISON_PY';
86	END IF;
87	
88	--Pull the prior year's evaluation score. Prior year is defined as the CURR_YEAR - 1
89	SQLSTMT := 'CREATE TABLE STAGE_EVAL_COMPARISON_PY AS ('
90	|| 'SELECT B.CALENDAR_YEAR, '
91	|| 'A.KEY_EVALUATION_RECIPIENT, '
92	|| 'SUM(A.ACTUAL_SCORE)/ '
93	|| 'SUM(A.POSSIBLE_SCORE) EVALSCORE '
94	|| 'FROM FACT_EVALUATION A, '
95	|| 'DIM_DAY B '
96	|| 'WHERE A.KEY_EVALUATION_DATE = B.KEY_DAY '
97	|| 'AND B.CALENDAR_YEAR = ' || TO_CHAR(CURR_YEAR - 1) || ' '
98	|| 'GROUP BY B.CALENDAR_YEAR, '
99	|| 'A.KEY_EVALUATION_RECIPIENT) ';
100	
101	EXECUTE IMMEDIATE SQLSTMT;
102	

Lines 73 – 87 will drop the STAGE_EVAL_COMPARISON_PY table if it exists. Lines 89 – 99 will select the actual evaluation score and the possible evaluation score for the year prior to the current year of the loop and place the results into the STAGE_EVAL_COMPARISON_PY table.

Measure: On lines 92 and 93, the FACT_EVALUATION.ACTUAL_EVAL_SCORE is divided by the FACT_EVALUATION.POSSIBLE_EVAL_SCORE to get the evaluation score as a percentage.

Natural Key to DIM_CALENDAR_YEAR: DIM_DAY.CALENDAR_YEAR – Because the FACT_EVALUATION (line 90) star stores data at a daily grain, and does not include the KEY_CALENDAR_YEAR in that fact table, we are not able to simply extract the KEY_CALENDAR_YEAR from that star. The only alternative is to include the DIM_DAY.CALENDAR_YEAR in this staging table and then translate that into the KEY_CALENDAR_YEAR value later.

Surrogate Key to DIM_EMPLOYEE: FACT_EVALUATION.KEY_EVAL_RECIPIENT – The only instance in which a surrogate key can be pulled in this way (line 91) occurs when the data warehouse itself acts as the source system. This is the case, which allows us to pull this surrogate key in the extract step and avoid having to join to the dimension using the natural key later.

Lines 103 – 134

Line	Code
103	--If the table exists, drop it. If not, do nothing. The table will be
104	--created below.
105	SELECT COUNT(*) INTO TBLCOUNT
106	FROM ALL_TABLES
107	WHERE TABLE_NAME = 'STAGE_PAY_COMPARISON_PY'
108	AND OWNER =
109	(
110	SELECT SYS_CONTEXT('USERENV', 'CURRENT_SCHEMA')
111	FROM DUAL
112	);
113	
114	IF TBLCOUNT > 0 THEN
115	EXECUTE IMMEDIATE 'DROP TABLE STAGE_PAY_COMPARISON_PY';
116	END IF;
117	
118	--Pull the prior year's salary data
119	SQLSTMT := 'CREATE TABLE STAGE_PAY_COMPARISON_PY AS '

Line	Code
120	|| ' (SELECT B.CALENDAR_YEAR, '
121	|| 'A.KEY_EMPLOYEE, '
122	|| 'SUM(A.AMOUNT) SALARY '
123	|| 'FROM FACT_SALARY A, '
124	|| 'DIM_MONTH B, '
125	|| 'DIM_PAY_TYPE C '
126	|| 'WHERE A.KEY_MONTH = B.KEY_MONTH '
127	|| 'AND A.KEY_PAY_TYPE = C.KEY_PAY_TYPE '
128	--Must use upper
129	|| 'AND UPPER(C.COMPONENT_OF_GROSS_PAY) = "YES" '
130	|| 'AND B.CALENDAR_YEAR = ' || TO_CHAR(CURR_YEAR - 1) || ' '
131	|| 'GROUP BY B.CALENDAR_YEAR, A.KEY_EMPLOYEE) ';
132	
133	EXECUTE IMMEDIATE SQLSTMT;
134	

Lines 103 – 117 will drop the STAGE_PAY_COMPARISON_PY table if it exists. Lines 119 – 134 will select the actual salary amount paid for the year prior to the current year of the loop and place the results into the STAGE_PAY_COMPARISON_PY table. Line 129 is important, since the requirements specify that the total gross pay will be used.

Measure: FACT_SALARY.AMOUNT (line 122)

Natural Key to DIM_CALENDAR_YEAR: DIM_MONTH.CALENDAR_YEAR – The FACT_SALARY (line 120) star stores data at a monthly grain and does not include the KEY_CALENDAR_YEAR in that fact table. As a result, we are not able to simply extract the KEY_CALENDAR_YEAR from that star. The only alternative is to include the CALENDAR_YEAR in this staging table and then translate that into the KEY_CALENDAR_YEAR value later.

Surrogate Key to DIM_EMPLOYEE: FACT_SALARY.KEY_EMPLOYEE – As discussed with the FACT_EVALUATION star, the only instance in which a surrogate key can be pulled in this way (line 121) occurs when the data warehouse itself acts as the source system. This is the case, which allows us to pull this surrogate key in the extract step and avoid having to join to the dimension using the natural key later.

Lines 135 – 165

Line	Code
135	--If the table exists, drop it. If not, do nothing. The table will be
136	--created below.
137	SELECT COUNT(*) INTO TBLCOUNT
138	FROM ALL_TABLES
139	WHERE TABLE_NAME = 'STAGE_EVAL_COMPARISON_CY'
140	AND OWNER =
141	(
142	SELECT SYS_CONTEXT('USERENV', 'CURRENT_SCHEMA')
143	FROM DUAL
144	);
145	
146	IF TBLCOUNT > 0 THEN
147	EXECUTE IMMEDIATE 'DROP TABLE STAGE_EVAL_COMPARISON_CY';
148	END IF;
149	
150	--Pull the current year's evaluation data. The current year is stored in
151	--the CURR_YEAR variable.
152	SQLSTMT := 'CREATE TABLE STAGE_EVAL_COMPARISON_CY AS ('
153	|| 'SELECT B.CALENDAR_YEAR, '
154	|| 'A.KEY_EVALUATION_RECIPIENT, '
155	|| 'SUM(A.ACTUAL_SCORE)/ '
156	|| 'SUM(A.POSSIBLE_SCORE) EVALSCORE '
157	|| 'FROM FACT_EVALUATION A, '
158	|| 'DIM_DAY B '
159	|| 'WHERE A.KEY_EVALUATION_DATE = B.KEY_DAY '
160	|| 'AND B.CALENDAR_YEAR = ' || TO_CHAR(CURR_YEAR) || ' '
161	|| 'GROUP BY B.CALENDAR_YEAR, '
162	|| 'A.KEY_EVALUATION_RECIPIENT) ';
163	
164	EXECUTE IMMEDIATE SQLSTMT;
165	

Lines 135 – 149 will drop the STAGE_EVAL_COMPARISON_CY table if it exists. Lines 152 – 165 will select the actual evaluation score and the possible evaluation score for the year equal to the current year of the loop and place the results into the STAGE_EVAL_COMPARISON_CY table.

Measure: On lines 155 and 156, the FACT_EVALUATION.ACTUAL_EVAL_SCORE is divided by the FACT_EVALUATION.POSSIBLE_EVAL_SCORE to get the evaluation score as a percentage.

Natural Key to DIM_CALENDAR_YEAR: DIM_DAY.CALENDAR_YEAR – As mentioned previously, because the FACT_EVALUATION (line 153) star stores data at a daily grain, and does not include the KEY_CALENDAR_YEAR in that fact table, we are not able to simply extract the KEY_CALENDAR_YEAR from that star. The only alternative is to include the DIM_DAY.CALENDAR_YEAR in this staging table and then translate that into the KEY_CALENDAR_YEAR value later.

Surrogate Key to DIM_EMPLOYEE: FACT_EVALUATION.KEY_EVAL_RECIPIENT – The only instance in which a surrogate key can be pulled in this way (line 154) occurs when the data warehouse itself acts as the source system. This is the case, which allows us to pull this surrogate key in the extract step and avoid having to join to the dimension using the natural key later.

Lines 166 – 196

Line	Code
166	--If the table exists, drop it. If not, do nothing. The table will be
167	--created below.
168	SELECT COUNT(*) INTO TBLCOUNT
169	FROM ALL_TABLES
170	WHERE TABLE_NAME = 'STAGE_PAY_COMPARISON_CY'
171	AND OWNER =
172	(
173	SELECT SYS_CONTEXT('USERENV', 'CURRENT_SCHEMA')
174	FROM DUAL
175	);
176	
177	IF TBLCOUNT > 0 THEN
178	EXECUTE IMMEDIATE 'DROP TABLE STAGE_PAY_COMPARISON_CY';
179	END IF;
180	
181	--Pull the current year's salary data.

Line	Code
182	SQLSTMT := 'CREATE TABLE STAGE_PAY_COMPARISON_CY AS '
183	|| '(SELECT B.CALENDAR_YEAR, '
184	|| 'A.KEY_EMPLOYEE, '
185	|| 'SUM(A.AMOUNT) SALARY '
186	|| 'FROM FACT_SALARY A, '
187	|| 'DIM_MONTH B, '
188	|| 'DIM_PAY_TYPE C '
189	|| 'WHERE A.KEY_MONTH = B.KEY_MONTH '
190	|| 'AND A.KEY_PAY_TYPE = C.KEY_PAY_TYPE '
191	|| 'AND UPPER(C.COMPONENT_OF_GROSS_PAY) = "YES" '
192	|| 'AND B.CALENDAR_YEAR = ' || TO_CHAR(CURR_YEAR) || ' '
193	|| 'GROUP BY B.CALENDAR_YEAR, A.KEY_EMPLOYEE) ';
194	
195	EXECUTE IMMEDIATE SQLSTMT;
196	

Lines 166 – 180 will drop the STAGE_PAY_COMPARISON_CY table if it exists. Lines 181 – 196 will select the actual salary amount paid for the year equal to the current year of the loop and place the results into the STAGE_PAY_COMPARISON_CY table. Similar to line 29, line 191 is important, since the requirements specify that the total gross pay will be used.

Measure: FACT_SALARY.AMOUNT (line 185)

Natural Key to DIM_CALENDAR_YEAR: DIM_DAY.CALENDAR_YEAR – Similar to the FACT_EVALUATION star, the FACT_SALARY (line 183) star stores data at a monthly grain and does not include the KEY_CALENDAR_YEAR in that fact table. As a result, we are not able to simply extract the KEY_CALENDAR_YEAR from that star. The only alternative is to include the CALENDAR_YEAR in this staging table and then translate that into the KEY_CALENDAR_YEAR value later.

Surrogate Key to DIM_EMPLOYEE: FACT_SALARY.KEY_EMPLOYEE – As discussed with the FACT_EVALUATION star, the only instance in which a surrogate key can be pulled in this way (line 184) occurs when the data warehouse itself acts as the source system. This is the case, which allows us to pull this surrogate key in the extract step and avoid having to join to the dimension using the natural key later.

Transform The Data

Now that the current year's salary and prior year's salary as well as the current year's evaluation and prior year's evaluation data has been extracted, it is time to consolidate that data. This will be accomplished in the transform portion of the job. Consider this code.

261

Lines 197 – 224

Line	Code
197	--If the table exists, drop it. If not, do nothing. The table will be
198	--created below.
199	SELECT COUNT(*) INTO TBLCOUNT
200	FROM ALL_TABLES
201	WHERE TABLE_NAME = 'STAGE_EVAL_PAY_COMPARISON_PY'
202	AND OWNER =
203	(
204	SELECT SYS_CONTEXT('USERENV', 'CURRENT_SCHEMA')
205	FROM DUAL
206	);
207	
208	IF TBLCOUNT > 0 THEN
209	EXECUTE IMMEDIATE 'DROP TABLE STAGE_EVAL_PAY_COMPARISON_PY';
210	END IF;
211	
212	--Combine the prior year evaluation and salary data
213	SQLSTMT := 'CREATE TABLE STAGE_EVAL_PAY_COMPARISON_PY AS ('
214	|| 'SELECT '
215	|| 'NVL(B.CALENDAR_YEAR, A.CALENDAR_YEAR) PRIOR_YEAR, '
216	|| 'NVL(B.KEY_EMPLOYEE, A.KEY_EVALUATION_RECIPIENT) KEY_EMPLOYEE, '
217	|| 'A.EVALSCORE, '
218	|| 'B.SALARY '
219	|| 'FROM STAGE_EVAL_COMPARISON_PY A FULL OUTER JOIN STAGE_PAY_COMPARISON_PY B '
220	|| 'ON B.CALENDAR_YEAR = A.CALENDAR_YEAR '
221	|| 'AND B.KEY_EMPLOYEE = A.KEY_EVALUATION_RECIPIENT) ';
222	
223	EXECUTE IMMEDIATE SQLSTMT;
224	

Lines 197 – 211 will drop the STAGE_EVAL_PAY_COMPARISON_PY table if it exists. Lines 212 – 224 will select the prior year's evaluation and salary data from the

STAGE_EVAL_COMPARISON_PY table and the STAGE_PAY_COMPARISON_PY table respectively for each individual. Because the data for some individuals may exist in one table and not the other, a full outer join is used. The NVL() function on lines 215 and 216 is important since the data returned by either table may be null. For example, if the CURR_YEAR variable is 1994, then the STAGE_EVAL_COMPARISON_PY table will contain this row for Manuel Madsen (your KEY_EMPLOYEE value may differ):

```
SELECT          B.KEY_EMPLOYEE,
                B.FULL_NAME,
                C.CALENDAR_YEAR,
                SUM(A.ACTUAL_SCORE)
FROM            FACT_EVALUATION A,
                DIM_EMPLOYEE B,
                DIM_DAY C
WHERE           A.KEY_EVALUATION_RECIPIENT = B.KEY_EMPLOYEE
                AND A.KEY_EVALUATION_DATE = C.KEY_DAY
                AND B.EMPLOYEE_NUMBER = '1048707'
                AND C.CALENDAR_YEAR = 1993
GROUP BY        B.KEY_EMPLOYEE,
                B.FULL_NAME,
                C.CALENDAR_YEAR
ORDER BY        1,2
```

KEY_EMPLOYEE	FULL_NAME	CALENDAR_YEAR	SUM(A.ACTUAL_SCORE)
48270	Manuel Madsen	1993	34

Under the same conditions, the STAGE_PAY_COMPARISON_PY table will contain nothing for Manuel Madsen due to her having no salary data for the year 1993.

```
SELECT      B.KEY_EMPLOYEE,
            B.FULL_NAME,
            C.CALENDAR_YEAR,
            SUM(A.AMOUNT)
FROM        FACT_SALARY A,
            DIM_EMPLOYEE B,
            DIM_MONTH C
WHERE       A.KEY_EMPLOYEE = B.KEY_EMPLOYEE
            AND A.KEY_MONTH = C.KEY_MONTH
            AND B.EMPLOYEE_NUMBER = '1048707'
            AND C.CALENDAR_YEAR = 1993
GROUP BY    B.KEY_EMPLOYEE,
            B.FULL_NAME,
            C.CALENDAR_YEAR
```

KEY_EMPLOYEE	FULL_NAME	CALENDAR_YEAR	SUM(A.AMOUNT)
(null)	(null)	(null)	(null)

The full outer join will allow us to merge the two result sets even if an individual appears in one and not the other and place the following row into the STAGE_EVAL_PAY_COMPARISON_PY table.

PRIOR_YEAR	KEY_EMPLOYEE	EVAL_SCORE	SALARY
1993	48270	0.85	(null)

Lines 225 – 253

Line	Code
225	--If the table exists, drop it. If not, do nothing. The table will be
226	--created below.
227	SELECT COUNT(*) INTO TBLCOUNT
228	FROM ALL_TABLES
229	WHERE TABLE_NAME = 'STAGE_EVAL_PAY_COMPARISON_CY'
230	AND OWNER =
231	(
232	SELECT SYS_CONTEXT('USERENV', 'CURRENT_SCHEMA')
233	FROM DUAL
234	);
235	
236	IF TBLCOUNT > 0 THEN
237	EXECUTE IMMEDIATE 'DROP TABLE STAGE_EVAL_PAY_COMPARISON_CY';
238	END IF;
239	
240	--Combine the current year's evaluation and salary data
241	SQLSTMT := 'CREATE TABLE STAGE_EVAL_PAY_COMPARISON_CY AS ('
242	|| 'SELECT '
243	|| 'NVL(B.CALENDAR_YEAR, A.CALENDAR_YEAR) CURRENT_YEAR, '
244	|| 'NVL(B.KEY_EMPLOYEE, A.KEY_EVALUATION_RECIPIENT) KEY_EMPLOYEE, '
245	|| 'A.EVALSCORE, '
246	|| 'B.SALARY '
247	|| 'FROM STAGE_EVAL_COMPARISON_CY A FULL OUTER JOIN '

Line	Code
248	||'STAGE_PAY_COMPARISON_CY B '
249	|| 'ON B.CALENDAR_YEAR = A.CALENDAR_YEAR '
250	|| 'AND B.KEY_EMPLOYEE = A.KEY_EVALUATION_RECIPIENT) ';
251	
252	EXECUTE IMMEDIATE SQLSTMT;
253	

Lines 225 - 239 will drop the STAGE_EVAL_PAY_COMPARISON_CY table if it exists. Using similar logic as was used with the prior year data, lines 240 – 253 will select the current year's evaluation and salary data from the STAGE_EVAL_COMPARISON_CY table and the STAGE_PAY_COMPARISON_CY table respectively for each individual. Because the data for some individuals may exist in one table and not the other, a full outer join is used. The importance of the NVL() function applies here just as it did in the prior section. The example above, illustrating Manuel Madsen's data, can apply to this section as well by simply changing the CURR_YEAR variable, in that example, to be a value of 1993.

Load The Data

This portion of the job will delete the existing rows (for the applicable time frame) from the FACT_EVAL_PAY_COMPARISON table and load the new rows. Because some individuals may have only prior year data, some may have only current year data, and some may have both prior year and current year data, there are three separate loads into the fact table. The details of each load are explained below. Consider the following code.

Lines 254 – 264

Line	Code
254	--Delete the current year's data from the fact table
255	SQLSTMT := 'DELETE FROM FACT_EVAL_PAY_COMPARISON '
256	|| 'WHERE KEY_CURRENT_CALENDAR_YEAR IN '
257	|| '(SELECT KEY_CALENDAR_YEAR '
258	|| 'FROM DIM_CALENDAR_YEAR '
259	|| 'WHERE CALENDAR_YEAR = ' || TO_CHAR(CURR_YEAR) || ')';
260	
261	EXECUTE IMMEDIATE SQLSTMT;
262	
263	COMMIT;
264	

These lines delete the data from the FACT_EVAL_PAY_COMPARISON table that pertain to the current year in the loop.

Lines 265 – 290

Line	Code
265	--Place the data into the fact table for individuals who have data
266	--in both the prior year and current year.
267	SQLSTMT := 'INSERT INTO FACT_EVAL_PAY_COMPARISON '
268	|| 'SELECT A.KEY_EMPLOYEE, '
269	|| 'D.KEY_CALENDAR_YEAR KEY_CURRENT_CALENDAR_YEAR, '
270	|| 'C.KEY_CALENDAR_YEAR KEY_PRIOR_CALENDAR_YEAR, '
271	|| 'A.EVALSCORE PRIOR_YEAR_EVAL_SCORE, '
272	|| 'A.SALARY PRIOR_YEAR_SALARY, '
273	|| 'B.EVALSCORE CURRENT_YEAR_EVAL_SCORE, '
274	|| 'B.SALARY CURRENT_YEAR_SALARY, '
275	|| 'ROUND((B.EVALSCORE - A.EVALSCORE) / A.EVALSCORE,2) '
276	|| 'EVAL_PERCENTAGE_CHANGE, '
277	|| 'ROUND((B.SALARY - A.SALARY) / A.SALARY,2) '
278	||'SALARY_PERCENTAGE_CHANGE '
279	|| 'FROM STAGE_EVAL_PAY_COMPARISON_PY A, '
280	|| 'STAGE_EVAL_PAY_COMPARISON_CY B, '
281	|| 'DIM_CALENDAR_YEAR C, '
282	|| 'DIM_CALENDAR_YEAR D '
283	|| 'WHERE A.KEY_EMPLOYEE = B.KEY_EMPLOYEE '
284	|| 'AND A.PRIOR_YEAR = C.CALENDAR_YEAR '
285	|| 'AND B.CURRENT_YEAR = D.CALENDAR_YEAR ';
286	
287	EXECUTE IMMEDIATE SQLSTMT;
288	
289	COMMIT;
290	

As discussed above, the STAGE_EVAL_PAY_COMPARISON_PY table contains the prior year's evaluation data and salary data for each individual. Also, the STAGE_EVAL_PAY_COMPARISON_CY table contains the current year's evaluation data and salary data for each individual. Joining these two tables on KEY_EMPLOYEE will allow an ETL developer to easily populate the FACT_EVAL_PAY_COMPARISON table with both the current and prior data for each individual. Lines 265 – 290 accomplish this. Lines 275 – 278 specifically calculate the percentage increase or decrease between the current year's data and prior year's data. However, this will not populate the FACT_EVAL_PAY_COMPARISON table with data for individuals who have no data in the current year (i.e., individuals who recently resigned) nor will it populate the FACT_EVAL_PAY_COMPARISON table with data for individuals who had no data in the prior year (i.e., new hires).

Lines 291 – 315

Line	Code
291	--Place the data into the fact table for individuals who have data
292	--in the prior year but not the current year.
293	SQLSTMT := 'INSERT INTO FACT_EVAL_PAY_COMPARISON '
294	|| 'SELECT A.KEY_EMPLOYEE, '
295	|| 'D.KEY_CALENDAR_YEAR KEY_CURRENT_CALENDAR_YEAR, '
296	|| 'C.KEY_CALENDAR_YEAR KEY_PRIOR_CALENDAR_YEAR, '
297	|| 'A.EVALSCORE PRIOR_YEAR_EVAL_SCORE, '
298	|| 'A.SALARY PRIOR_YEAR_SALARY, '
299	|| 'B.EVALSCORE CURRENT_YEAR_EVAL_SCORE, '
300	|| 'B.SALARY CURRENT_YEAR_SALARY, '
301	|| 'null, '
302	|| 'null '
303	|| 'FROM STAGE_EVAL_PAY_COMPARISON_PY A, '
304	|| 'STAGE_EVAL_PAY_COMPARISON_CY B, '
305	|| 'DIM_CALENDAR_YEAR C, '
306	|| 'DIM_CALENDAR_YEAR D '
307	|| 'WHERE A.KEY_EMPLOYEE = B.KEY_EMPLOYEE(+) '
308	|| 'AND A.PRIOR_YEAR = C.CALENDAR_YEAR '
309	|| 'AND D.CALENDAR_YEAR = C.CALENDAR_YEAR + 1 '
310	|| 'AND B.KEY_EMPLOYEE IS NULL ';
311	
312	EXECUTE IMMEDIATE SQLSTMT;
313	
314	COMMIT;
315	

These lines of code will populate the FACT_EVAL_PAY_COMPARISON table with the prior year's data for those individuals who had prior year data but have no current year data (i.e., individuals who recently resigned). Notice the following nuances of the select statement that make this possible:

1.) Lines 301 and 302 place null values into columns that calculate the percentage increase or decrease. If left alone, these calculations will always show a drop of 100%, which may be misleading since there is no current year data for this individual.

2.) Line 307 specifies an outer join between the STAGE_EVAL_PAY_COMPARISON_PY and the STAGE_EVAL_PAY_COMPARISON_CY tables. Line 310 specifies that only those individuals with a null value in the STAGE_EVAL_PAY_COMPARISON_CY table will return, which will only include those with prior year results in the result set.

3.) Although there is no current year data the KEY_CURRENT_CALENDAR_YEAR value is still needed. As a result, the join on line 309 will grab that key from the DIM_CALENDAR_YEAR table by finding the key that corresponds to the prior year plus one.

Lines 316 – 340

Line	Code
316	--Place the data into the fact table for individuals who have data
317	--in the current year but not the prior year.
318	SQLSTMT := 'INSERT INTO FACT_EVAL_PAY_COMPARISON '
319	|| 'SELECT B.KEY_EMPLOYEE, '
320	|| 'D.KEY_CALENDAR_YEAR KEY_CURRENT_CALENDAR_YEAR, '
321	|| 'C.KEY_CALENDAR_YEAR KEY_PRIOR_CALENDAR_YEAR, '
322	|| 'A.EVALSCORE PRIOR_YEAR_EVAL_SCORE, '
323	|| 'A.SALARY PRIOR_YEAR_SALARY, '
324	|| 'B.EVALSCORE CURRENT_YEAR_EVAL_SCORE, '
325	|| 'B.SALARY CURRENT_YEAR_SALARY, '
326	|| 'null, '
327	|| 'null '
328	|| 'FROM STAGE_EVAL_PAY_COMPARISON_PY A, '
329	|| 'STAGE_EVAL_PAY_COMPARISON_CY B, '
330	|| 'DIM_CALENDAR_YEAR C, '
331	|| 'DIM_CALENDAR_YEAR D '
332	|| 'WHERE A.KEY_EMPLOYEE(+) = B.KEY_EMPLOYEE '
333	|| 'AND C.CALENDAR_YEAR = D.CALENDAR_YEAR - 1 '
334	|| 'AND B.CURRENT_YEAR = D.CALENDAR_YEAR '

Line	Code
335	|| 'AND A.KEY_EMPLOYEE IS NULL';
336	
337	EXECUTE IMMEDIATE SQLSTMT;
338	
339	COMMIT;
340	

These lines of code will populate the FACT_EVAL_PAY_COMPARISON table with the current year data for those individuals who have current year data but had no prior year data (i.e., new hires). Notice the following nuances of the select statement that make this possible:

1.) Lines 326 and 327 place null values into columns that calculate the percentage increase or decrease. If these calculations were left in place of the null values, they would always result in an error since the denominator would be null.

2.) Line 332 specifies an outer join between the STAGE_EVAL_PAY_COMPARISON_PY and the STAGE_EVAL_PAY_COMPARISON_CY tables. Line 335 specifies that only those individuals with a null value in the STAGE_EVAL_PAY_COMPARISON_PY table will return, which will only include those with current year results in the result set.

3.) Although there is no prior year data the KEY_PRIOR_CALENDAR_YEAR value is still needed. As a result, the join on line 333 will grab that key from the DIM_CALENDAR_YEAR table by finding the key that corresponds to the current year minus one.

Lines 341 – 345

Line	Code
341	--The CURR_YEAR variable in incremented by 1
342	CURR_YEAR := CURR_YEAR + 1;
343	
344	END LOOP;
345	

This code signifies the end of the WHILE loop. The CURR_YEAR variable is incremented by one. If the new value of the CURR_YEAR variable does not exceed the value of the END_YEAR variable (see line 71), the loop begins again. Otherwise, it ends.

Lines 346 – 363

Line	Code
346	--Log the successful completion of the job.

Line	Code
347	INSERT INTO ETL_JOB_STATUS
348	(
349	ID,
350	ETL_JOB_NAME,
351	STATUS_NAME,
352	STATUS_TIMESTAMP
353	)
354	VALUES
355	(
356	SEQ_ETL_JOB_STATUS.NEXTVAL,
357	'LOAD_EVAL_PAY_COMPARISON_FACT',
358	'SUCCESSFULLY COMPLETED',
359	SYSTIMESTAMP
360	);
361	
362	COMMIT;
363	

The end of the job is logged.

Lines 364 – 436

Line	Code
364	--This is the equivalent of a catch block. Any errors are caught and logged.
365	
366	EXCEPTION
367	--The MULTIPLE_FLAGS exception is raised here
368	WHEN MULTIPLE_FLAGS THEN
369	ERR_MSG := 'The ENTIRE_REFRESH and DEFAULT_TIMEPERIOD flags are both set '
370	||'to "Y". Please set only one to "Y" or set both to "N" with two '
371	||'override years.';
372	
373	INSERT INTO ETL_JOB_STATUS
374	(

Line	Code
375	ID,
376	ETL_JOB_NAME,
377	STATUS_NAME,
378	ERROR_MESSAGE,
379	STATUS_TIMESTAMP
380	)
381	VALUES
382	(
383	SEQ_ETL_JOB_STATUS.NEXTVAL,
384	'LOAD_EVAL_PAY_COMPARISON_FACT',
385	'ERROR',
386	ERR_MSG,
387	SYSTIMESTAMP
388	);
389	
390	COMMIT;
391	
392	--The YEARS_OUT_OF_ORDER exception is raised here
393	WHEN YEARS_OUT_OF_ORDER THEN
394	ERR_MSG := 'The year provided for the BEGIN_YEAR_OVERRIDE falls after the '
395	|| 'END_YEAR_OVERRIDE.';
396	INSERT INTO ETL_JOB_STATUS
397	(
398	ID,
399	ETL_JOB_NAME,
400	STATUS_NAME,
401	ERROR_MESSAGE,
402	STATUS_TIMESTAMP
403	)
404	VALUES
405	(
406	SEQ_ETL_JOB_STATUS.NEXTVAL,
407	'LOAD_EVAL_PAY_COMPARISON_FACT',

Line	Code
408	'ERROR',
409	ERR_MSG,
410	SYSTIMESTAMP
411	);
412	
413	COMMIT;
414	
415	WHEN OTHERS THEN
416	ERR_MSG := SUBSTR(SQLERRM, 1, 200);
417	INSERT INTO ETL_JOB_STATUS
418	(
419	ID,
420	ETL_JOB_NAME,
421	STATUS_NAME,
422	ERROR_MESSAGE,
423	STATUS_TIMESTAMP
424	)
425	VALUES
426	(
427	SEQ_ETL_JOB_STATUS.NEXTVAL,
428	'LOAD_EVAL_PAY_COMPARISON_FACT',
429	'ERROR',
430	ERR_MSG,
431	SYSTIMESTAMP
432	);
433	
434	COMMIT;
435	
436	END;

These lines are written to catch any exceptions thrown by the job and log those exceptions in the ETL_JOB_STATUS table.

Review The ETL Job

Running this job should result in 550,895 rows being placed into the FACT_EVAL_PAY_COMPARISON table. Unlike the other ETL jobs, running this job so that the ENTIRE_REFRESH variable is set to 'Y' will refresh the data up through the current fiscal year. In this context, current refers to the date on which the job was run. So, depending on when the job is run (independent of the data that is in the source tables) the row count may be different. In order to establish some level of consistency, the 550,895 row count given above is appropriate for running the job for a 1985 – 2012 timeframe.

1.) This ETL job is designed to be run as many times as necessary. Running this job multiple times will not cause rows to be duplicated.
2.) By default, the prior year and the current year (based on the sysdate) are refreshed. However, variables may be passed that will cause the fact table to be refreshed for data between certain calendar years or the entire fact table to be refreshed.
3.) The EVAL_PERCENTAGE_CHANGE and the SALARY_PERCENTAGE_CHANGE columns contain the percent increase or decrease when compared to the prior year. This percentage will be rounded to two decimal places.

Verify the ETL Job

Because of the complexity of this ETL job, either a complex SQL statement or a couple of SQL statements are needed to verify the results. The statement below should help to verify the results by selecting the current year's and prior year's evaluation and salary data from both the FACT_EVAL_PAY_COMPARISON table as well as their respective fact tables. That data can be used to manually calculate the delta between the current year and the prior year for comparison to the FACT_EVAL_PAY_COMPARISON.EVAL_PERCENTAGE_CHANGE and the FACT_EVAL_PAY_COMPARISON.SALARY_PERCENTAGE_CHANGE columns.

The SQL statement, as it exists below, may be a bit much to run so that all rows will be returned. As a result, a developer may need to break it up into smaller pieces or run it for a subset of individuals.

```
SELECT       KEY_EMPLOYEE,
             KEY_PRIOR_CALENDAR_YEAR,
             PRIOR_YEAR_EVAL_SCORE,
             PRIOR_YEAR_SALARY,
             PY_EVAL_FROM_STAR,
             PY_PAY_FROM_STAR,
             KEY_CURRENT_CALENDAR_YEAR,
             CURRENT_YEAR_EVAL_SCORE,
             CURRENT_YEAR_SALARY,
             CY_EVAL_FROM_STAR,
             CY_PAY_FROM_STAR,
             EVAL_PERCENTAGE_CHANGE,
             SALARY_PERCENTAGE_CHANGE
FROM
             (
             SELECT    A.KEY_EMPLOYEE,
                       A.KEY_PRIOR_CALENDAR_YEAR,
                       A.PRIOR_YEAR_EVAL_SCORE,
                       A.PRIOR_YEAR_SALARY,

                   (
                   SELECT    SUM(B.AMOUNT)
                   FROM      FACT_SALARY B,
                             DIM_MONTH C,
                             DIM_CALENDAR_YEAR D,
                             DIM_PAY_TYPE E
                   WHERE     B.KEY_MONTH = C.KEY_MONTH
                             AND C.CALENDAR_YEAR = D.CALENDAR_YEAR
                             AND D.KEY_CALENDAR_YEAR = A.KEY_PRIOR_CALENDAR_YEAR
```

```
                AND B.KEY_EMPLOYEE = A.KEY_EMPLOYEE
                AND B.KEY_PAY_TYPE = E.KEY_PAY_TYPE
                AND UPPER(E.COMPONENT_OF_GROSS_PAY) = 'YES'
        ) PY_PAY_FROM_STAR,
        (
                SELECT    SUM(NVL(B.ACTUAL_SCORE,0))/SUM(NVL(B.POSSIBLE_SCORE,0))
                FROM      FACT_EVALUATION B,
                          DIM_DAY C,
                          DIM_CALENDAR_YEAR D
                WHERE     B.KEY_EVALUATION_DATE = C.KEY_DAY
                          AND C.CALENDAR_YEAR = D.CALENDAR_YEAR
                          AND D.KEY_CALENDAR_YEAR = A.KEY_PRIOR_CALENDAR_YEAR
                          AND B.KEY_EVALUATION_RECIPIENT = A.KEY_EMPLOYEE
        ) PY_EVAL_FROM_STAR,

                A.KEY_CURRENT_CALENDAR_YEAR,
                A.CURRENT_YEAR_EVAL_SCORE,
                A.CURRENT_YEAR_SALARY,

        (
                SELECT    SUM(B.AMOUNT)
                FROM      FACT_SALARY B,
                          DIM_MONTH C,
                          DIM_CALENDAR_YEAR D,
                          DIM_PAY_TYPE E
                WHERE     B.KEY_MONTH = C.KEY_MONTH
                          AND C.CALENDAR_YEAR = D.CALENDAR_YEAR
                          AND D.KEY_CALENDAR_YEAR = A.KEY_CURRENT_CALENDAR_YEAR
                          AND B.KEY_EMPLOYEE = A.KEY_EMPLOYEE
                          AND B.KEY_PAY_TYPE = E.KEY_PAY_TYPE
                          AND UPPER(E.COMPONENT_OF_GROSS_PAY) = 'YES'
        ) CY_PAY_FROM_STAR,
        (
                SELECT    SUM(NVL(B.ACTUAL_SCORE,0))/SUM(NVL(B.POSSIBLE_SCORE,0))
                FROM      FACT_EVALUATION B,
                          DIM_DAY C,
                          DIM_CALENDAR_YEAR D
                WHERE     B.KEY_EVALUATION_DATE = C.KEY_DAY
                          AND C.CALENDAR_YEAR = D.CALENDAR_YEAR
                          AND D.KEY_CALENDAR_YEAR = A.KEY_CURRENT_CALENDAR_YEAR
                          AND B.KEY_EVALUATION_RECIPIENT = A.KEY_EMPLOYEE
        ) CY_EVAL_FROM_STAR,

                A.EVAL_PERCENTAGE_CHANGE,
                A.SALARY_PERCENTAGE_CHANGE

        FROM      FACT_EVAL_PAY_COMPARISON A
    )
```

Analyzing the data will show that it appears to match the source. The LOAD_EVAL_PAY_COMPARISON_FACT procedure in its entirety is below.

Line	Code
1	CREATE OR REPLACE PROCEDURE LOAD_EVAL_PAY_COMP_FACT
2	(
3	BEGIN_YEAR_OVERRIDE NUMBER,
4	END_YEAR_OVERRIDE NUMBER,
5	DEFAULT_TIMEPERIOD VARCHAR2,

Line	Code
6	ENTIRE_REFRESH VARCHAR2
7	)
8	
9	AS
10	
11	SQLSTMT VARCHAR2(3000);
12	TBLCOUNT NUMBER := 0;
13	BEGIN_YEAR NUMBER;
14	END_YEAR NUMBER;
15	ERR_MSG VARCHAR2(200);
16	YEARS_OUT_OF_ORDER EXCEPTION;
17	MULTIPLE_FLAGS EXCEPTION;
18	CURR_YEAR NUMBER;
19	
20	BEGIN
21	--Log the beginning of the job
22	INSERT INTO ETL_JOB_STATUS
23	(
24	ID,
25	ETL_JOB_NAME,
26	STATUS_NAME,
27	STATUS_TIMESTAMP
28	)
29	VALUES
30	(
31	SEQ_ETL_JOB_STATUS.NEXTVAL,
32	'LOAD_EVAL_PAY_COMPARISON_FACT',
33	'IN PROGRESS',
34	SYSTIMESTAMP
35	);
36	
37	COMMIT;
38	

Line	Code
39	--The job cannot execute an entire refresh and the default time period at the
40	--same time, so if both flags are set to 'Y' then an exception is raised.
41	IF DEFAULT_TIMEPERIOD = 'Y' AND ENTIRE_REFRESH = 'Y' THEN
42	RAISE MULTIPLE_FLAGS;
43	END IF;
44	
45	--If the DEFAULT_PERIOD variable is set to 'Y', then the prior year and the
46	--current year are loaded or reloaded into the fact table. If the
47	--ENTIRE_REFRESH variable is set to 'Y', then the entire fact table is
48	--truncated and reloaded. Otherwise, the overrides are used.
49	IF DEFAULT_TIMEPERIOD = 'Y' THEN
50	SELECT EXTRACT(YEAR FROM SYSDATE) - 1 INTO BEGIN_YEAR FROM DUAL;
51	SELECT EXTRACT(YEAR FROM SYSDATE) INTO END_YEAR FROM DUAL;
52	ELSIF ENTIRE_REFRESH = 'Y' THEN
53	SELECT MIN(CALENDAR_YEAR) INTO BEGIN_YEAR FROM DIM_CALENDAR_YEAR;
54	SELECT EXTRACT(YEAR FROM TRUNC(SYSDATE)) INTO END_YEAR FROM DUAL;
55	ELSE
56	--If the BEGIN_YEAR_OVERRIDE variable is larger than the END_YEAR_OVERRIDE
57	--then an exception is raised
58	IF BEGIN_YEAR_OVERRIDE > END_YEAR_OVERRIDE THEN
59	RAISE YEARS_OUT_OF_ORDER;
60	END IF;
61	
62	BEGIN_YEAR := BEGIN_YEAR_OVERRIDE;
63	END_YEAR := END_YEAR_OVERRIDE;
64	END IF;
65	
66	--The fact table is loaded one year at a time using a while loop. The
67	--CURR_YEAR is set to the first year in the range before entering the loop.
68	CURR_YEAR := BEGIN_YEAR;
69	

Line	Code
70	--The WHILE LOOP begins
71	WHILE CURR_YEAR <= END_YEAR
72	LOOP
73	--If the table exists, drop it. If not, do nothing. The table will be
74	--created below.
75	SELECT COUNT(*) INTO TBLCOUNT
76	FROM ALL_TABLES
77	WHERE TABLE_NAME = 'STAGE_EVAL_COMPARISON_PY'
78	AND OWNER =
79	(
80	SELECT SYS_CONTEXT('USERENV', 'CURRENT_SCHEMA')
81	FROM DUAL
82	);
83	
84	IF TBLCOUNT > 0 THEN
85	EXECUTE IMMEDIATE 'DROP TABLE STAGE_EVAL_COMPARISON_PY';
86	END IF;
87	
88	--Pull the prior year's evaluation score. Prior year is defined as the CURR_YEAR - 1
89	SQLSTMT := 'CREATE TABLE STAGE_EVAL_COMPARISON_PY AS ('
90	|| 'SELECT B.CALENDAR_YEAR, '
91	|| 'A.KEY_EVALUATION_RECIPIENT, '
92	|| 'SUM(A.ACTUAL_SCORE)/'
93	|| 'SUM(A.POSSIBLE_SCORE) EVALSCORE '
94	|| 'FROM FACT_EVALUATION A, '
95	|| 'DIM_DAY B '
96	|| 'WHERE A.KEY_EVALUATION_DATE = B.KEY_DAY '
97	|| 'AND B.CALENDAR_YEAR = ' || TO_CHAR(CURR_YEAR - 1) || ' '
98	|| 'GROUP BY B.CALENDAR_YEAR, '
99	|| 'A.KEY_EVALUATION_RECIPIENT) ';
100	
101	EXECUTE IMMEDIATE SQLSTMT;
102	

Line	Code
103	--If the table exists, drop it. If not, do nothing. The table will be
104	--created below.
105	SELECT COUNT(*) INTO TBLCOUNT
106	FROM ALL_TABLES
107	WHERE TABLE_NAME = 'STAGE_PAY_COMPARISON_PY'
108	AND OWNER =
109	(
110	SELECT SYS_CONTEXT('USERENV', 'CURRENT_SCHEMA')
111	FROM DUAL
112	);
113	
114	IF TBLCOUNT > 0 THEN
115	EXECUTE IMMEDIATE 'DROP TABLE STAGE_PAY_COMPARISON_PY';
116	END IF;
117	
118	--Pull the prior year's salary data
119	SQLSTMT := 'CREATE TABLE STAGE_PAY_COMPARISON_PY AS '
120	|| ' (SELECT B.CALENDAR_YEAR, '
121	|| 'A.KEY_EMPLOYEE, '
122	|| 'SUM(A.AMOUNT) SALARY '
123	|| 'FROM FACT_SALARY A, '
124	|| 'DIM_MONTH B, '
125	|| 'DIM_PAY_TYPE C '
126	|| 'WHERE A.KEY_MONTH = B.KEY_MONTH '
127	|| 'AND A.KEY_PAY_TYPE = C.KEY_PAY_TYPE '
128	--Must use upper
129	|| 'AND UPPER(C.COMPONENT_OF_GROSS_PAY) = "YES" '
130	|| 'AND B.CALENDAR_YEAR = ' || TO_CHAR(CURR_YEAR - 1) || ' '
131	|| 'GROUP BY B.CALENDAR_YEAR, A.KEY_EMPLOYEE) ';
132	
133	EXECUTE IMMEDIATE SQLSTMT;
134	
135	--If the table exists, drop it. If not, do nothing. The table will be

Line	Code
136	--created below.
137	SELECT COUNT(*) INTO TBLCOUNT
138	FROM ALL_TABLES
139	WHERE TABLE_NAME = 'STAGE_EVAL_COMPARISON_CY'
140	AND OWNER =
141	(
142	SELECT SYS_CONTEXT('USERENV', 'CURRENT_SCHEMA')
143	FROM DUAL
144	);
145	
146	IF TBLCOUNT > 0 THEN
147	EXECUTE IMMEDIATE 'DROP TABLE STAGE_EVAL_COMPARISON_CY';
148	END IF;
149	
150	--Pull the current year's evaluation data. The current year is stored in
151	--the CURR_YEAR variable.
152	SQLSTMT := 'CREATE TABLE STAGE_EVAL_COMPARISON_CY AS ('
153	|| 'SELECT B.CALENDAR_YEAR, '
154	|| 'A.KEY_EVALUATION_RECIPIENT, '
155	|| 'SUM(A.ACTUAL_SCORE)/ '
156	|| 'SUM(A.POSSIBLE_SCORE) EVALSCORE '
157	|| 'FROM FACT_EVALUATION A, '
158	|| 'DIM_DAY B '
159	|| 'WHERE A.KEY_EVALUATION_DATE = B.KEY_DAY '
160	|| 'AND B.CALENDAR_YEAR = ' || TO_CHAR(CURR_YEAR) || ' '
161	|| 'GROUP BY B.CALENDAR_YEAR, '
162	|| 'A.KEY_EVALUATION_RECIPIENT) ';
163	
164	EXECUTE IMMEDIATE SQLSTMT;
165	
166	--If the table exists, drop it. If not, do nothing. The table will be
167	--created below.
168	SELECT COUNT(*) INTO TBLCOUNT

Line	Code
169	FROM ALL_TABLES
170	WHERE TABLE_NAME = 'STAGE_PAY_COMPARISON_CY'
171	AND OWNER =
172	(
173	SELECT SYS_CONTEXT('USERENV', 'CURRENT_SCHEMA')
174	FROM DUAL
175	);
176	
177	IF TBLCOUNT > 0 THEN
178	EXECUTE IMMEDIATE 'DROP TABLE STAGE_PAY_COMPARISON_CY';
179	END IF;
180	
181	--Pull the current year's salary data.
182	SQLSTMT := 'CREATE TABLE STAGE_PAY_COMPARISON_CY AS '
183	|| '(SELECT B.CALENDAR_YEAR, '
184	|| 'A.KEY_EMPLOYEE, '
185	|| 'SUM(A.AMOUNT) SALARY '
186	|| 'FROM FACT_SALARY A, '
187	|| 'DIM_MONTH B, '
188	|| 'DIM_PAY_TYPE C '
189	|| 'WHERE A.KEY_MONTH = B.KEY_MONTH '
190	|| 'AND A.KEY_PAY_TYPE = C.KEY_PAY_TYPE '
191	|| 'AND UPPER(C.COMPONENT_OF_GROSS_PAY) = "YES" '
192	|| 'AND B.CALENDAR_YEAR = ' || TO_CHAR(CURR_YEAR) || ' '
193	|| 'GROUP BY B.CALENDAR_YEAR, A.KEY_EMPLOYEE) ';
194	
195	EXECUTE IMMEDIATE SQLSTMT;
196	
197	--If the table exists, drop it. If not, do nothing. The table will be
198	--created below.
199	SELECT COUNT(*) INTO TBLCOUNT
200	FROM ALL_TABLES
201	WHERE TABLE_NAME = 'STAGE_EVAL_PAY_COMPARISON_PY'

Line	Code
202	AND OWNER =
203	(
204	SELECT SYS_CONTEXT('USERENV', 'CURRENT_SCHEMA')
205	FROM DUAL
206	);
207	
208	IF TBLCOUNT > 0 THEN
209	EXECUTE IMMEDIATE 'DROP TABLE STAGE_EVAL_PAY_COMPARISON_PY';
210	END IF;
211	
212	--Combine the prior year evaluation and salary data
213	SQLSTMT := 'CREATE TABLE STAGE_EVAL_PAY_COMPARISON_PY AS ('
214	|| 'SELECT '
215	|| 'NVL(B.CALENDAR_YEAR, A.CALENDAR_YEAR) PRIOR_YEAR, '
216	|| 'NVL(B.KEY_EMPLOYEE, A.KEY_EVALUATION_RECIPIENT) KEY_EMPLOYEE, '
217	|| 'A.EVALSCORE, '
218	|| 'B.SALARY '
219	|| 'FROM STAGE_EVAL_COMPARISON_PY A FULL OUTER JOIN STAGE_PAY_COMPARISON_PY B '
220	|| 'ON B.CALENDAR_YEAR = A.CALENDAR_YEAR '
221	|| 'AND B.KEY_EMPLOYEE = A.KEY_EVALUATION_RECIPIENT) ';
222	
223	EXECUTE IMMEDIATE SQLSTMT;
224	
225	--If the table exists, drop it. If not, do nothing. The table will be
226	--created below.
227	SELECT COUNT(*) INTO TBLCOUNT
228	FROM ALL_TABLES
229	WHERE TABLE_NAME = 'STAGE_EVAL_PAY_COMPARISON_CY'
230	AND OWNER =
231	(
232	SELECT SYS_CONTEXT('USERENV', 'CURRENT_SCHEMA')
233	FROM DUAL

Line	Code
234	);
235	
236	IF TBLCOUNT > 0 THEN
237	EXECUTE IMMEDIATE 'DROP TABLE STAGE_EVAL_PAY_COMPARISON_CY';
238	END IF;
239	
240	--Combine the current year's evaluation and salary data
241	SQLSTMT := 'CREATE TABLE STAGE_EVAL_PAY_COMPARISON_CY AS ('
242	|| 'SELECT '
243	|| 'NVL(B.CALENDAR_YEAR, A.CALENDAR_YEAR) CURRENT_YEAR, '
244	|| 'NVL(B.KEY_EMPLOYEE, A.KEY_EVALUATION_RECIPIENT) KEY_EMPLOYEE, '
245	|| 'A.EVALSCORE, '
246	|| 'B.SALARY '
247	|| 'FROM STAGE_EVAL_COMPARISON_CY A FULL OUTER JOIN '
248	||'STAGE_PAY_COMPARISON_CY B '
249	|| 'ON B.CALENDAR_YEAR = A.CALENDAR_YEAR '
250	|| 'AND B.KEY_EMPLOYEE = A.KEY_EVALUATION_RECIPIENT) ';
251	
252	EXECUTE IMMEDIATE SQLSTMT;
253	
254	--Delete the current year's data from the fact table
255	SQLSTMT := 'DELETE FROM FACT_EVAL_PAY_COMPARISON '
256	|| 'WHERE KEY_CURRENT_CALENDAR_YEAR IN '
257	|| '(SELECT KEY_CALENDAR_YEAR '
258	|| 'FROM DIM_CALENDAR_YEAR '
259	|| 'WHERE CALENDAR_YEAR = ' || TO_CHAR(CURR_YEAR) || ')';
260	
261	EXECUTE IMMEDIATE SQLSTMT;
262	
263	COMMIT;
264	
265	--Place the data into the fact table for individuals who have data

Line	Code
266	--in both the prior year and current year.
267	SQLSTMT := 'INSERT INTO FACT_EVAL_PAY_COMPARISON '
268	|| 'SELECT A.KEY_EMPLOYEE, '
269	|| 'D.KEY_CALENDAR_YEAR KEY_CURRENT_CALENDAR_YEAR, '
270	|| 'C.KEY_CALENDAR_YEAR KEY_PRIOR_CALENDAR_YEAR, '
271	|| 'A.EVALSCORE PRIOR_YEAR_EVAL_SCORE, '
272	|| 'A.SALARY PRIOR_YEAR_SALARY, '
273	|| 'B.EVALSCORE CURRENT_YEAR_EVAL_SCORE, '
274	|| 'B.SALARY CURRENT_YEAR_SALARY, '
275	|| 'ROUND((B.EVALSCORE - A.EVALSCORE) / A.EVALSCORE,2) '
276	|| 'EVAL_PERCENTAGE_CHANGE, '
277	|| 'ROUND((B.SALARY - A.SALARY) / A.SALARY,2) '
278	||'SALARY_PERCENTAGE_CHANGE '
279	|| 'FROM STAGE_EVAL_PAY_COMPARISON_PY A, '
280	|| 'STAGE_EVAL_PAY_COMPARISON_CY B, '
281	|| 'DIM_CALENDAR_YEAR C, '
282	|| 'DIM_CALENDAR_YEAR D '
283	|| 'WHERE A.KEY_EMPLOYEE = B.KEY_EMPLOYEE '
284	|| 'AND A.PRIOR_YEAR = C.CALENDAR_YEAR '
285	|| 'AND B.CURRENT_YEAR = D.CALENDAR_YEAR ';
286	
287	EXECUTE IMMEDIATE SQLSTMT;
288	
289	COMMIT;
290	
291	--Place the data into the fact table for individuals who have data
292	--in the prior year but not the current year.
293	SQLSTMT := 'INSERT INTO FACT_EVAL_PAY_COMPARISON '
294	|| 'SELECT A.KEY_EMPLOYEE, '
295	|| 'D.KEY_CALENDAR_YEAR KEY_CURRENT_CALENDAR_YEAR, '
296	|| 'C.KEY_CALENDAR_YEAR KEY_PRIOR_CALENDAR_YEAR, '
297	|| 'A.EVALSCORE PRIOR_YEAR_EVAL_SCORE, '
298	|| 'A.SALARY PRIOR_YEAR_SALARY, '

Line	Code
299	|| 'B.EVALSCORE CURRENT_YEAR_EVAL_SCORE, '
300	|| 'B.SALARY CURRENT_YEAR_SALARY, '
301	|| 'null, '
302	|| 'null '
303	|| 'FROM STAGE_EVAL_PAY_COMPARISON_PY A, '
304	|| 'STAGE_EVAL_PAY_COMPARISON_CY B, '
305	|| 'DIM_CALENDAR_YEAR C, '
306	|| 'DIM_CALENDAR_YEAR D '
307	|| 'WHERE A.KEY_EMPLOYEE = B.KEY_EMPLOYEE(+) '
308	|| 'AND A.PRIOR_YEAR = C.CALENDAR_YEAR '
309	|| 'AND D.CALENDAR_YEAR = C.CALENDAR_YEAR + 1 '
310	|| 'AND B.KEY_EMPLOYEE IS NULL ';
311	
312	EXECUTE IMMEDIATE SQLSTMT;
313	
314	COMMIT;
315	
316	--Place the data into the fact table for individuals who have data
317	--in the current year but not the prior year.
318	SQLSTMT := 'INSERT INTO FACT_EVAL_PAY_COMPARISON '
319	|| 'SELECT B.KEY_EMPLOYEE, '
320	|| 'D.KEY_CALENDAR_YEAR KEY_CURRENT_CALENDAR_YEAR, '
321	|| 'C.KEY_CALENDAR_YEAR KEY_PRIOR_CALENDAR_YEAR, '
322	|| 'A.EVALSCORE PRIOR_YEAR_EVAL_SCORE, '
323	|| 'A.SALARY PRIOR_YEAR_SALARY, '
324	|| 'B.EVALSCORE CURRENT_YEAR_EVAL_SCORE, '
325	|| 'B.SALARY CURRENT_YEAR_SALARY, '
326	|| 'null, '
327	|| 'null '
328	|| 'FROM STAGE_EVAL_PAY_COMPARISON_PY A, '
329	|| 'STAGE_EVAL_PAY_COMPARISON_CY B, '
330	|| 'DIM_CALENDAR_YEAR C, '
331	|| 'DIM_CALENDAR_YEAR D '

Line	Code
332	|| 'WHERE A.KEY_EMPLOYEE(+) = B.KEY_EMPLOYEE '
333	|| 'AND C.CALENDAR_YEAR = D.CALENDAR_YEAR - 1 '
334	|| 'AND B.CURRENT_YEAR = D.CALENDAR_YEAR '
335	|| 'AND A.KEY_EMPLOYEE IS NULL';
336	
337	EXECUTE IMMEDIATE SQLSTMT;
338	
339	COMMIT;
340	
341	--The CURR_YEAR variable in incremented by 1
342	CURR_YEAR := CURR_YEAR + 1;
343	
344	END LOOP;
345	
346	--Log the successful completion of the job.
347	INSERT INTO ETL_JOB_STATUS
348	(
349	ID,
350	ETL_JOB_NAME,
351	STATUS_NAME,
352	STATUS_TIMESTAMP
353	)
354	VALUES
355	(
356	SEQ_ETL_JOB_STATUS.NEXTVAL,
357	'LOAD_EVAL_PAY_COMPARISON_FACT',
358	'SUCCESSFULLY COMPLETED',
359	SYSTIMESTAMP
360	);
361	
362	COMMIT;
363	
364	--This is the equivalent of a catch block. Any errors are caught and logged.

Line	Code
365	
366	EXCEPTION
367	--The MULTIPLE_FLAGS exception is raised here
368	WHEN MULTIPLE_FLAGS THEN
369	ERR_MSG := 'The ENTIRE_REFRESH and DEFAULT_TIMEPERIOD flags are both set '
370	||'to "Y". Please set only one to "Y" or set both to "N" with two '
371	||'override years.';
372	
373	INSERT INTO ETL_JOB_STATUS
374	(
375	ID,
376	ETL_JOB_NAME,
377	STATUS_NAME,
378	ERROR_MESSAGE,
379	STATUS_TIMESTAMP
380	)
381	VALUES
382	(
383	SEQ_ETL_JOB_STATUS.NEXTVAL,
384	'LOAD_EVAL_PAY_COMPARISON_FACT',
385	'ERROR',
386	ERR_MSG,
387	SYSTIMESTAMP
388	);
389	
390	COMMIT;
391	
392	--The YEARS_OUT_OF_ORDER exception is raised here
393	WHEN YEARS_OUT_OF_ORDER THEN
394	ERR_MSG := 'The year provided for the BEGIN_YEAR_OVERRIDE falls after the '
395	|| 'END_YEAR_OVERRIDE.';
396	INSERT INTO ETL_JOB_STATUS
397	(

Line	Code
398	ID,
399	ETL_JOB_NAME,
400	STATUS_NAME,
401	ERROR_MESSAGE,
402	STATUS_TIMESTAMP
403	)
404	VALUES
405	(
406	SEQ_ETL_JOB_STATUS.NEXTVAL,
407	'LOAD_EVAL_PAY_COMPARISON_FACT',
408	'ERROR',
409	ERR_MSG,
410	SYSTIMESTAMP
411	);
412	
413	COMMIT;
414	
415	WHEN OTHERS THEN
416	ERR_MSG := SUBSTR(SQLERRM, 1, 200);
417	INSERT INTO ETL_JOB_STATUS
418	(
419	ID,
420	ETL_JOB_NAME,
421	STATUS_NAME,
422	ERROR_MESSAGE,
423	STATUS_TIMESTAMP
424	)
425	VALUES
426	(
427	SEQ_ETL_JOB_STATUS.NEXTVAL,
428	'LOAD_EVAL_PAY_COMPARISON_FACT',
429	'ERROR',
430	ERR_MSG,
431	SYSTIMESTAMP

Line	Code
432	);
433	
434	COMMIT;
435	
436	END;

11
CONCLUSION

Congratulations! The following list was presented in chapter one as a list of areas to which you will be exposed. Now, this list represents some areas in which you have developed some familiarity.

1.) Populating conformed dimensions
2.) Populating type one and type two slowly changing dimensions
3.) Populating junk dimensions
4.) Recognizing when it is appropriate to refresh a table entirely as opposed to updating existing records and inserting new ones
5.) Creating a job so that the data in a star schema can be refreshed entirely, refreshed according to a default timeframe (only the current month, for example), or refreshed with dates provided
6.) Comparing the newly warehoused data to the source system to ensure that the ETL job is working correctly
7.) Creating tables in the staging area to make the job optimal for debugging when the data warehouse does not match the source
8.) Using the staging tables in number seven above to identify where in the ETL a problem may lie and possible solutions
9.) Changing the grain of a fact table
10.) Considering ways to make a job run more efficiently when it is discovered that it is taking too much time to complete

The star schemas that you have just created are not the only star schemas that can be created from the source data. Feel free to alter some of the business requirements as well as some of the source data itself in order to continue practicing. As stated in chapter one, business intelligence is a growing field with huge potential. However, treat this experience as only step one on your journey into this exciting field. In addition to your continued practice with this dataset, consider these additional steps as you move forward:

Practice
While only some people have job responsibilities that revolve entirely around data management, everybody touches data in some area of their lives. Begin to notice where you touch data and

practice these skills by warehousing some of that data. Examples may include warehousing your checkbook register or your grocery receipts. In these cases, nobody will be architecting the solutions for you. You will have to design the solution as well as write the ETL, which will necessitate that you get some training in architecture as well.

Business Processes

A star schema should be designed around a business process. As a result, it is important for a data warehouse professional to be familiar with the business processes within his/her organization. While an ETL developer fills a technical role, a data warehouse effort is not solely a technical effort. Listening to payroll, accounting, inventory, and other experts discuss the ways that they go about doing business will be invaluable as you move forward.

New Techniques

While a traditional data warehouse provides immense value to an organization, some other technologies are emerging to help with business intelligence as well. For example, the use of Big Data is a promising trend that is permeating the marketplace. In addition to the ETL skills discussed in the preceding chapters, learn about these new techniques also.

Market Yourself

Gaining this new experience is great; however, your ultimate goal is to offer these skills to others. How can you market yourself as someone who is interested in and capable of ETL development? Of course, there is no one right answer to this. Networking with business intelligence professionals and sharing your desire is a great idea. If your organization has not begun a business intelligence effort, consider helping it to move in that direction. In other words, consider looking at the data used by your current employer in a new way. What kinds of stars may help you or your leaders to make better decisions? Finally, putting together a portfolio of some sort may help in this area. A book entitled *The Data Warehouse Portfolio* describes one possible structure to such a portfolio.

For those who are detail oriented, a career in ETL development can provide a great deal of fulfillment. While it is important to become familiar with the details of the technologies being used in the marketplace, it is important to remember that those technologies themselves are not the end-all-be-all. The value of a business intelligence professional does not lie in knowing how to write ETL. That is only a means used to reach the ultimate goal. The ultimate goal is to enable excellent decision making.

ABOUT THE AUTHOR

Brian Ciampa is a business intelligence developer who loves to write about the power of data. Feel free to check out his blog at http://valuabledata.blogspot.com.

20617683R00165

Printed in Great Britain
by Amazon

Line	Code
234	);
235	
236	IF TBLCOUNT > 0 THEN
237	EXECUTE IMMEDIATE 'DROP TABLE STAGE_EVAL_PAY_COMPARISON_CY';
238	END IF;
239	
240	--Combine the current year's evaluation and salary data
241	SQLSTMT := 'CREATE TABLE STAGE_EVAL_PAY_COMPARISON_CY AS ('
242	|| 'SELECT '
243	|| 'NVL(B.CALENDAR_YEAR, A.CALENDAR_YEAR) CURRENT_YEAR, '
244	|| 'NVL(B.KEY_EMPLOYEE, A.KEY_EVALUATION_RECIPIENT) KEY_EMPLOYEE, '
245	|| 'A.EVALSCORE, '
246	|| 'B.SALARY '
247	|| 'FROM STAGE_EVAL_COMPARISON_CY A FULL OUTER JOIN '
248	||'STAGE_PAY_COMPARISON_CY B '
249	|| 'ON B.CALENDAR_YEAR = A.CALENDAR_YEAR '
250	|| 'AND B.KEY_EMPLOYEE = A.KEY_EVALUATION_RECIPIENT) ';
251	
252	EXECUTE IMMEDIATE SQLSTMT;
253	
254	--Delete the current year's data from the fact table
255	SQLSTMT := 'DELETE FROM FACT_EVAL_PAY_COMPARISON '
256	|| 'WHERE KEY_CURRENT_CALENDAR_YEAR IN '
257	|| '(SELECT KEY_CALENDAR_YEAR '
258	|| 'FROM DIM_CALENDAR_YEAR '
259	|| 'WHERE CALENDAR_YEAR = ' || TO_CHAR(CURR_YEAR) || ')';
260	
261	EXECUTE IMMEDIATE SQLSTMT;
262	
263	COMMIT;
264	
265	--Place the data into the fact table for individuals who have data

Line	Code
202	AND OWNER =
203	(
204	SELECT SYS_CONTEXT('USERENV', 'CURRENT_SCHEMA')
205	FROM DUAL
206	);
207	
208	IF TBLCOUNT > 0 THEN
209	EXECUTE IMMEDIATE 'DROP TABLE STAGE_EVAL_PAY_COMPARISON_PY';
210	END IF;
211	
212	--Combine the prior year evaluation and salary data
213	SQLSTMT := 'CREATE TABLE STAGE_EVAL_PAY_COMPARISON_PY AS ('
214	|| 'SELECT '
215	|| 'NVL(B.CALENDAR_YEAR, A.CALENDAR_YEAR) PRIOR_YEAR, '
216	|| 'NVL(B.KEY_EMPLOYEE, A.KEY_EVALUATION_RECIPIENT) KEY_EMPLOYEE, '
217	|| 'A.EVALSCORE, '
218	|| 'B.SALARY '
219	|| 'FROM STAGE_EVAL_COMPARISON_PY A FULL OUTER JOIN STAGE_PAY_COMPARISON_PY B '
220	|| 'ON B.CALENDAR_YEAR = A.CALENDAR_YEAR '
221	|| 'AND B.KEY_EMPLOYEE = A.KEY_EVALUATION_RECIPIENT) ';
222	
223	EXECUTE IMMEDIATE SQLSTMT;
224	
225	--If the table exists, drop it. If not, do nothing. The table will be
226	--created below.
227	SELECT COUNT(*) INTO TBLCOUNT
228	FROM ALL_TABLES
229	WHERE TABLE_NAME = 'STAGE_EVAL_PAY_COMPARISON_CY'
230	AND OWNER =
231	(
232	SELECT SYS_CONTEXT('USERENV', 'CURRENT_SCHEMA')
233	FROM DUAL